Pfeiffer
& COMPANY

THE
1993 ANNUAL:
DEVELOPING
HUMAN RESOURCES

(The Twenty-Second Annual)

Edited by
J. WILLIAM PFEIFFER, Ph.D., J.D.

Amsterdam • Johannesburg • London
San Diego • Sydney • Toronto

Printed in the United States of America

Published by

Amsterdam
Pfeiffer & Company
Roggestraat 15
2153 GC Nieuw-Vennep
The Netherlands
31-2526-89840, FAX 31-2526-86885

San Diego
Pfeiffer & Company
8517 Production Avenue
San Diego, California 92121
United States of America
1-619-578-5900, FAX 1-619-578-2042

Johannesburg
Pfeiffer & Company
P.O. Box 4684, Randberg, 2145
9 Langwa Street, Strijdom Park
Republic of South Africa
27-11-792-8465/6/7, FAX 27-11-792-8046

Sydney
Pfeiffer & Company
6/1 Short Street
Chatswood NSW 2067
Australia
61-2-417-5551, FAX 61-2-417-5621

London
Pfeiffer & Company
862 Garratt Lane
London, SW17 0NB
England
44-81-682-1766, FAX 44-81-682-1729

Toronto
Pfeiffer & Company
4190 Fairview Street
Burlington, Ontario L7L 4Y8
Canada
1-416-632-5832, FAX 1-416-333-5675

PREFACE

The contents of this *Annual,* the twenty-second volume in our series, confirm that human resource development (HRD)—which includes training, career development, personnel, management development, and organization development functions—continues to thrive. The changes in the title of the *Annual* over the past twenty-two years reflect the evolution of HRD as well as the intention of Pfeiffer & Company to remain at the cutting edge of this field.

The central purpose of the *Annual* has always been to keep readers aware of and involved in current developments in the field. Consequently, each year the contents of the *Annual* are selected and edited to reflect these developments as we at Pfeiffer & Company perceive them. For several years now the HRD function in most organizations has grown in terms of visibility and has exerted a stronger and more valuable influence in such efforts as strategic planning. The individual pieces selected for this *Annual* exemplify the depth of the field today. They not only serve as cause for optimism about the future of HRD; they also offer food for thought about the needs and requirements of that future.

In this year's *Annual,* the Lecturette, Theory and Practice, and Resources sections again are combined into a single Professional Development section. This format, established in 1984, allows greater flexibility in selection and facilitates a more coherent overview of what is occurring in the field of HRD.

In the Instrumentation section, Pfeiffer & Company intends to continue to publish practical measurement devices that are useful for trainers, consultants, and managers. Moreover, as has been the case in the last several *Annuals,* both the theoretical background for each instrument and practical suggestions for its administration and application are included. These features have been added to make the instruments easier to use and to increase their value to our readers. Those people who intend to submit instruments and other materials to the *Annual* are advised to take these standards into account.

There are several aspects of the *Annual* series that have not changed over the years. One is a continuing bias that everything in the *Annual* be potentially useful to the professional trainers, consultants, and facilitators who read it. The content of this *Annual* focuses on increasing each reader's professional competence and, therefore, his or her impact on the field of HRD. In keeping with this objective, users are allowed to duplicate and modify materials from the *Annuals* for *educational and training* purposes, so long as the credit statement found on the copyright page of the particular volume is included on all copies. However, if Pfeiffer & Company materials are to be reproduced in publications for sale or are intended for large-scale distribution (more than one hundred copies per event), *prior written permission* is required. Also, if a footnote indicates that the material is copyrighted by some source other than Pfeiffer & Company, no reproduction is allowed without the written permission of that designated copyright holder.

We at Pfeiffer & Company continue to solicit materials from our readers—especially materials with a clear organizational focus and those that reflect the changing nature of the HRD field. The success of the *Annual* as a clearing house for HRD professionals depends on the continual flow of materials from our readers. We encourage and welcome the submission of structured experiences, instruments, and articles, including both innovative methods and tried-and-true procedures. Our guidelines for contributors are available from the Editorial Department at the San Diego address listed on the copyright page of this volume, and submissions should be sent to the managing editor at the same address.

I want to express my appreciation to the capable and talented people at Pfeiffer & Company who have produced this volume: Marian K. Prokop and Carol Nolde, joint project managers; Arlette C. Ballew, developmental senior editor; Mary Kitzmiller, managing editor; Steffany N. Parker, editor; Jennifer O. Bryant, editor; Katharine A. Munson, editor; Heidi Erika Callinan, editor; Judy Whalen, page compositor; Nicola Ruskin, graphic designer; and Heather Kennedy, graphic designer. Also, I particularly want to thank Dr. Beverly Byrum-Robinson, whose review of our structured experiences always enhances the usefulness of these training designs. As always, I extend my deepest gratitude to our authors for their generosity in sharing their professional ideas, materials, and techniques so that HRD practitioners may benefit.

J. William Pfeiffer

San Diego, California
September, 1992

About Pfeiffer & Company

Pfeiffer & Company (formerly University Associates, Inc.) is engaged in publishing in the broad field of human resource development (HRD). The organization has earned an international reputation as the leading source of practical publications that are immediately useful to today's facilitators, trainers, consultants, and managers. A distinct advantage of these publications is that they are designed by practicing professionals who are continually experimenting with new techniques. Thus, readers benefit from the fresh but thoughtful approach that underlies Pfeiffer & Company's experientially based materials, resources, books, workbooks, instruments, and tape-assisted learning programs. These materials are designed for the HRD practitioner who wants access to a broad range of training and intervention technologies as well as background in the field.

The wide audience that Pfeiffer & Company serves includes training and development professionals, internal and external consultants, managers and supervisors, team leaders, and those in the helping professions. Pfeiffer & Company offers its customers a practical approach aimed at increasing people's effectiveness on an individual, group, and organizational basis.

TABLE OF CONTENTS

---

*See Structured Experience Categories, p.5, for an explanation of numbering.

PROFESSIONAL DEVELOPMENT

GENERAL INTRODUCTION TO THE 1993 *ANNUAL*

The 1993 Annual: Developing Human Resources is the twenty-second volume in the *Annual* series. The series is a collection of practical and useful materials for human resource development (HRD) practitioners—materials written by and for professionals. As such, the series continues to provide a publication outlet for HRD professionals who wish to share their experiences, their viewpoints, and their procedures with their colleagues.

In accordance with the changes made in the *Annual* format in 1984, there are now three rather than five sections: Structured Experiences, Instrumentation, and Professional Development. The Professional Development section combines the Lecturettes, Theory and Practice, and Resources sections that appeared in the first twelve volumes of the series.

As has been the case with each volume of the *Annual* series, the materials for the 1993 *Annual* have been selected for their quality of conceptualization, applicability to the real-world concerns of HRD practitioners, relevance to today's HRD issues, and ability to provide readers with assistance in their own professional development. In addition to using these criteria for selecting valuable tools, we were also able to choose structured experiences that will create a high degree of enthusiasm among the participants and add a great deal of enjoyment to the learning process. In this volume, as in previous editions, readers will notice a focus on organizational issues, which reflects the fact that a large number of our readers are organizationally based or are consultants and trainers for organizations. Thus, there is a need for more structured experiences that have organizational relevance or that can be used with intact groups, especially work teams. A description of the structured experiences selected for this volume is given in the "Introduction to the Structured Experiences Section."

The order of the structured experiences in the 1993 *Annual* is dictated by the categorization scheme of our *Structured Experience Kit* and the *Reference Guide to Handbooks and Annuals.* We believe that this order is logical and easy to use, particularly for those readers who regularly use structured experiences in their work and who select them from the *Reference Guide* or the *Structured Experience Kit.*

The Instrumentation section of this *Annual* contains four new paper-and-pencil, instrumented-feedback scales, questionnaires, or inventories. These instruments are described in the "Introduction to the Instrumentation Section."

The Professional Development section is intended to assist readers of the *Annual* in their own professional development. The articles in the 1992 *Annual* cover a range of issues that confront HRD professionals today. These articles are described in the "Introduction to the Professional Development Section."

The editor of this *Annual* and the Pfeiffer & Company editorial staff continue to be pleased with the high quality of submitted materials. Nevertheless, just as we cannot publish every manuscript that is submitted, readers may find that not all of the works we include in the *Annual* are equally useful to them. We actively solicit feedback from our readers so that we may continue to select manuscripts that meet their needs.

Pfeiffer & Company follows the stylistic guidelines established by the American Psychological Association, particularly with regard to the use and format of references. Potential contributors to our publications may wish to purchase copies of the APA's Publication Manual from: American Psychological Association, P.O. Box 2710, Hyattsville, MD 20784, phone (202) 955-7600. Pfeiffer & Company also publishes guidelines for potential authors. These guidelines are available from Pfeiffer & Company's Editorial Department.

Biographies of *Annual* authors are published at the end of each structured experience, instrument, and professional development article. In addition, at the end of each *Annual* is a list of contributors' names, affiliations, addresses, and telephone numbers. This information is intended to contribute to the "networking" function that is so valuable in the field of HRD.

INTRODUCTION TO THE
STRUCTURED EXPERIENCES SECTION

Adults need more active involvement in the learning process than children do. Using structured experiences is an effective way to add experiential learning to a training design. Experiential learning gives the participants the opportunity to do something, to look back at it critically, to gain insight from the analysis, and to put the results to work.

Note that the structured experiences in the 1993 *Annual,* as in recent *Annuals,* are presented in an order that reflects their classification into categories, according to their focus and intent. A list of the six major categories and their subcategories can be found immediately following this introduction, and an explanation of the categorization scheme can be found in the "User's Guide" to the *Structured Experience Kit,* in the discussion beginning on page 27 of the *Reference Guide to Handbooks and Annuals* (1992 Edition), and in the "Introduction to the Structured Experiences Section" of the 1981 *Annual.*

The structured experiences in this *Annual* represent all six major categories: Personal, Communication, Group Characteristics, Group Task Behavior, Organizations, and Facilitating Learning. The first two structured experiences represent the Personal category. In "A Note to My Teammate," the participants practice giving and receiving positive feedback with members of their work teams, thereby improving the working climate. In the second activity, "Career Visioning," the participants have the opportunity to generate various career-development options for themselves, to select from among those options, and to develop plans to achieve their goals. Through this process, the participants also become acquainted with the techniques of "visioning" and gap analysis.

The third structured experience, "Time Flies," represents the Communication category. This activity offers participants the opportunity to role play the use of assertive behavior in managing their time and to receive feedback about how effectively they use assertion.

The fourth and fifth activities belong to the Group Characteristics category. The fourth, "Yours, Mine, and Ours," is designed to be used with an intact work team. It allows the participants to clarify which tasks and responsibilities belong to individual team members and which belong to the group as a whole. The fifth activity, "People Are Electric," helps participants to enhance creativity. By imagining a different way of life, the participants discover heuristics and selective perception in their thinking patterns.

The sixth, seventh, and eighth activities belong to the Group Task Behavior category. The sixth, "The Real Meaning," and the seventh, "Stating the Issue," both involve problem solving. In "The Real Meaning," a series of statements forms the basis for creative thinking and for devising creative solutions to problems. "Stating the Issue" focuses on how participants can describe personal and organizational issues accurately and specifically, thereby practicing the skills needed for effective communication. The eighth activity, "Organizational Structures," examines the interrelationships of organic and mechanistic organizational structures with problem-solving performance and organizational climate.

The ninth and tenth structured experiences are from the Organizations category. "The Hundredth Monkey" explores the concept of four types of shared mind-sets and offers participants the opportunity to promote a shared organizational mind-set. In "International Equity Claims Department," the participants develop a work design that is driven by customer and employee needs as well as by measurable work-process goals.

The last two of the twelve structured experiences represent the Facilitating Learning category. Both are designed for use with practicing or prospective facilitators. In "Color Me," the participants introduce themselves on the basis of characteristics associated with a color. In "Zodiac for Trainers," the participants identify the attitudes and skills that they feel are essential to being an effective human resource development (HRD) professional and then assess their own competencies, using the framework of horoscopes.

All of the structured experiences in this *Annual* include a description of the goals of the activity, the size of the group and/or subgroups that can be accommodated, the time required to do and to *process*[1] the activity, the materials and handouts required, the physical setting, step-by-step instructions for facilitating both the experiential task and discussion phases of the activity, and variations of the design that the facilitator might find useful. All of these activities are complete; the content of all handouts is provided.

For several years we cross-referenced the materials in the *Annuals* and the *Handbooks* by providing suggestions after each structured experience for "similar structured experiences," "suggested instruments," and "lecturette sources." With the 1987 *Annual* we discontinued this process for several reasons. In response to a questionnaire, our sample of readers indicated that the cross-references were not being used as frequently as we had anticipated. In addition, because older volumes do not reflect material in later volumes, the cross-referencing in any particular volume is incomplete as soon as a later volume is published. Finally, the *Reference Guide to Handbooks and Annuals*, which is revised periodically, is apparently much more beneficial to our readers. It provides the type of help that the cross-referencing was originally intended to give. With each revision, the *Reference Guide* is completely updated and provides an easy way to select appropriate materials from *all* of the *Annuals* and *Handbooks*.

---

[1] It would be redundant to print here a caveat for the use of structured experiences, but HRD professionals who are not experienced in the use of this training technology are strongly urged to read the "Introduction to the Structured Experiences Section" of the 1980 *Annual* or the "Introduction" to the *Reference Guide to Handbooks and Annuals* (1992 Edition). Both of these articles present the theory behind the experiential-learning cycle and explain the necessity of adequately completing each phase of the cycle in order to allow effective learning to occur.

STRUCTURED EXPERIENCE CATEGORIES

Pfeiffer & Company

497. A NOTE TO MY TEAMMATE: POSITIVE FEEDBACK

Goals

   I. To provide the participants with an opportunity to experience positive feedback.

  II. To offer the participants an opportunity to practice giving specific positive feedback.

 III. To offer the participants a method for improving their working climate.

Group Size

All members of an intact work team.

Time Required

Thirty minutes or less, depending on the size of the group.

Materials

   I. Several sheets of colored paper for each participant.

  II. Colored pens for each participant.

 III. A clipboard or other portable writing surface for each participant.

 IV. A newsprint poster prepared in advance with the following information:

- Take responsibility for the perception—use "I."
- Make it personal—use "you" or the person's name.
- Use the present tense.
- Use positive, active verbs (has, can, chooses, deserves, sees).
- Focus on specific, concrete, observable behaviors, as opposed to general, abstract personality qualities that are inferred from behavior.

  V. A copy of A Note to My Teammate Theory Sheet for the facilitator.

Physical Setting

Any room in which the group can meet comfortably.

Process

   I. The facilitator explains that the participants will have an opportunity to write and to share positive phrases, to develop the habit of thinking positively, and to experience receiving positive feedback. He or she then presents a lecturette based on A Note to My Teammate Theory Sheet. (Ten minutes.)

II. The facilitator distributes paper, pencils, and portable writing surfaces to the participants and instructs each person to write his or her name on the paper.

III. The participants are asked to circulate and to write a positive phrase on every person's paper. (Five to ten minutes.)

IV. The facilitator leads a concluding discussion based on the following questions:

1. How do you feel about yourself right now?

2. What do you notice about the phrases that others use to describe you? What themes do you recognize? What does that tell you about yourself? What does that tell you about your contribution to the team?

3. How can you use positive feedback on yourself to help break a habit or overcome a limitation?

4. How might the group use this process during its work? How will this kind of experience aid the group in being more productive?

(Fifteen minutes.)

Variations

I. This activity can be conducted during each meeting of the group, becoming a regular programming practice. It can be carried into the general work place, with co-workers writing phrases on posted sheets or on a community board.

II. The group can brainstorm a group or team phrase.

III. Rather than circulate the notes, each participant could write a separate note to every other team member. Each team member could be given a big envelope to serve as a mailbox.

Submitted by Deborah M. Fairbanks.

Deborah M. Fairbanks *is a Certified Self-Talk trainer through the Self-Talk Institute. Ms. Fairbanks teaches courses in developing positive thought patterns and designs instructional programs. She contracts with Pfeiffer & Company as an acquisitions reviewer and developmental editor.*

A NOTE TO MY TEAMMATE
THEORY SHEET

Throughout a person's personal and professional life, he or she gives and receives feedback. Some feedback comes from other people; other feedback can be self-feedback, based on one's own observations and evaluations of experiences. A person's feelings, thoughts, and behavior are shaped by this feedback, whether it be positive or negative.

Self-feedback influences behavior. For example, when a person makes a mistake, his or her self-feedback might take the form of "What a dunce I am! I can't seem to do anything right!" On the other hand, the self-feedback might sound more like "That didn't work the way that I wanted it to work. Next time I'll try something else." The phrasing of the self-feedback makes a difference in how this person will react to the experience of making the mistake.

Feedback from others also influences behavior. For instance, if another person sees the mistake and judges it to be the result of a lack of experience, he or she might say, "That's O.K. What works best for me is to do it this way." However, if that person perceives the mistake to be a careless one, he or she might say, "Why can't you be more careful? You must pay more attention to what you're doing!" Once again, the phrasing of the feedback from others makes a difference in how a person reacts to an experience.

A person's tendency to respond positively or negatively— constructively or destructively—is a pattern that can be modified. Positive feedback empowers, supports, and informs. It is a technique for managing one's thoughts and making conscious choices about how to respond to people and to situations. Learning to use positive feedback appropriately can alter a person's responses and can create a more positive and supportive environment.

One form for giving positive feedback is "I think/perceive/sense that you, (name), (general quality), because (specific description). For example, a person might say "I think that you, Chris, are a dedicated worker because I see the quality of the work you produce." Another example might be to say, "I perceive that you, Robin, are a careful listener because I hear you ask insightful questions."

In summary, key characteristics of positive feedback include the following:

- Take responsibility for the perception—use "I."
- Make it personal—use "you" or the person's name.
- Use the present tense.
- Use positive, active verbs (has, can, chooses, deserves, sees).
- Focus on specific, concrete, observable behaviors, as opposed to general, abstract personality qualities that are inferred from behavior.

498. CAREER VISIONING:
STRATEGIC PROBLEM SOLVING

Goals

I. To offer participants an opportunity to generate various career-development options for themselves, to select among those options, and develop a plan to achieve them.

II. To acquaint participants with techniques of "visioning" and gap analysis.

Group Size

Up to thirty participants.

Time Required

Approximately three hours.

Materials

I. Several sheets of blank paper and a pencil for each participant.

II. A newsprint flip chart and felt-tipped markers in various colors.

III. Masking tape for posting newsprint.

IV. A copy of the Career Visioning Theory Sheet for the facilitator's use. (Optional: The facilitator may choose to distribute copies of the Career Visioning Theory Sheet; in this case, one copy for each participant would be necessary.)

Physical Setting

A room large enough for participants to work comfortably—both in groups and as individuals.

Process

I. The facilitator explains the goals of the activity and distributes paper and pencils to the participants. (Five minutes.)

II. The facilitator asks for a volunteer who is "willing to model the career-planning process." The volunteer is asked to envision his or her career one year from today and to verbally brainstorm everything that he or she would like to be true of his or her career at that time. The facilitator lists all ideas on newsprint, labeling the sheet with the volunteer's name and the date.

The volunteer should be encouraged to "create a career dream," that is, to identify everything that he or she would like, without considering relative importance or current likelihood. (Ten minutes.)

III. The volunteer is asked to look at these visions and to star with a marking pen the three visions with which he or she would be satisfied if only three could be accomplished in the next year. The volunteer then rank orders the visions. The facilitator lists the volunteer's first-priority vision on a separate sheet of newsprint. (Five minutes.)

IV. The facilitator asks each participant to repeat the process in Steps II and III individually: to envision his or her own work life one year from today, listing everything he or she would like to be true then (including specifics about the career), and then to identify the three most important visions, rank order them, and list the first-priority item on a separate sheet of paper. (Fifteen minutes.)

V. The facilitator delivers a lecturette on the strategic problem-solving approach to career development based on the Career Visioning Theory Sheet. Copies of the Career Visioning Theory Sheet may be distributed to participants or key points may be listed on newsprint. (Ten minutes.)

VI. Each participant is asked to write about his or her *current* career situation, listing any information that might help an outsider to understand it. The original volunteer writes his or her description on a sheet of newsprint and posts it. (Ten minutes.)

VII. The facilitator refers to the original volunteer's first-priority item and current situation and leads the volunteer through the process of "gap analysis," that is, identifying the differences between the desired future and the current situation. The other participants are encouraged to participate in this process, asking questions, making comments, and so on, to assess the reality of the desired outcome. This continues until the majority believe that the gap between the volunteer's vision and the current reality is realistic. (Ten minutes.)

VIII. The facilitator asks the entire group (including the volunteer) to think of what the volunteer might need to bridge the gap. The facilitator can make suggestions, such as training, on-the-job experiences, mentors, expanding one's network, and so on. The items are listed on newsprint. (Five minutes.)

IX. The facilitator then asks all participants to brainstorm all of the possible, specific actions—based on the items in the list generated previously—that the volunteer might need to take in the next twelve months to achieve the first-priority vision. Everything is listed on newsprint, regardless of its importance or likelihood at the present time. (Ten minutes.)

X. Once all suggested actions are listed, the volunteer is asked to examine the list of specific actions and to mark those actions that would have the most impact in helping to reach the vision. Then the volunteer is asked to commit to those actions and to list dates for accomplishment beside each one as an action plan. (Ten minutes.)

XI. Each participant is asked to look at his or her own first-priority vision, to compare it with his or her current reality, to determine the size of the gap, and to address the gap realistically. Each participant then is to list what he or she would need to achieve in order to reach the vision and to jot down any actions that he or she might take to achieve it. (Ten minutes.)

XII. The facilitator directs the participants to form small discussion groups of approximately five members each. The facilitator tells the small groups to look at each group member's first-priority vision, current situation, and gap analysis, and to suggest additional actions that the person might take to reach his or her vision. (Fifteen to twenty-five minutes.)

XIII. Once these lists are complete, each person is directed to review his or her own list to identify high-impact actions, to establish time lines, and to commit to them. (Ten minutes.)

XIV. The facilitator asks each participant to look at his or her completed plans and to consider, and then discuss with fellow group members, the following questions:

1. How does this differ from what you came to the session with?

2. When might you want to reconsider the plan again?

3. How can participants help one another in achieving their goals?

(Fifteen minutes.)

XV. The facilitator asks the participants to consider the strategic problem-solving process in general and to discuss the following:

1. What conclusions about the strategic problem-solving process might be drawn from reviewing the result of the gap analysis of current reality and the desired-outcome vision?

2. What conclusions might be drawn about the strategic problem-solving process from looking at so many different approaches to the same situation?

3. What does this say about entering a problem-solving process individually or in a group effort? What are the advantages and disadvantages of each approach?

4. How else can you apply what you have learned in this experience to your future work and personal situations?

(Fifteen minutes.)

Variations

I. If time permits, the session can be divided into two parts: At the end of part 1, the participants take away their preliminary plans (before committing to specific actions) and obtain further ideas from other people in their lives (both inside and outside the workplace) before the session is resumed.

II. Participants can be asked to generate "life" visions or to include "personal" goals in their desired visions. The facilitator can encourage the process by asking if there is anything that the person would like to add about relationships inside or outside work, free time, personal interests, and so on. This will take more time to process.

III. The total group may meet later at a specified date to check the members' progress toward achieving their first-priority visions and to make any desired changes in plans. They also may work through the members' other two starred visions from Step III at this time.

IV. The process can be completed with just one person and a facilitator, with the facilitator actively offering additional ideas.

Submitted by Neil Johnson and Jason Ollander-Krane.

Neil Johnson is a managing partner of Ollander-Krane/Johnson, a consulting company specializing in practical, innovative ways to grow and plan business growth, develop people, deliver the best products, and improve sales and service. He designs and delivers custom programs in management development, selling and service, visioning, and planning for groups and individuals. Organizations also draw on his expertise in facilitating, team building, and other interventions.

Jason Ollander-Krane is also a managing partner of Ollander-Krane/Johnson. He has held training and development positions with Wells Fargo Bank, Young and Rubicam, Macy's, and Adia Personnel Services.

Neil Johnson and Jason Ollander-Krane have been working together for twelve years. Their current clients include Hewlett Packard, Saatchi & Saatchi DFS, Procter and Gamble, The City of San Francisco, Bermuda Department of Tourism, and Remedy Temporaries.

CAREER VISIONING
THEORY SHEET

One way to look at planning career development is that it is solving a problem. Generally, there are two different ways to solve problems. Try to determine which way might produce better results for career-development planning.

Short-Term Problem-Solving Model

One method of problem solving is to describe the problem first and then to generate a number of solutions and decide on one (or more). This method of problem solving produces a single picture of the problem and solutions that radiate in different directions from the problem.

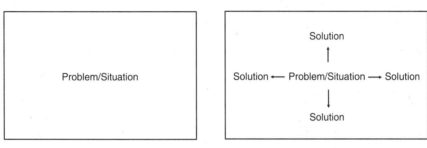

Step 1:
Describe the problem or situation

Step 2:
Devise solution(s) to the problem or situation

Figure 1. Short-Term Problem-Solving Model

Strategic Problem-Solving Model

A different way to solve problems might be called "strategic problem solving." It starts with the creation of a vision of the desired outcome—how you would like the situation to be—at a specific time in the future. Then describe the current situation or problem. After this, you perform a "gap analysis," that is, you determine the differences between the desired situation and the current one.

The gap analysis is a *feasibility* analysis or reality test. It is important to be absolutely honest about the current reality if the gap analysis is to be accurate. If the differences between the desired future and the current situation are too great, the description of the desired outcome needs to be revised. It is important—and may be difficult—at this point to be realistic without limiting one's vision more than is necessary. Factors to be considered may include actual possibilities of advancement within the targeted organization, family concerns, location and access, education and training, financial concerns, trade-offs, and resources.

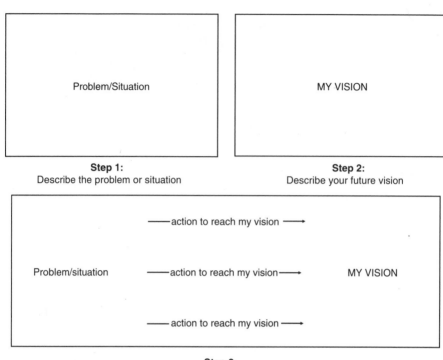

Figure 2. Strategic Problem-Solving Model

Once the gap is of a realistic size, you can begin to explore possible solutions—things that need to be done to get from your current situation to your desired vision of the future. These solutions should specify exactly what is required (obstacles to be overcome, actions to be taken, support and resources needed, time lines, and so on) in order to move from the current situation to the desired one. We say "solutions" rather than "solution" because there may be more than one gap, and more than one line of action or strategy may be required. On the other hand, if little is required, you may want to consider returning to the visioning stage and setting slightly higher goals.

This process requires both openness and honesty. It also requires recognition of the possible need to back off from one direction and to go in another. The resulting action plan may be quite different from what originally was envisioned. The overall purpose is to develop a plan that has a reasonable probability of success.

Using this problem-solving technique, you obtain results that are more focused on your desired future, and that future is likely to be more realistic and more suited to your actual preferences and abilities.

499. TIME FLIES: NEGOTIATING PERSONAL EFFECTIVENESS THROUGH ASSERTION

Goals

I. To demonstrate to the participants the importance of assertive behavior in managing one's time.

II. To give the participants an opportunity to practice assertive behavior.

III. To give the participants an opportunity to receive feedback about their use of assertion in interpersonal issues that concern time management.

Group Size

Any number of triads.

Time Required

Two hours and twenty minutes to two and one-half hours.

Materials

I. A copy of the Time Flies Instruction Sheet for each participant.

II. A copy of the Time Flies Situations Sheet for each participant.

III. A copy of the Time Flies Partner Characteristics Sheet for each participant.

IV. A copy of the Time Flies Observer Sheet for each participant.

V. A copy of the Time Flies Assertion Theory Sheet for each participant.

VI. A copy of the Time Flies Action Plan for each participant.

VII. A pencil for each participant.

VIII. A clipboard or other portable writing surface for each participant.

IX. A newsprint poster prepared in advance showing the following chart:

	Role Player	Partner	Observer
First Role Play	A	B	C
Second Role Play	B	C	A
Third Role Play	C	A	B

X. A stopwatch for the facilitator's use.

XI. A newsprint flip chart and felt-tipped marker.

XII. Masking tape for posting newsprint.

Physical Setting

A room in which the subgroups can work without distracting one another. Movable chairs should be provided.

Process

    I. The facilitator introduces the role play as an effective way of practicing new skills and explains that the participants will be role playing situations that deal with assertiveness in time management (that is, being able to say "no" without losing one's job or ruining a relationship). (Five minutes.)

    II. The facilitator assembles the participants into triads and asks each triad to designate one member as "A," another member as "B," and the third member as "C." *Note to facilitator: If there are two participants without a group, they may do the activity as a dyad; similarly, if a single person is without a group, he or she may form a dyad with the facilitator.* (Five minutes.)

    III. The facilitator posts the newsprint chart of role-play assignments and explains that each person in the triad will have the opportunity to be a role player, a partner, and an observer. *Note to facilitator: In the case of a dyad, the role of observer is omitted and the dyad conducts three role plays among themselves.* The facilitator distributes one copy of the Time Flies Instruction Sheet, one copy of the Time Flies Situations Sheet, one copy of the Time Flies Partner Characteristics Sheet, and one copy of the Time Flies Observer Sheet to each participant. The facilitator instructs the participants to read the Time Flies Instruction Sheet. (Ten minutes.)

    IV. The facilitator instructs the subgroups to read the Time Flies Situations Sheet and to select a role-play situation from it. (Five minutes.)

    V. The facilitator directs Person A (Role Player) in each subgroup to complete the Time Flies Partner Characteristics Sheet, to hand it to Person B (Partner), and to relate any information about the situation that would be helpful to Person B (Partner), such as, "When I talk to my boss, she doesn't pay attention after the first few moments and she interrupts me." Person B (Partner) may take notes on the completed Time Flies Participant Characteristics Sheet. Person C (Observer) is instructed to review the questions on the Time Flies Observer Sheet and to take notes while the role players are sharing information. (Five minutes.)

    VI. The participants are directed to role play the two people in their selected situations. Person A is instructed to attempt to manage Person B's time demands, and Person B is instructed to attempt to achieve his or her demands. (Five minutes.)

VII. The facilitator calls time and instructs the observers to summarize for the others in their subgroup their observations and reactions to the role plays. (Five minutes.)

VIII. The facilitator reconvenes the total group and leads a discussion based on the following questions from the Time Flies Observer Sheet:

1. How did the role-play partner make demands on the first role player? What behaviors appeared to be demanding?

2. How successful was the first role player in managing the demands? What did he or she do that worked? What did not work?

3. How would you describe the role players' communication patterns? What might the patterns indicate about their relationship?

4. How was the situation resolved? Was it a "win-win" situation or a "win-lose" situation? If it appeared to be a win-lose situation, who was the loser? What could the person who lost have done to balance the outcome? If it appeared to be a win-win situation, how was that achieved?

(Ten minutes.)

IX. The facilitator instructs the members of each subgroup to switch roles and to repeat the exercise two more times, choosing the same situation or other situations and sharing information as in Step V, until each member has held the roles of the role player, the partner, and the observer. The facilitator calls time after each role-play segment and instructs the participants to debrief as directed in Steps VII-VIII. (Twenty-five minutes.)

X. Copies of the Time Flies Theory Sheet are distributed, and the participants are asked to read this sheet. Then the facilitator leads a discussion of assertion theory, clarifying points as necessary and relating them to the comments made during Step VIII. (Ten to fifteen minutes.)

XI. The facilitator then instructs the participants to complete three more role plays, thus repeating Steps V-IX. (Thirty minutes.)

XII. The facilitator reconvenes the total group and leads a discussion based on the following questions:

1. What were the differences between the first and second group of role plays? How do you account for these differences?

2. What new questions or statements did you, as the first role player, make during the second group of role plays?

3. Which of the rights listed in the Time Flies Theory Sheet did you find yourself exercising? How were they appropriate to the situation? What level of difficulty did you experience in asserting these rights? How could the assertion of these rights be beneficial in a work situation?

4. In your role-play situations, did you find that you needed to negotiate with your role-play partners to ensure the best use of your and your

partners' time? Did negotiation prove to be a time saver? How did it save time? Waste time? Are there instances in your work situation in which negotiation could be a time saver?

5. What have you learned about the skills necessary to behave assertively? In what other situations, both related and unrelated to time management, might assertive behavior be beneficial? What could you do differently to manage your time as a result of this experience?

(Fifteen to twenty minutes.)

XIII. The facilitator distributes copies of the Time Flies Action Plan and leads the group in a brainstorming session on tips to enhance effective use of assertiveness. (Ten minutes.)

Variations

I. To shorten the time and to proceed directly to the activity's focus, the first set of role plays may be eliminated.

II. Participants may be instructed to think of "real-life" situations to role play and to develop action plans for them based on question 5 in Step XII.

Submitted by Michael Lee Smith.

Michael Lee Smith is the director of training and development for the Air & Water Technologies Corporation (AWT). He develops and conducts management and sales training (which he refers to as nontechnical survival skills) for the nine AWT environmental-engineering companies. He has published more than twenty-five articles. Mr. Smith is certified as a Senior Professional in Human Resources (SPHR) and as a Professional Services Manager in Human Resources (CPM).

TIME FLIES
INSTRUCTION SHEET

You will be asked to choose a situation and then to role play it with one of the members of your group. The member designated as "observer" will watch your role play and will give you feedback when you have finished.

Role Player: You are to take the part of the "you" described in the situation (the person with the problem). Think of what you would say to the other person in this situation. You may write out your response if you wish to do so.

Partner: You are to take the part of the "other person" described in the situation (the person who is making demands on the first role player). Think of what you would say or what approach you would take if you were the "other person" in this situation. You may write notes if you wish. It is important that you not take an extreme position at this point. Allow the Role Player to negotiate a resolution if what he or she says is reasonable.

TIME FLIES
SITUATIONS SHEET

Situation 1: Your manager literally looks over your shoulder, continually checks on your progress, and asks for details about your dealings with clients and with other managers. His or her behavior is a continual drain on your time.

Situation 2: You ask one of your staff members to do a task. He or she replies that your manager has just assigned an urgent, "top-priority" project to him or her. You were unaware of this assignment.

Situation 3: Your manager, who seems to have difficulty planning ahead, has begun to schedule frequent department meetings before or after normal working hours. It is 6:00 in the evening, and you have just been informed that tomorrow morning's meeting will commence at 7:00 a.m.

Situation 4: A co-worker begins to talk to you about last night's sporting event; you do not wish to listen.

Situation 5: Your manager often calls you into his or her office. During your meetings, your manager frequently takes phone calls and makes you wait until he or she is finished.

Situation 6: You often find yourself doing tasks, such as making copies, collating, and proofreading, that other people should be doing. You are hesitant to delegate these tasks because the others seem so busy and because they seem to resent being assigned "drudge work."

Situation 7: One of your subordinates frequently asks you to make decisions that he or she should be willing and able to make.

Situation 8: On short notice, you learn that the manager of a department on which you depend to get your work done has scheduled you for a meeting. You already are scheduled to visit the site of a major project and to meet with a client on that date.

Situation 9: Every assignment from your manager is "ASAP," or "Number 1 Priority." You are expected to complete all of your assignments, but you believe that that is not humanly possible.

Situation 10: Your manager gives you work that is really his or her own job. You are expected to do this work while keeping your own work on schedule. Although there are people to whom you could delegate the work, you are expected to complete it yourself.

Pfeiffer & Company

TIME FLIES
PARTNER CHARACTERISTIC SHEET

Instructions: When it is your turn as the role player, use this checklist to mark the characteristics that your partner should display during the role play. In this way, the role-play situation will more closely resemble situations that you face in back-home situations.

_____ Interrupts me.

_____ Talks down to me.

_____ "Listens" but does not hear what I say.

_____ Only talks about his or her needs.

_____ Labels my explanations as excuses.

_____ Talks about things that are not related to my concerns.

_____ Appears to be angry when I talk.

_____ Displays no emotions.

_____ Repeats his or her demands without variation.

_____ Questions my commitment, loyalty, or competence.

_____ Summarizes what I have said, but repeats the same demands.

_____ Ignores what I say.

_____ Allows telephone interruptions.

_____ Refuses to look me in the eye.

_____ Always agrees with me, but presses his or her own demands.

_____ Always ends with "What are you going to do about this?"

_____ Other (please specify):

TIME FLIES
OBSERVER SHEET

Instructions: Two members of your subgroup are about to role play one of the situations outlined on the Time Flies Situations Sheet.

Your task is to observe the role play between the two members. While you are observing the role play, think about and/or jot down answers to the following questions. Also keep track of "quotable quotes" or any "emotionally loaded" words or phrases used by either participant (for example, unreasonable, ridiculous, and so on). Later you will be asked to share the questions and your answers with the members of your subgroup.

1. How did the role-play partner make demands on the first role player? What behaviors appeared to be demanding?

2. How successful was the first role player in managing the demands? What did he or she do that worked? What did not work?

3. How would you describe the role players' communication patterns? What might the patterns indicate about their relationship?

4. How was the situation resolved? Was it a "win-win" situation or a "win-lose" situation? If it appeared to be a win-lose situation, who was the loser? What could the person who lost have done to balance the outcome? If it appeared to be a win-win situation, how was that achieved?

TIME FLIES
ASSERTION THEORY SHEET[1]

Assertion theory is based on the premise that every person is entitled to certain basic human rights. These rights include the right to refuse requests without feeling guilty or selfish, the right to believe that one's own needs are as important as the needs of others, and the right to make mistakes.

People relate to these basic human rights with one of three general response styles: *nonassertion, aggression,* and *assertion.*

Nonassertion

Nonassertion represents an inability to maintain adequate boundaries between one's own rights and those of others. When one of her friends asked to borrow Jan's new sports car for a trip, Jan lent the car, fearing that her friend would perceive her as petty or distrustful; however, she spent the rest of the afternoon wishing that she had not done so. Thus, by being nonassertive, Jan did not act on her right to say no.

Aggression

A second response style, aggression, occurs when one person invades the other's individual rights. If Jan had reacted aggressively to her friend's request, she might have said "Certainly not!" or "You've *got* to be kidding!" In this case, Jan would have violated her friend's right to make the request and her right to be treated with courtesy and respect.

Assertion

Standing up for one's basic human rights without violating the rights of others is assertion (Jakubowski-Spector, 1973). This response style recognizes boundaries between one's own rights and those of others and operates to keep the boundaries stabilized.

In Jan's case, an assertive response might have been to say, "I appreciate your need for some transportation, but the car is too valuable to me to lend." By this response, Jan would have respected both her friend's right to make the request and her own right to refuse it.

Components of an Assertive Situation

Basic human rights include the right to say yes and no with conviction, to give and to receive criticism, to initiate and to conclude conversations, to allow or to resist interruptions, to give and to receive compliments, to demand fair deals, to deal with discriminatory remarks, and to negotiate win-win arrangements.

---

[1] Adapted from C. Kelley, "Assertion Theory," in J.W. Pfeiffer & J.E. Jones, *The 1976 Annual Handbook for Group Facilitators.* San Diego, CA: Pfeiffer & Company.

A person may feel capable of being assertive in a situation but may decide not to because of factors such as power or time or effort. Before deciding to be assertive, it is helpful to examine the six components of an assertive situation:

1. The basic human rights and the level of confidence in both the potential asserter and the other person;

2. The specific behavior to which the potential asserter is responding;

3. The potential asserter's feeling reactions to this specific behavior;

4. The specific behaviors that the potential asserter would prefer;

5. The possible positive and negative consequences for the other person if he or she behaves as the potential asserter wishes; and

6. The possible consequences of the assertive response for the potential asserter.

Conclusion

Assertiveness offers a model for those who wish to stand up for their own rights without violating the rights of others. Such a model can be used in all types of situations—personal, professional, and social—to facilitate honest, direct, functional communication.

Reference

Jakubowski-Spector, P. (1973). Facilitating the growth of women through assertive training. *The Counseling Psychologist, 4*(1), 75-86.

TIME FLIES
ACTION PLAN

Instructions: List some examples of new behaviors that you would like to use in situations you typically encounter. Be sure to set target dates at which to reassess the behaviors.

Typical Situation	Behavioral Goals	Reassessment Date

500. YOURS, MINE, AND OURS: CLARIFYING TEAM RESPONSIBILITIES

Goal

To assist the participants in clarifying and establishing agreements about which activities are their group's responsibilities and which are the responsibilities of individual members (including the formal leader).

Group Size

All members of an intact work group. The process works best with a minimum of three members and a maximum of eight members.

Time Required

Approximately three to three and one-half hours for a group with five or six members. The facilitator should add or subtract ten minutes for each member above or below that number.

Materials

   I. A set of colored 3" x 5" index cards for each participant. There should be as many colors of index cards as there are participants, plus one; for example, if there are four group members, there should be five different colors of index cards. The set of cards that each participant receives should include six cards of each color. *Note:* If there are more participants than there are colors of index cards available, the facilitator may use white cards and code them with different colors of felt-tipped markers, making a colored stripe along the top edge of each card.

   II. A pencil for each participant.

   III. Two sheets of newsprint and a felt-tipped marker for each participant.

   IV. A newsprint flip chart and a felt-tipped marker for the facilitator's use.

   V. Masking tape for posting newsprint.

Physical Setting

A room with tables and movable chairs for the participants. Each participant must have enough tabletop surface to create stacks of index cards and prepare two newsprint posters.

Process

I. The facilitator describes the goal of the structured experience, emphasizing that when group members establish agreements about which activities are the group's responsibilities and which are the responsibilities of individual members, they can enhance not only the effectiveness of their group but also their individual security and motivation as members of that group.

II. Each participant is assigned a color of 3" x 5" index cards, and one color is reserved for the group; these color assignments are announced and written on newsprint. Each participant is given a set of index cards and a pencil.

III. The facilitator gives instructions as follows:

1. Using the cards of the color assigned to him or her, each participant (1) writes brief descriptions of *six work activities* (one activity description per card) that are his or her *most important* responsibilities and prerogatives; and (2) rank orders the activities, writing the rank of each on its card.

2. Using the cards of the color assigned to another group member, each participant (1) writes brief descriptions of *six work activities* (one activity description per card) that are the *most important* responsibilities and prerogatives of that group member; and (2) rank orders the activities, writing the rank of each on its card. This procedure is completed for every other member of the group.

3. Using the cards of the color assigned to the group, each participant (1) writes brief descriptions of *six work activities* (one activity description per card) that are the *most important* responsibilities and prerogatives of the group as a whole; and (2) rank orders the activities, writing the rank of each on its card.

The facilitator elicits and answers questions about the task and then asks the participants to begin. (Approximately forty minutes.)

IV. After the participants have completed the task, they are instructed to distribute their completed cards to the appropriate group members and to give the cards identifying group activities to the facilitator.

V. The facilitator gives each participant two sheets of newsprint and a felt-tipped marker and then explains the process for reviewing and analyzing the content of the cards:

1. Each participant reviews the cards received and compares them with the ones that he or she wrote.

2. Each participant sorts the cards into stacks that reflect the same basic intent.

3. Each participant summarizes his or her conclusions on two newsprint sheets: one listing *activities and rankings* about which there is widespread agreement and the other listing *activities and rankings* about which there is not widespread agreement. On the latter sheet, the participant writes "S" (for "self") beside activities that he or she identified and others did

not and writes "O" (for "others") beside activities that others identified and he or she did not; discrepancies in rankings are similarly identified. (Thirty minutes.)

VI. The members are instructed to take turns posting their newsprint sheets and sharing their conclusions with the group. The facilitator explains that the purpose of each presentation and the ensuing discussion is to try to reach agreement on each participant's six most important activities and their rankings. The members are told that each presentation should follow this pattern:

1. The participant summarizes activities and rankings on which he or she and fellow group members generally agreed and then asks the group members if they concur with this analysis. If there is disagreement, the facilitator assists in a discussion intended to help the group to move toward clarity and agreement regarding activities and their rankings. If the group members are unable to reach clarity and/or agreement, the activities and rankings under dispute are listed on a separate sheet of newsprint.

2. The participant summarizes activities and rankings on which he or she and fellow group members disagreed. Again, the facilitator assists in a discussion intended to move the group toward clarity and agreement. Where disagreements persist, the activities and rankings in question are added to the separate sheet of newsprint, which is then set aside.

After all participants have taken a turn, the group is asked whether it might be useful to set up another time to meet and address the activities and rankings that require further clarification and/or agreement. If the participants want a follow-up session, the details of that session are determined, including the process to be followed. The separate sheets of newsprint listing activities and rankings in dispute are given to one of the group members to retain or transcribe into handout form for use at the follow-up session. (Approximately fifteen minutes per participant.)

VII. The participants are asked to be seated around one of the tables. The facilitator gives them the group cards, and they separate the cards into two stacks: (1) activities and rankings representing general agreement, either according to the cards or as a result of discussion, and (2) activities and rankings that represent disagreement. The two sets of activities are listed on separate newsprint sheets and are posted. The facilitator leads a discussion about the activities and rankings that represent disagreement, helping the group members to move toward clarity and agreement regarding the group's six most important activities and their rankings. If disagreement persists, the facilitator encourages the participants to set up another follow-up session and to determine a process to follow during that session. The newsprint list of activities and rankings in dispute is given to one of the participants to keep or transcribe for use at the follow-up session. (Forty-five minutes.)

VIII. The facilitator leads a concluding discussion based on questions such as the following:

1. How are you feeling about your group at this moment? How do you feel about being a member of this group?

2. In what ways has this experience been helpful to you and to the group as a whole? What have you learned? What surprised you?

3. When are activities best completed by the group? When are they best completed by individual members?

4. In your day-to-day work with your group, how will you use what you have learned as a result of this experience?

Variations

I. If this structured experience is being conducted as a result of prior diagnosis and team-member agreement regarding the need to distinguish team activities from individual-member activities, in Step I the facilitator should review information about the diagnosis and agreement.

II. The facilitator may request in advance that the group members bring with them to the activity any existing documentation that could be useful, such as written job descriptions.

III. If extra time is available, the individual and group activities and rankings that remain in dispute may be addressed in the same session.

IV. This structured experience may be used to identify the kinds of decisions that should be made by individual members or by the group.

Submitted by Mike M. Milstein.

Mike M. Milstein, Ph.D., *is a professor of educational administration at the University of New Mexico in Albuquerque. He has been an organization development consultant for educational and business organizations for twenty years. His current research and consultation efforts focus on employee "plateauing" and restructuring of educational organizations.*

501. PEOPLE ARE ELECTRIC: UNDERSTANDING HEURISTICS IN THE CREATIVE PROCESS

Goals

I. To encourage the participants to think creatively.

II. To help the participants to discover heuristics in their thinking patterns.

III. To assist the participants in recognizing their own selective perception patterns.

IV. To improve team effectiveness by uncovering judgmental thinking and biases.

Group Size

Three to six groups of five members each.

Time Required

One hour and fifteen minutes to one and one-half hours.

Materials

I. A copy of the People Are Electric Scenario Sheet for each participant.

II. A pen or pencil and a clipboard or other portable writing surface for each participant.

III. Several sheets of newsprint and a felt-tipped marker for each subgroup.

IV. A newsprint flip chart and a felt-tipped marker for the facilitator.

V. Masking tape for posting newsprint.

Physical Setting

A room large enough for subgroups to work without disturbing one another, with plenty of wall space for posting newsprint. Movable chairs should be provided.

Process

I. The facilitator introduces the goals of the activity and presents an explanation in words similar to the following:

"Team effectiveness is sometimes limited by the judgmental thinking of team members. Especially in ambiguous or uncertain circumstances, people tend to use heuristics (rules of thumb) to make judgments or decisions. Examples of heuristics might be certain opening moves in chess or arriving at this year's budget by adding 10 percent to last year's budget. Essentially heuristics are ways that people simplify thinking and decision making. Problems occur when these heuristics lead to wrong inferences and conclusions. Selective perception, or viewing problems from one's own perspective, is an example of a heuristic that can lead to problems. A person's perspectives and views of life are influenced by education, personality, and life experiences. However, in an uncertain situation, that person tends to make decisions based on his or her own perspective, which may not be apparent to others. This activity is intended to bring out thinking patterns and experiences that influence your decisions."

(Five minutes.)

II. The participants are instructed to form subgroups of five members each and to share information among themselves about their education and work experience. (Ten minutes.)

III. Each subgroup is given several sheets of newsprint, a felt-tipped marker, and masking tape for posting the newsprint. The facilitator distributes copies of the People Are Electric Scenario Sheet, pencils, and clipboards or other portable writing surfaces. Each participant is instructed to read the handout. (Five minutes.)

IV. The facilitator reviews the instructions with the participants and directs the subgroups to begin the activity. (Twenty-five minutes.)

V. After the time has elapsed, the facilitator reconvenes the total group. Each subgroup in turn notes how the group reached consensus, presents its answers to the scenario questions, and posts its newsprint sheets. (Ten to fifteen minutes.)

VI. The facilitator leads a concluding discussion based on questions such as the following:

1. In what ways were your thinking patterns in this activity influenced by the information presented about heuristics? In what ways were your thinking patterns in this activity influenced by previous experiences?

2. How was your subgroup's thinking influenced by education or work experiences?

3. How was the consensus process affected by the subgroup's thinking process?

4. How did you feel about members of your subgroup whose ideas matched yours? What about those whose ideas were different from yours?

5. Have your ideas about the scenario changed as a result of group discussion? How?

6. What have you learned about heuristics and selective perception? What situations can you think of in which the use of heuristics was an obstacle to creativity or effective decision making? How might you apply what you learned in personal or professional situations?

(Twenty minutes.)

Variations

I. When a subgroup member introduces himself or herself, the other members may write down the information that is shared and record any expectations they have about how that person may respond during the activity.

II. Participants may be asked to note selective perception patterns that they observe in themselves and to design actions plans to modify these patterns if they choose.

III. The facilitator may obtain information about the backgrounds of the participants in advance and use that information to structure the subgroups. Half the subgroups may be formed of participants with similar backgrounds and interests and half of those with different backgrounds and interests. The responses of the two types of groups may be compared as part of the concluding discussion.

IV. The activity could be conducted before information on heuristics is presented, with a similar but different activity following. The resulting creativity in the two situations then could be compared.

Submitted by Taggart Smith, Ed.D.

Taggart Smith, Ed.D., is a professor in the School of Technology at Purdue University. Dr. Smith's applied research interests are in first-level management, small-business management, and work patterns in bureaucracies. Her academic credentials include a B.S. from Indiana State, an M.A. from the University of South Florida, and an Ed.D. from Indiana University. Her nearly twenty-five years of teaching experience ranges from media management for public schools to communication skills at Subic Bay Naval Station in the Republic of the Philippines. Prior to becoming a university professor, Dr. Smith also established a law library for a maximum security prison.

PEOPLE ARE ELECTRIC
SCENARIO SHEET

Instructions: Begin by answering the questions on this page individually. Then discuss your answers with the other members of your subgroup. When you reach consensus on your subgroup's answers, write the answers on the sheets of newsprint. Take particular note of how your subgroup's thinking process affects consensus. You will have about twenty minutes for this activity.

What if human beings were electrically powered rather than having their energy supplied through food, water, and rest?

1. How would your personal life be affected?

2. How would your professional life be affected?

3. How would the following systems be changed:
   Employment?

   Education?

   Family?

   Leisure activities?

   Government programs?

   Global affairs?

   Other?

502. THE REAL MEANING: CREATIVE PROBLEM SOLVING

Goals

I. To encourage participants to think creatively.

II. To help participants identify ways to stimulate creativity.

III. To help participants find methods for obtaining creative solutions to problems.

Group Size

Two to twelve subgroups of three participants each. (One or two subgroups can contain four participants.)

Time Required

One and one-half hours to two and one-half hours, depending on the size of the group.

Materials

I. A copy of The Real Meaning Problem Sheet for each participant.

II. A clipboard or other portable writing surface for each participant.

III. A pencil and a blank sheet of paper for each participant.

IV. A newsprint flip chart and a felt-tipped marker for the facilitator.

V. Two sheets of newsprint and a felt-tipped marker for each subgroup.

VI. Masking tape for posting newsprint.

Physical Setting

A room with movable chairs. The room must be large enough to allow small groups to work without disturbing one another.

Process

I. The following is a sufficient explanation for the activity:

"It is often difficult to understand exactly what an author means by a certain phrase, even when we read it within the context of the book or article; and it is even more difficult to determine what an author means when a statement is taken *out* of context. But I am sure you are up to this challenge.

"We are going to have a contest. You will be divided into subgroups that will compete with one another. You will be given a list of statements, and each subgroup will choose four statements and decide on the most likely meaning of each statement. Each subgroup will write its answers on newsprint. The subgroup that has the highest number of points wins."

(Five minutes.)

II. The participants are asked to form subgroups of three members each. If necessary, one or more subgroups of four members may be formed. Each subgroup is instructed to select a spokesperson to report the answers.

III. The facilitator distributes The Real Meaning Problem Sheet and reviews the instructions with the participants. The facilitator explains that "consensus" does not necessarily mean "unanimous agreement," but that—in this case—it means that all members of a subgroup prefer to accept a solution in an attempt to gain points for the subgroup. (Five minutes.)

IV. The portable writing surfaces, pencils, blank paper, newsprint, and felt-tipped markers are distributed to the subgroups.

V. The facilitator tells the participants they will have thirty minutes to work on the activity and that they will be apprised of the time ten minutes and twenty minutes into the process. The facilitator gives them a signal to start and then moves from one subgroup to another to observe the process. The facilitator gives no help during the activity except to clarify the instructions. (Ten minutes.)

VI. The facilitator interrupts the process to tell participants that they have been working ten minutes. The subgroups then continue the process. (Ten minutes.)

VII. The facilitator interrupts the process to tell the participants that they have only ten minutes left to work. The subgroups then continue the process. (Ten minutes.)

VIII. The facilitator calls time and reconvenes the entire group. Each spokesperson is asked to post the newsprint from his or her subgroup and to read the answers. After all answers are read, the facilitator tells the participants that they will have a group discussion before the winners are announced. (Five minutes per subgroup.)

IX. The facilitator explains the goals of the activity and leads a group discussion based on the following questions:

1. What processes did you use in generating the meaning of your first statement? How did they seem to work? How difficult was it to develop a meaning for the statement? What was difficult? What was easy?

2. What different processes did you use with your other statements? Which processes seemed to stimulate discussion and new ideas? Why?

3. In what ways did the competitive element help or hinder you in generating meanings?

4. How can the processes you used help you to find creative alternatives and solutions in your work situations? What can you do to make sure you try these processes in your work situations?

5. How can you encourage one another to continue to work on processes to find creative solutions?

(Twenty to thirty minutes, depending on the size of the group.)

X. Before calculating the scores, the facilitator asks volunteers to comment on meanings that they are especially proud of.

XI. The facilitator assigns points to each subgroup's answers, basing the points solely on whether the answer was a consensus decision (five points), a majority decision (three points), or an individual decision (one point). If a subgroup reached consensus on all four statements that it selected, it will also be given one point for each additional consensus decision it reached on the remaining four statements. The facilitator totals the points for each subgroup and announces the subgroup or subgroups with the highest score. The facilitator leads the applause for the winners. (Five minutes.)

XII. The facilitator then announces that all participants are "winners" in this activity because they discovered creative solutions—and creativity is a prize to treasure and to use the rest of their lives. The facilitator explains that the author wrote the statements specifically for this type of activity in order to inspire people to think creatively; the author had no one interpretation in mind. Therefore each meaning is significant to the subgroup that developed it.

XIII. The facilitator encourages participants to express how they feel about the activity and how they would change it to increase creativity in problem solving. (Fifteen minutes.)

Variations

I. The facilitator can show an actual prize (such as a box of candy) that will be given to the winning subgroup.

II. Participants or subgroups can develop their own statements and give them to another subgroup to generate meanings.

Submitted by Mary Harper Kitzmiller.

Mary Harper Kitzmiller is the managing editor at Pfeiffer & Company, where she is also a member of the organization's strategic planning team. Her previous editorial experience has been in diverse areas, such as college textbooks (Harcourt Brace Jovanovich), early-childhood education (University of Illinois Press), ecology (Oceanic Library), and dairy cattle (U.S. Department of Agriculture). Mary has received awards for excellence in industrial editing and is a member of American Mensa. Formerly she was a fingerprint "expert" for the FBI.

THE REAL MEANING
PROBLEM SHEET

Instructions: The object of this activity is to determine the most likely meaning of four of the eight statements listed below. Your subgroup must decide which four you want to tackle. None of these statements is any easier or harder to decipher than the others are, so choose the ones that look most interesting to you. (Remember, the quicker you make your selections, the more time you will have for the main task.) You will have thirty minutes for this activity. The facilitator will keep you apprised of the time.

Try to reach consensus on your answers and write them down on the newsprint. An acceptable subgroup answer will receive five points. If you cannot reach consensus within a reasonable time, write down your individual answers on the newsprint and mark each with an asterisk. An acceptable individual answer will receive one point for the subgroup. If the majority of members of your subgroup agrees on an answer that is acceptable, your subgroup will receive three points. Mark these answers with two asterisks.

If you reach consensus on meanings of all four statements in less than thirty minutes, work on additional statements for extra credit. Your subgroup can receive one point by reaching consensus on an acceptable answer for any of the remaining statements. Therefore, the highest score possible for this activity is twenty-four (five points each for four answers and one point each for the remaining four answers).

What is the meaning of each of the following statements?

1. All good things go together.

2. There is never space for mirth nor treasure.

3. If time were fixed, we could ascend.

4. The person is the portrait.

5. An introduction is like a house.

6. Was there ever a day when fruit ripened on bare trees?

7. The value of an asset depends on the angle of the moon.

8. The fifth well will quench your thirst.

Pfeiffer & Company

503. STATING THE ISSUE: PRACTICING "OWNERSHIP"

Goals

I. To present participants with a method for describing personal and organizational issues accurately and specifically.

II. To help participants to recognize when and how they may hinder problem solving by disowning responsibility for their part in the issue.

III. To offer participants the opportunity to practice the skills needed for non-defensive, open (self-disclosing), and effective communication.

Group Size

Up to thirty participants.

Time Required

Approximately three hours.

Materials

I. One copy of the Stating the Issue Participant Workbook for each participant.

II. One copy of the Stating the Issue Lessons Learned Work Sheet for each participant.

III. A pencil and a portable writing surface for each participant.

IV. Five newsprint posters prepared in advance:

1. On the first poster: The information contained in Figure 1. Examples of Transforming Stage I to Stage II Statements.

2. On the second poster: The information contained in Figure 2. Examples of Transforming Stage II to Stage III Statements.

3. On the third poster: The information contained in Figure 3. Examples of Transforming Stage III to Stage IV Statements.

4. On the fourth poster: The information contained in Figure 4. Examples of Transforming Stage IV to Stage V Statements.

5. On the fifth poster: The information contained in Figure 5. The Evolution of a Well-Formed Statement of an Issue

V. One copy of the Stating the Issue Theory Sheet for the facilitator's use.

VI. A newsprint flip chart and a felt-tipped marker.

VII. Masking tape for posting newsprint.

Physical Setting

A room large enough so that the subgroups can work without disturbing one another.

Process

I. The facilitator presents the goals of the activity and presents a short lecturette based on the Stating the Issue Theory Sheet. (Ten minutes.)

II. The participants are asked to form subgroups of three or four participants each. One copy of the Stating the Issue Participant Workbook is distributed to each participant. (Five minutes.)

III. The facilitator describes the process for defining an issue in words similar to the following:

"An issue can be a problem that interferes with achieving goals or objectives or something that obstructs or reduces the efficiency and effectiveness of work activities and processes. Alternatively, the issue may be an opportunity to improve conditions by increasing efficiency, productivity, or quality in your own work, the work of your team, or that of your company. Improvement opportunities may also include ways to reduce or contain operational costs.

"Most people describe issues in terms of their most obvious elements: goals or objectives, strategic and operational plans, finances, time lines, technology, structures, procedures, or policies. These tend to be the most obvious and easily acknowledged elements of business and organizational life. Most people are familiar, competent, comfortable, and confident in discussing these elements. Less obvious and less likely to be acknowledged are the cultural, political, and social dynamics that either confound or facilitate achieving effective, innovative solutions.

"Each of you should now select an issue. It should be a significant work relationship issue that either has caused or has perpetuated organizational problems or improvement opportunities. The issue should satisfy the following four criteria:

1. The issue must involve you personally. That is, you and your work or your work relationships must be affected by the problem or opportunity in some way.

2. The issue that you select must involve at least one other person. The other involved party or parties may be colleagues, peers, subordinates, supervisors, managers, suppliers, providers of resources, investors, regulators, customers, or users of your products or services.

3. The issue must be something about which you are personally concerned. It must be a problem or opportunity with which you are dissatisfied.

4. The issue must be something into which you are willing to invest some of your time and energy in an effort to solve the problem or to capitalize on the opportunity to improve conditions.

For example, an issue could be a relationship in which one person frequently misunderstands what another person tries to communicate. An issue also could be a conflict situation in which two or more persons have become adversaries who advocate quite different, competing situational analyses, conclusions, goals, plans, methods, positions, or preferences." (Ten minutes.)

IV. Individually, the participants are instructed to write initial, provisional descriptions of their personal issues on Work Sheet 1. (Five minutes.)

V. The facilitator posts the newsprint poster of Figure 1 and reviews it with the participants. The facilitator presents information to the participants about ways to move from Stage I to Stage II, in words similar to the following:

"What stage does your statement represent? If you have described the issue as something that is wrong or unacceptable, as something taking place 'out there,' as something that affects other people but not you, and as something in which you are not personally involved, then you are in Stage I.

"If your description clearly indicates how you are personally involved in and affected by the issue, then you are probably in Stage II.

"Notice the examples listed on the newsprint. Including yourself in the description makes each statement more personal and more useful for problem-solving and decision-making. In other words, if the issue is out there and only involves others, you have very little control of the situation.

"However, when you place yourself within the situation as a part of the issue, you enable yourself to see and to understand more clearly that you have at least two leverage points: (1) the actions you choose to take; and (2) the interactions you have with others who are involved in and concerned about the issue."
(Ten minutes.)

VI. The facilitator asks participants to compare their initial issue descriptions with the examples of Stage I and Stage II statements in Figure 1. The facilitator invites participants to rewrite their issue descriptions in a Stage II manner using Work Sheet 2. The facilitator invites participants to share their restated issue descriptions with members of their subgroups. Each participant reads his or her restated issue description to the other members of the subgroup. Subgroup members share their reactions to each participant's issue description in terms of "Is this a Stage II statement? If not, how can we make it one?" (Fifteen minutes.)

VII. The facilitator posts the newsprint poster of Figure 2 and reviews it with the participants. The facilitator presents information about moving from Stage II to Stage III in words like the following:

"Now that you have the issue stated in terms of how you are impacted, we will focus on what you think about the issue. How you think about an issue is based in part on how you perceive the situation. What you perceive depends on your personal perceptual filters, preferences, current preoccupations, expectations, opinions, beliefs, values, and attitudes. If some event or condition does not match your expectations, you have several choices of how to perceive it. First, you might choose to ignore it, unconsciously refusing to allow it to pass through your perceptual filter to become part of your conscious awareness. Second, you might choose to distort it to fit your expectations. Your conscious perceptions, therefore, are whatever registers in your conscious mind. You are to state your conscious perceptions now. In other words, what do you think is going on with the issue?"

(Ten minutes.)

VIII. The facilitator asks participants to compare their Work Sheet 2 descriptions with the examples of Stage II and Stage III statements in Figure 2. The facilitator invites participants to rewrite their issue descriptions in a Stage III manner on Work Sheet 3. The facilitator invites participants to share their restated issue descriptions with members of their subgroups. Each participant reads his or her restated issue description to the other members of the subgroup. Subgroup members share their reactions to each participant's issue description and help to rewrite it, asking "Is this a Stage III statement? If not, how can we make it one?" (Fifteen minutes.)

IX. The facilitator posts the newsprint poster of Figure 3 and reviews it with the participants. The facilitator presents information about moving from Stage III to Stage IV in words like the following:

"Compare your revised statement with the examples listed in Figure 3. As instructed at Stage III, you probably described the issue as something about which you had no feelings whatsoever. You probably described the issue as something that was totally objective and emotionally neutral. We do this because, in most organizations, what we think about an issue is accepted and valued far more highly than how we might feel about it. However, feelings are essential elements of effective problem solving and decision making.

"The perceptions and thoughts that you recorded will either support or interfere with satisfying your goals and personal interests. What you perceive may also fulfill or violate your beliefs and values about organizational and business life. If your perception of a situation matches how you believe people should behave in their corporate interactions, or if the situation supports your goals and interests, you are likely to experience positive emotions. However, when there is a mismatch or an apparent threat, you are likely to experience unpleasant, negative feelings.

"You can progress to Stage IV by rewriting your statement to show how you feel about your involvement in the situation."

(Ten minutes.)

X. The facilitator asks participants to compare their Work Sheet 3 descriptions with the examples of Stage III and Stage IV statements in Figure 3. The facilitator invites participants to rewrite their issue descriptions in a Stage IV manner on Work Sheet 4. The facilitator invites participants to share their restated issue descriptions with members of their subgroups. Each participant reads his or her restated issue description to the other members of the subgroup. Subgroup members share their reactions to each participant's issue description by asking "Is this a Stage IV statement? If not, how can we make it one?" (Fifteen minutes.)

XI. The facilitator posts the newsprint poster of Figure 4 and reviews it with the participants. The facilitator presents information about moving from Stage IV to Stage V in words like the following:

"Stage V is a critical stage in understanding and coping with most interpersonal, group, and intergroup issues. Stage V is achieved when each person involved recognizes and accepts his or her own personal contribution to the issue. That is, when each party accepts personal ownership of the ways in which his or her behaviors may have added to the problem or detracted from discovering some effective means for dealing with the issue.

"Look over your last revision (Stage IV) of your statement of the issue. Ask yourself now how you can fully explore and write down your personal contributions to the cause or perpetuation of the situation. Are there things that you do, intentionally or not, that seem to add to the difficulties? Are there things that you could but refrain from doing that could help your organization to deal with the opportunities or the difficulties?

"When your statement describes how your behavior has helped to create or how you personally may be perpetuating the issue, you have reached the point at which you are capable of describing issues at a Stage V level."

(Ten minutes.)

XII. The facilitator asks participants to compare their Work Sheet 4 descriptions with the examples of Stage IV and Stage V statements and invites them to rewrite their issue descriptions in a Stage V manner on Work Sheet 5. (Five minutes.)

XIII. The facilitator invites participants to share their restated (Stage V) issue descriptions with members of their subgroups. Before allowing them to begin, the facilitator offers the following guidelines:

"Before you return to work with your subgroup, I want to offer one caution. Many subgroup members change the topic and detour their subgroups at this point because they move beyond stating the issue to offering solutions to it. Most often members do this because they are accustomed to functioning as problem-solvers. This happens particularly with people who have been rewarded for being effective as organizational problem-solvers; for such people, the issues being discussed may represent an irresistible invitation to do what they do so well. Although it is important to move into problem solving, remember that we are here first to learn how to state the issue in order to make problem solving easier and more efficient. At other times members of a subgroup will collude with each other and change the topic in order to shift the focus of attention away from an issue that is believed to be too difficult, sensitive, or embarrassing.

"To derive the greatest benefit from this activity, it is important to keep the subgroup on track. You can help your subgroup and its members by describing the observable behaviors that you think indicate that people are digressing or topic jumping. You may choose to select one member to perform the function of challenging the relevance of discussions that seem to be moving in the direction of problem solving."

(Ten minutes.)

XIV. Each participant reads his or her restated issue description to the other members of the subgroup. Subgroup members share their reactions to each participant's issue description and ask "Is this a Stage V statement? If not, how can we make it one?" During this time, the facilitator should circulate and remind participants, where necessary, to focus on simply describing the issue. (Ten minutes.)

XV. The facilitator posts the newsprint poster of Figure 5 and presents summary material in words similar to the following:

"To summarize, a well-formed statement of an issue has several components (Figure 5). It is stated in terms of what I think is taking place right here in the present situation and right now at this time among all parties involved. It is as objective a description as possible of the transactions and interactions that are taking place. In addition, a well-formed statement includes my assessment of the impact of my behaviors and those of others on the current situation. Further, a well-formed statement includes a description of what I feel about all the involved parties and our behaviors, both positive and negative. Finally, a well-formed statement includes a description of what I actually do in response to my perceptions, my assessments, and my feelings.

"At this point, you are probably beginning to see and understand your issue in a new way. As a result, you may become aware that you have some feelings about yourself and how you have been dealing with the issue and the situation. You may discover that once you have taken enough time to fully discuss an issue, you can be more relaxed and open to considering new ways of understanding or looking at the situation. With this new perspective, you may find that you and your colleagues are more likely to create new, effective ways to deal with difficult issues."

(Ten minutes.)

XVI. The facilitator distributes copies of the Stating the Issue Lessons Learned Work Sheet and instructs the participants, individually, to finish the sentences in writing. The participants then are instructed to share and to discuss their responses with the other members of their subgroups. (Ten minutes.)

XVII. The facilitator reconvenes the entire group and invites participants to share information and observations from the Stating the Issue Lessons Learned Work Sheet. (Ten minutes.)

XVIII. The facilitator leads a concluding discussion based on questions such as the following:

1. Which stage is most like your normal pattern of communicating? Which stage is least like your normal pattern? How do you feel about this discovery?

2. What have you learned about stating an issue responsibly? What implications do these learnings have for your problem-solving communication skills? What might you do differently in the future?

3. How can you use these skills in back-home or back-on-the-job situations?

(Fifteen minutes.)

Variations

I. The facilitator may choose to add a Stage VI to the process, in which participants and the other members of their subgroups explore what they can do to improve the situations.

II. The facilitator instructions can be added to the workbook and used as prework. Participants then would come together to review their Stage V descriptions.

Submitted by Arthur M. Freedman, Ph.D.

Arthur M. Freedman, Ph.D., *is a former clinician who now functions exclusively as an independent Organization Development (OD) and Human Resource Management (HRM) consultant. He works with organizations in the United States, Sweden, and the former Soviet Union. As a long-term member of the National Training Laboratories (NTL) Institute, he has conducted public workshops and has been a frequent presenter at such conferences as the World OD Congress, Society of Psychologists in Management, the OD Network, and the Association for Quality and Productivity. He has served as a Visiting or Adjunct Faculty Professor at graduate institutions such as the American University/NTL Masters Program in Human Resource Development, the Institute for Organizational Dynamics at George Williams College and Aurora University, and the Stockholm School of Economics.*

STATING THE ISSUE
THEORY SHEET

Traditional solutions are effective with well-known, repetitive problems. However, modern society requires people to be problem-solving pioneers who address more and more one-of-a-kind "issues" in life. This demands an inquisitive attitude, realistic expectations, and flexible problem-solving approaches that can be adapted to a variety of problems and improvement opportunities.

Organizational change usually results from designing and installing "solutions" in response to challenging problems. Alternatively, change may also result from attempts to capitalize on opportunities to improve current conditions. However, a solution or an opportunity for one person or organizational group often becomes a problem for other involved parties.

Effective problem-solving is a process for creating practical solutions that are mutually understood, accepted, and satisfying to all involved parties. When enacted, practical solutions must result in desirable, observable consequences that satisfy the demands of the original issue as well as being acceptable to the parties involved.

The first phase of effective problem-solving is to state the issue. The goal is for all involved parties to understand the issue in the same way. People must progress through five specific stages in order for an issue to be stated in a high quality, well-formed style. These stages, which will be explained as the activity progresses, are not always recognized by those who use them or by those who are affected by them. With practice, some people can skip the early stages and state issues directly in Stage IV or Stage V terms. Other people tend not to see or understand the practicality of working beyond Stage I.

Those who become proficient in consistently working at Stage V contribute to the creation of useful ways of studying and responding to both personal and organizational issues. Working at Stage V brings issues into a focus that makes efficient and effective use of scarce problem-solving resources.

You will be invited to follow a series of instructions in order to complete the Stating the Issue process. To derive the greatest value from this exercise, follow these instructions and express your thoughts and feelings honestly and openly.

Although this skill-development exercise can be done alone, you will derive greater benefits by working with others in a small group. You do not need to have a great deal in common with these subgroup members. Remember that they are—or will be—confronted with similar problems and opportunities and will participate in this exercise for reasons like yours.

There are two elements of this skill-development exercise:

1. First you will be asked to work individually and with the other members of your subgroup on each of the five stages of Stating the Issue, in sequence. Subgroup members will provide and receive assistance from other members at each stage.

2. When your subgroup has completed all five stages of the Stating the Issue process, you will be invited to share your reactions to the entire Stating the Issue process with the members of the other subgroups. It will be up to you to determine how much of your work you are willing to share with others.

Instructions: Write down a draft statement that describes the issue as you currently understand it. Use Work Sheet 1, provided below. Write quickly, putting your thoughts down on paper just as they come to you. Put everything on paper first—you will have plenty of time to review and revise what you have written later. At this stage, the organization of your thoughts, coherence, grammar, and spelling are unimportant.

Statement of the Issue: Initial Version.

Work Sheet 1. Issues Work Sheet for Initial Statement

STOP HERE. DO NOT TURN THE PAGE UNTIL YOU ARE INSTRUCTED TO DO SO.

Stage I: "What is going on is..."	Stage II: "The impact that this has on me is..."
Supervisors do not let their subordinates try new ideas. Their philosophy is "Don't fix it if it isn't broken."	My supervisor does not let me or my people try any new ideas if it means breaking with our company's traditional work practices.
Governmental regulators expect the companies to instantly comply with all of their new regulations and guidelines.	Government regulators expect me to get my people to comply, instantly, to all of their new, constantly changing regulations.
Supervisors never listen to their subordinates' concerns or suggestions.	My supervisor does not ask me for my input when she has to make a decision. She also does not take my concerns or suggestions seriously.
People only hang around with others of their own race. Other kinds of people cannot break into their cliques so they never know what concerns they discuss.	People of different races with whom I work do not invite me into their conversations. They seem to avoid me except when we work together directly.
The consultant is too "academic" and uses too much technical jargon. Nobody understands what he's talking about.	Sometimes I don't understand the consultant's complex way of expressing concepts that are new to me. He often uses terms that I do not understand.

Figure 1. Examples of Transforming Stage I to Stage II Statements

Use Work Sheet 2 below to make your first revision of your initial statement.

Statement of the Issue: Revision #1.

Work Sheet 2. Issues Work Sheet for Stage II Statement

STOP HERE. DO NOT TURN THE PAGE UNTIL YOU ARE INSTRUCTED TO DO SO.

Stage II: "The impact that this has on me is..."	Stage III: "What I think is..."
My supervisor does not let me or my people try any new ideas if it means breaking with our company's traditional work practices.	I think my boss is much too conservative. I see many opportunities to reduce costs and improve quality in our work. I believe in "improving things before they break."
Government regulators expect me to get my people to comply, instantly, to all of their new, constantly changing regulations.	I think the regulators expect too much from those of us whose work has to be changed because of their unrealistic standards and demands.
My supervisor does not ask me for my input when she has to make a decision. She also does not take my concerns or suggestions seriously.	I think my input would help my supervisor and her management team to make better, more informed decisions. I also think I have legitimate concerns and useful suggestions.
People of different races with whom I work do not invite me into their conversations. They seem to avoid me except when we work together directly.	I think all of us can learn a lot from one other. It is unnecessary and wasteful to put up barriers between us.
Sometimes I don't understand the consultant's complex way of expressing concepts that are new to me. He often uses terms that I do not understand.	I think it is up to the consultant to find a way to make himself understood to the average employee. We should not have to learn his jargon; he should learn and use ours!

Figure 2. Examples of Transforming Stage II to Stage III Statements

Use Work Sheet 3 below to make your second revision of your issues statement.

Statement of the Issue: Revision #2.

Work Sheet 3. Issues Work Sheet for Stage III Statement

STOP HERE. DO NOT TURN THE PAGE UNTIL YOU ARE INSTRUCTED TO DO SO.

Pfeiffer & Company

Stage III: "What I think is..."	Stage IV: "How I feel is..."
I think my boss is much too conservative. I see many opportunities to reduce costs and improve quality in our work. I believe in "improving things before they break."	I feel disappointed and frustrated with my boss because his limits deny me the opportunity to demonstrate the innovative contributions I can make to this company.
I think the regulators expect too much from those of us whose work has to be changed because of their unrealistic standards and demands. They don't trust us to do things right.	I feel unappreciated and misunderstood by the regulators. I feel angry that they can impose their demands arbitrarily. I am angry with myself because I have no hope of influencing them. I feel helpless.
I think my input would help my supervisor and her management team to make better, more informed decisions. I also think I have legitimate concerns and useful suggestions.	I feel like my supervisor thinks I'm criticizing her. I'm really trying to improve conditions of work around here. I feel misunderstood and frightened that she will make trouble for me.
I think all of us can learn a lot from each other. It is unnecessary and wasteful to put up barriers between us.	I like many of these people and I want them to like me. When I feel excluded and ignored, I feel rejected, insecure, and threatened.
I think it is up to the consultant to find a way to make himself understood to the average employee. We should not have to learn his jargon; he should learn and use ours!	I feel a lot of self-doubt. I'm afraid my boss, colleagues, and subordinates think I should understand the jargon. I don't and I'm afraid to admit it. I feel inadequate and angry with myself and with my consultant.

Figure 3. Examples of Transforming Stage III to Stage IV Statements

Use Work Sheet 4 to make your third revision of your issues statement.

Statement of the Issue: Revision #3.

Work Sheet 4. Issues Work Sheet for Stage IV Statement

STOP HERE. DO NOT TURN THE PAGE UNTIL YOU ARE INSTRUCTED TO DO SO.

Stage IV: "How I feel is..."	Stage V: "And, so, I act..."
I feel disappointed and frustrated with my boss because his limits deny me the opportunity to demonstrate the innovative contributions I can make to this company.	Because I can't seem to get anywhere with my boss, I gripe about his arbitrary, shortsighted, and unproductive limits to anyone who will listen.
I feel unappreciated and misunderstood by the regulators. I feel angry that they can impose their demands arbitrarily. I am angry with myself because I have no hope of influencing them. I feel helpless.	When I have to talk with regulators, I try to act extremely professional. I overuse my technical jargon, hoping they will feel intimidated. I guess I sound pompous, like I'm talking down to them.
I feel like my supervisor thinks I'm criticizing her. I'm really trying to improve conditions of work around here. I feel misunderstood and afraid that she will make trouble for me.	I figure that as long as she is making my life miserable, I might as well give her some reason for thinking that I'm trying to undermine her authority. Knowing how little it takes for her to lose her self-control, I bait her.
I like many of these people and I want them to like me. When I feel excluded and ignored, I feel rejected, insecure, and threatened.	I avoid them and shut them out of my social activities. I also find myself not disagreeing with associates of my race when they express bigoted opinions about these other people.
I feel a lot of self-doubt. I'm afraid my boss, colleagues, and subordinates think I should understand the jargon. I don't and I'm afraid to admit it. I feel inadequate and angry with myself and with my consultant.	I avoid discussing this issue. Instead I criticize my consultant when I talk with my colleagues and my boss. I complain about his "smug superiority" and how he acts like he thinks he's too good for us.

Figure 4. Examples of Transforming Stage IV to Stage V Statements

If you wish, you may use Work Sheet 5 to make a final revision of your statement. Please include all elaborations and clarifications.

Statement of the Issue: Revision #4.

Work Sheet 5. Issues Work Sheet for Stage V Statement

Pfeiffer & Company

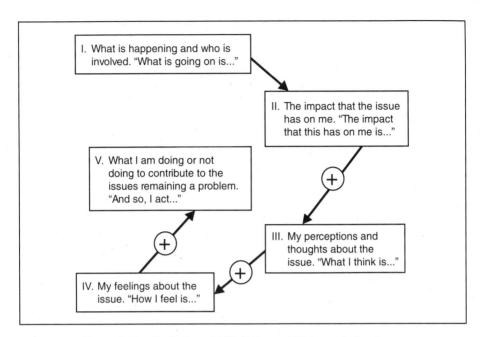

Figure 5. The Evolution of a Well-Formed Statement of an Issue

STATING THE ISSUE
LESSONS LEARNED WORK SHEET

Instructions: First complete each of the following statements on your own. When everyone in your subgroup has finished, discuss the results, one statement at a time.

1. My ideas and feelings about the role that I generally play in dealing with problems or opportunities to improve conditions at work are...

2. In the future, there are a few things that I intend to do differently when dealing with organizational issues so that I can become more effective and contribute to producing higher quality, more gratifying work results. That is, I am willing to:

   a. Stop doing.../Do less...

   b. Start doing.../Do more...

   c. Continue to do...

504. ORGANIZATIONAL STRUCTURES: A SIMULATION

Goals

I. To assist participants in their efforts to understand the relationships between organizational structure, problem-solving performance, and organizational climate.

II. To provide participants with an opportunity to experience and explore these relationships in a simulated environment.

III. To encourage participants to examine the structures that prevail in their own work environments.

Group Size

At least two groups of eight members each. (The activity can be conducted with seven in a group, but it is preferable to have eight.)

Time Required

Approximately two hours to two hours and fifteen minutes.

Materials

I. One set of index cards for each group, one card per member. [If there are more than seven members in the group other than the observer(s), repeat the information on one or more of the cards.] The information displayed on each card is as follows.

Card 1:
(a) The problem you have to solve is to figure out the total cost of Project X.
(b) Is Maslow's theory applicable here?
(c) Try to reach consensus
(d) $e = mc^2$

Card 2:
(a) $S = m$
(b) The fixed cost is 50 (Project X)
(c) $TC = F + n \times V$
(d) a = number of units produced in Project B

Card 3:
(a) Deadline for Project B is tomorrow
(b) F = Fixed cost
(c) Total cost of Project A = PA
(d) b = 184

Card 4:
(a) Use the PC
(b) We have tried that before!
(c) The correct oil is SAE 40
(d) $NaCL + H_2O$?

Card 5:
(a) n = Number of parts
(b) PA = a + bx - 12
(c) The company has a good EEO policy
(d) The variable cost per part is 0.2 (Project X)

Card 6:
(a) The machine uses roller bearings
(b) E = 12
(c) The total cost of Project X = TC
(d) M

Card 7:
(a) $X = M^{-2} \log y$
(b) You need to produce 1000 parts for Project X (i.e., n = 1000)
(c) V = Variable cost per part
(d) E + M = L

II. Copies of the Organizational Structures Mechanistic Task Sheet for half of the groups (one copy per member) and one for each observer.

III. Copies of the Organizational Structures Organic Task Sheet for the other half of the groups (one copy per member) and one for each observer.

IV. One copy of the Organizational Structures Background Sheet for each participant.

V. An Organizational Structures Observer Sheet for each observer.

VI. Blank paper and a pencil for each participant.

VII. A clipboard or other portable writing surface for each participant.

VIII. A newsprint flip chart and felt-tipped markers.

Physical Setting

A room that is large enough so that all groups can work without distracting one another or several smaller rooms. A chair should be provided for each participant.

Process

I. Participants are formed into groups of eight members each. One person in each group is selected to serve as the leader, and one person in each group is selected to serve as the observer. Any additional participants also can be assigned to groups as observers. (Five minutes.)

II. To half of the groups, the facilitator gives copies of the Organizational Structures: Mechanistic Task Sheet (one copy for each member, including observers). To the other half of the groups, the facilitator gives copies of the Organizational Structures: Organic Task Sheet (one copy for each member, including observers). Each observer also receives a copy of the Organizational Structures Observer Sheet. The facilitator tells the participants to read their task sheets and to arrange themselves as directed. (Five minutes.)

III. After the group members have occupied their respective positions, the facilitator allots a set of seven cards to each group, distributing the cards randomly among the group members. The members are instructed not to exchange cards or to discuss their content. [Note to facilitator: Some of the information on the cards is relevant (R) and some is irrelevant (I), as follows: Card 1: a-R, b-I, c-I, d-I; Card 2: a-I, b-R, c-R, d-I; Card 3: a-I, b-R, c-I, d-I; Card 4: a-I, b-I, c-I, d-I; Card 5: a-R, b-I, c-I, d-R; Card 6: a-I, b-I, c-R, d-I; Card 7: a-I, b-R, c-R, d-I. The pieces of information distributed across the six "relevant" cards together allow the correct solution to be determined.] (Five minutes.)

IV. The facilitator introduces the activity by announcing that the groups will be in competition with one another in an attempt to solve the problem that is contained in the set of cards. The winner will be the group that produces the correct solution first. Each group is to work according to its task instructions. No further clues are provided. (Five minutes.)

V. The groups work separately on the problem. The facilitator checks any proposed solutions and records on a newsprint flip chart the time taken by each group to produce the correct answer. If a group arrives at the correct solution before time is called, its members are instructed to discuss among themselves the reasons that they finished the task satisfactorily. The simulation is terminated after forty-five minutes. (Forty-five minutes.)

VI. The total group is reassembled (with the members of each work group seated together) for a debriefing session. The facilitator posts the solution to the problem on a newsprint flip chart. The solution is as follows:

Total Cost of Project X = TC	(extracted from cards 1 and 6)
TC = F + n x V	(extracted from card 2)
F = Fixed Cost = 50	(extracted from cards 2 and 3)
n = Number of Parts = 1000	(extracted from cards 5 and 7)
V = Variable Cost per Part = 0.2	(extracted from cards 7 and 5)

Therefore:

Total Cost of Project X = 50 + 1000 x 0.2 = 250

(Five minutes.)

VII. The facilitator leads the following discussion:

1. Which members felt satisfaction with the experience? What was it about the roles or tasks that contributed to that? How did that affect the organizational climate?

2. Which members felt dissatisfied? What was it about the roles or tasks that contributed to that? How did that affect the organizational climate?

3. How did members learn (a) what the problem was, (b) who had relevant and useful information, and (c) who was most capable of solving this type of (algebraic) problem? Did this latter recognition affect the leadership role? If so, how?

4. Did member(s) who held the card that contained the problem statement recognize the key to potential success? If not, why not? [Typically, the person either did not expect it or was awaiting instructions from the leader.]

(Fifteen minutes.)

VIII. The facilitator distributes a copy of the Organizational Structures Background Sheet to each participant. The facilitator explains the information on the sheet. An important part of the debriefing at this point is to reassure the participants, particularly those who played the role of leaders, that their performance was not a function of their ability but, rather, of the structures they had to work under. (Ten minutes.)

IX. Observers are asked to report their findings, particularly in relation to differences they observed in the behaviors of the various groups. (Ten minutes.)

X. The facilitator leads a discussion of the recorded outcomes of the simulation. Participants are asked to discuss the following items and their responses are recorded on a newsprint flip chart:

1. Reasons that the organic structure(s) performed more successfully.

2. Under what conditions the different types of structures are effective or ineffective.

(Ten minutes.)

XI. The facilitator then informs the participants that the simulation has been used with numerous participants in organizational training programs. The performance of groups working in an organic structure on uncertain problem situations was vastly superior to that of groups working within the constraints of a mechanistic structure. This superiority is evident in terms of both the rate of success and the time taken to arrive at the correct solution. The results also suggest that oral communication is more effective than written irrespective of the type of structure utilized, but that changing a mechanistic structure to an organic one while maintaining only written communication is more conducive to success than trying to achieve the same end by allowing members of the mechanistic structure to communicate orally. In other words, a suitable structure appears to be more critical to success than the communication mode under conditions of uncertainty. These findings are compatible with those obtained in classical studies of communication networks (for example, Leavitt, 1951; Shaw & Rothschild, 1956). However, they go beyond these contributions inasmuch as they also account for the concept of uncertainty. (Five minutes.)

XII. The participants are asked to form small discussion groups of four to five members each. Utilizing the experience as a "trigger," participants are encouraged to offer examples from their own work environments that demonstrate dynamics similar to those observed in the simulation and to develop possible solutions or recommendations for improvement. (Fifteen minutes.)

Variations

I. In addition to the groups, individual participants can be given complete sets of cards and allowed to complete the task in competition with the groups. Such participants will sit outside the groups. Individuals will process the experience along with the group members. In the processing discussion, it can be pointed out that, typically, individuals working on their own are even more successful than the organic/oral communication group in terms of the average time taken to solve the problem—probably because they have all the information they need and do not have to rely on others for information exchange—but they tend to have a lower success rate, probably because incorrect assumptions cannot be checked by others.

II. Compromise structures (for instance, a basically mechanistic structure within which members are allowed to talk with one another or an essentially organic structure in which members have to communicate in writing) also can be utilized. This approach is most useful with a large number of participants.

III. Steps X, XI, and XII can be replaced with a total-group discussion of back-home applications.

References

Leavitt, H.J. (1951). Some effects of certain communication patterns on group performance. *Journal of Abnormal and Social Psychology, 46*, pp. 38-50.

Shaw, M.E., & Rothschild, G.H. (1956). Some effects of prolonged experience in communication nets. *Journal of Applied Psychology, 40*, pp. 281-286.

Submitted by Rudi E. Weber, Ph.D.

Rudi E. Weber, Ph.D., *is an associate professor of management in the School of Business and Public Administration at Charles Sturt University—Mitchell in Bathurst, New South Wales, Australia. He lectures in the fields of general management, human resource development, and organizational theory and behavior. He also consults with a variety of organizations in the areas of management development, organizational change, creativity and innovation, and strategy. His research is centered on small group behavior, problem solving and decision making, and occupational stress; and he has a strong interest in experiential and action learning.*

ORGANIZATIONAL STRUCTURES
MECHANISTIC TASK SHEET

Instructions: Quickly pick a leader for your group. Arrange yourselves in the following configuration:

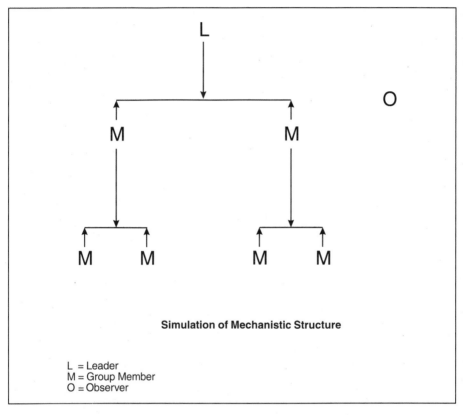

Simulation of Mechanistic Structure

L = Leader
M = Group Member
O = Observer

During this activity, your group is to function in a strictly hierarchical and bureaucratic fashion. That is, you are allowed to communicate only through the formal channels shown on your organizational chart and only in writing. You are not allowed to talk. You are not allowed to bypass anyone in the system.

Let the facilitator know when you have found the solution to the problem.

ORGANIZATIONAL STRUCTURES
ORGANIC TASK SHEET

Instructions: Quickly pick a leader for your group. Arrange yourselves in the following configuration:

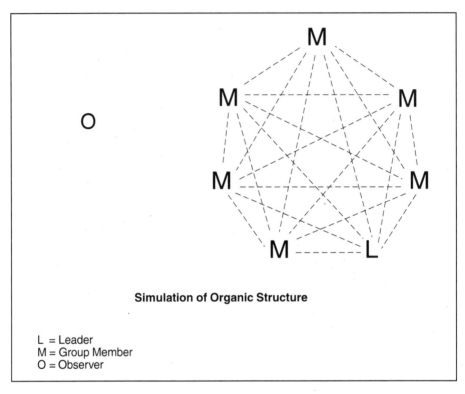

Simulation of Organic Structure

L = Leader
M = Group Member
O = Observer

During this activity, you are allowed to communicate within your group in any way you like, that is, with anyone and in any form (oral or written) that you wish to use. (The dashed lines above show possible patterns of communication.)

Let the facilitator know when you have found the solution to the problem.

ORGANIZATIONAL STRUCTURES
OBSERVER SHEET

During this activity, you are encouraged to move about and observe the various groups, in order to allow yourself to become aware of major characteristics of and differences in the groups' working patterns.

Make notes about the primary characteristics of the various groups' working patterns in the following space:

Try to answer the following questions:

1. What happened to the leaders in the mechanistic group(s)?

2. What happened to communication in the mechanistic group(s)?

3. What happened to the participants situated at the lower levels of the mechanistic group(s)?

4. Did the leader of the mechanistic group(s) ask for all of the information to be transmitted to him/her and then proceed to solve the problem singlehandedly or did he/she delegate?

5. Did the members of the organic group(s) engage in a multi-directional exchange of information? Did the members share their perceptions, test their ideas, and either verify or correct their assumptions and solutions?

6. What happened to the role of leader in the organic group(s)?

ORGANIZATIONAL STRUCTURES
BACKGROUND SHEET

In order to ensure success, organizations need to be structured to be prepared for environmental contingencies. Burns and Stalker (1961) suggest that mechanistic structures work best under stable environmental conditions and that organic structures are needed in times of rapid change (for the characteristics of both types of structure, see Table 1). More generally, Kanter (1983) shows that organizations operating in our changing environment need to maintain "structural flexibility."

Students of organizational behavior frequently find it difficult to understand these principles at a theoretical level. Other people are overwhelmed by the complexity of real-world organizational processes and their relationship to change. The purpose of the activity is to reduce this complexity to a simple, concrete experience—to a context and task situation that participants are familiar with and can relate to in a meaningful way.

Table 1. The Characteristics of Organic and Mechanistic Structures

Organic	Focus	Mechanistic (Bureaucratic)
Decentralized	HIERARCHY OF AUTHORITY	Centralized
Few	RULES AND PROCEDURES	Many
Ambiguous	DIVISION OF LABOR	Precise
Wide	SPAN OF CONTROL	Narrow
Informal and Personal	COORDINATION	Formal and Impersonal

The Effect of Structure on Problem Identification and Problem Solving

The type of the problem in this simulation frequently is observed in situations that arise in uncertain (that is, rapidly changing) organizational environments:

1. It is unique (it has never occurred before in its present form), undefined, and unexpected. Hence, the organization may not possess—or may not even be aware of—what expertise, experience, resources, structure, or procedures are needed to deal with the problem.

2. It may be recognized as a problem (or impact the organization) at any level—frequently at lower levels—or in any functional area. That is, top management—or management in general—might be unaware of its presence or may fail to interpret it as a problem.

3. Although some members of the organization may have certain skills, bits of information, or experiences that are useful in the definition or

solution of the problem, others may have no resources that could be employed in the problem-solving effort. Additionally, the types of personal resources required may be unknown to both employees and management.

The implications of such a problem situation are that:

1. Organizational members other than management may need to initiate appropriate action if the problem is to be solved; and

2. Members need to be able to communicate freely (without being hampered by undue structural barriers) to allow them to recognize that there is a problem; define it; discover who has the resources needed to solve it; and combine their skills, knowledge, and experience in an effort to generate a solution.

It clearly can be seen that an organic structure will facilitate this process while a mechanistic structure will interfere with it.

References

Burns, T., & Stalker, G.M. (1961). *The management of innovation*. London: Tavistock.

Kanter, R.M. (1983). *The change masters*. New York: Simon & Schuster.

505. THE HUNDREDTH MONKEY: SHARED MIND-SETS[1]

Goals

I. To introduce participants to the concept of shared mind-set.

II. To offer participants the opportunity to explore four types of shared mind-set.

III. To offer participants the opportunity to explore options for promoting a shared organizational mind-set.

Group Size

Twelve to twenty participants.

Time Required

Approximately two hours.

Materials

I. A copy of The Hundredth Monkey Story for each participant.

II. A copy of The Hundredth Monkey Figure 1 (from The Hundredth Monkey Theory Sheet), prepared in advance on newsprint.

III. A pencil and a portable writing surface for each participant.

IV. A copy of The Hundredth Monkey Work Sheet 1 for each member of the first subgroup.

V. A copy of The Hundredth Monkey Work Sheet 2 for each member of the second subgroup.

VI. A copy of The Hundredth Monkey Work Sheet 3 for each member of the third subgroup.

VII. A copy of The Hundredth Monkey Work Sheet 4 for each member of the fourth subgroup.

VIII. A newsprint flip chart and several felt-tipped markers.

IX. Masking tape for posting newsprint.

---

[1] The idea of shared mind-set is based on *Organizational Capability: Competing from the Inside Out*, by Dave Ulrich and Dale Lake, copyright © 1990 by John Wiley & Sons, Inc. Used with permission of John Wiley & Sons, Inc. *Organizational Capability* is available from Pfeiffer & Company, 8517 Production Avenue, San Diego, California 92121. (619) 578-5900.

X. A copy of The Hundredth Monkey Theory Sheet for the facilitator.

Physical Setting

A room with adequate space for the subgroups to work without disturbing one another.

Process

I. The facilitator presents the goals of the activity and asks the following question: "Do you like baseball?" The participants who respond "yes" are asked to form a group at one end of the room and those who respond "no" are asked to form a group at the opposite end of the room. *Note to facilitator: If more than twelve people choose the same subgroup, split that subgroup into two subgroups.* (Five minutes).

II. The facilitator distributes blank newsprint, felt-tipped markers, and masking tape to each subgroup. Both subgroups are given the following instructions: "Discuss the images—the thoughts, feelings, and especially the actions—that come to your mind when you think about baseball. List key phrases on the newsprint, and choose a representative to present your descriptions to the total group." (Ten minutes.)

III. The facilitator reconvenes the total group. Each representative in turn presents the conclusions of his or her subgroup. (Five to ten minutes).

IV. The facilitator leads a discussion of the similarities and the differences in the two descriptions. The facilitator asks the participants to think of something else that they love or hate and to imagine how someone else might see it differently. Volunteers are encouraged to make brief comments about the subjects they chose. (Twenty minutes.)

V. The facilitator then distributes copies of The Hundredth Monkey Story and instructs the participants to read the story. (Five minutes).

VI. The facilitator posts the newsprint copy of Figure 1 and presents a lecturette based on The Hundredth Monkey Theory Sheet. (Ten minutes).

VII. The participants are asked to form four subgroups of approximately equal size. Subgroup 1 is given a copy of The Hundredth Monkey Work Sheet 1; Subgroup 2 is given a copy of The Hundredth Monkey Work Sheet 2; Subgroup 3 is given a copy of The Hundredth Monkey Work Sheet 3; and Subgroup 4 is given a copy of The Hundredth Monkey Work Sheet 4. The facilitator distributes blank newsprint, felt-tipped markers, and masking tape to each subgroup. The subgroups are instructed to follow the instructions on their respective work sheets. (Twenty minutes).

VIII. The facilitator reconvenes the total group. Each subgroup in turn presents its conclusions. (Fifteen to twenty minutes).

IX. The facilitator leads a concluding discussion based on questions such as the following:

1. What were your reactions to exploring organizational mind-sets? What thoughts came to your mind?

2. What are the similarities among the four groups in terms of the importance of exploring the mind-sets? The differences?

3. What are the similarities among the four groups in terms of the ways an organization might promote a mind-set? The differences?

4. What have you learned about organizational mind-sets?

5. What can you do with that learning in your own organizational situation? What can you do to enhance or change your organization's mind-set?

(Fifteen to twenty minutes.)

Variations

I. Each subgroup could be given questions about all four mind-sets. Differences and similarities in their answers could be discussed.

II. The group could work from a case study about an organization to determine which mind-sets might need changes and how to go about making changes.

III. The activity could be shortened by beginning with stating the goals of the activity and moving on to Step V.

Submitted by Marian K. Prokop.

Marian K. Prokop is a senior editor for Pfeiffer & Company in San Diego, California. Ms. Prokop previously worked as a writer/trainer for migrant education programs in New York and California. She has been a frequent contributor to the Annuals *and is one of the co-authors of* Pfeiffer's Official Frequent Flyer Guide, *co-published by Pfeiffer & Company, Bonus Books, and Frequent Publications in 1989. Her latest book,* Managing to Be Green: An Environmental Primer, *was published by Pfeiffer & Company in 1993.*

THE HUNDREDTH MONKEY STORY[2]

"The Japanese monkey, *Macaca fuscata,* has been observed in the wild for a period of over 30 years. In 1952, on the island of Koshima scientists were providing monkeys with sweet potatoes dropped in the sand. The monkeys liked the taste of the sweet potatoes, but they found the dirt unpleasant.

"An 18-month-old female named Imo found she could solve the problem by washing the potatoes in a nearby stream. She taught this trick to her mother. Her playmates also learned this new way and they taught their mothers, too. This cultural innovation was gradually picked up by various monkeys before the eyes of the scientists.

"Between 1952 and 1958, all the young monkeys learned to wash the sandy sweet potatoes to make them more palatable. Only the adults who imitated their children learned this social improvement. Other adults kept eating the dirty sweet potatoes.

"Then something startling took place. In the autumn of 1958, a certain number of Koshima monkeys were washing sweet potatoes—the exact number is not known. Let us suppose that when the sun rose one morning there were 99 monkeys on Koshima Island who had learned to wash their sweet potatoes. Let's further suppose that later that morning, the hundredth monkey learned to wash potatoes.

"THEN IT HAPPENED!

"By that evening almost everyone in the tribe was washing sweet potatoes before eating them. The added energy of this hundredth monkey somehow created an ideological breakthrough! But notice.

"A most surprising thing observed by these scientists was that the habit of washing sweet potatoes then jumped over the sea—Colonies of monkeys on other islands and the mainland troop of monkeys at Takasakiyama began washing their sweet potatoes![3]

"Thus, when a certain critical number achieves an awareness, this new awareness may be communicated from mind to mind. Although the exact number may vary, the Hundredth Monkey Phenomenon means that when only a limited number of people know of a new way, it may remain the consciousness property of these people. But there is a point at which if only one more person tunes-in to a new awareness, a field is strengthened so that this awareness is picked up by almost everyone!"

---

[2] For the complete story of the hundredth monkey, see *The Hundredth Monkey,* by Ken Keyes, Jr., 1986, Coos Bay, OR: Vision Books. This book has sold more than one million copies.

[3] *Lifetide* by Lyall Watson, pp. 147-148. Bantam Books 1980. This book gives other fascinating details.

Pfeiffer & Company

THE HUNDREDTH MONKEY
WORK SHEET 1

Instructions: Your assignment, as members of Subgroup 1, is to look at Type I mind-sets: Internal Ends. A shared mind-set about internal ends means that employees feel an identity with the organization and that they understand the organization's mission and its competition.

Discuss Internal Ends with the other members of your subgroup and prepare answers on newsprint for the following questions:

1. Why is it important for employees within an organization to share a mind-set about internal ends?

2. How might an organization promote a shared mind-set about internal ends?

THE HUNDREDTH MONKEY
WORK SHEET 2

Instructions: Your assignment, as members of Subgroup 2, is to look at Type II mind-sets: Internal Means. A shared mind-set about internal means refers to a common understanding of how work is done in the organization, including such factors as decision making, information sharing, and so on.

Discuss Internal Means with the other members of your subgroup and prepare answers on newsprint for the following questions:

1. Why is it important for employees within an organization to share a mind-set about internal means?

2. How might an organization promote a shared mind-set about internal means?

THE HUNDREDTH MONKEY
WORK SHEET 3

Instructions: Your assignment, as members of Subgroup 3, is to look at Type III mind-sets: External Ends. A shared mind-set about external ends has to do with how well suppliers, customers, and other stakeholders understand and accept the goals of the organization.

Discuss External Ends with the other members of your subgroup and prepare answers on newsprint for the following questions:

1. Why is it important for suppliers, customers, and other stakeholders of an organization to share a mind-set about external ends?

2. How might an organization promote a shared mind-set about external ends?

THE HUNDREDTH MONKEY
WORK SHEET 4

Instructions: Your assignment, as members of Subgroup 4, is to look at Type IV mind-sets: External Means. A shared mind-set about external means refers to implementing processes by which suppliers, customers, and other stakeholders understand and agree with the processes by which an organization operates.

Discuss External Means with the other members of your subgroup and prepare answers on newsprint for the following questions:

1. Why is it important for suppliers, customers, and other stakeholders of an organization to share a mind-set about external means?

2. How might an organization promote a shared mind-set about external means?

THE HUNDREDTH MONKEY
THEORY SHEET[4]

The phenomenon of "the hundredth monkey" also occurs with organizational change. Successful management of change requires that a certain critical number achieves an awareness. How as leaders can we best promote awareness and acceptance of change as well as commitment to that change?

In *Organizational Capability: Competing from the Inside Out*, Ulrich and Lake (1990) present the concept of shared mind-set:

> Shared mind-sets stem from organizational culture; they exist within the overall corporation, or within businesses, departments, functions, or groups. They represent a uniform way of thinking, perceiving, and valuing both the goals of an organization and the processes used to reach those goals. They can be characterized as attitudes, values, or basic assumptions. If shared mind-sets exist, the employees within an organization and the stakeholders outside it experience strategic unity—a common understanding of the organization's goals as well as the process used to reach those goals. (p. 55)

Shared mind-set is a way of explaining that the reasons that people do what they do are a result of the ways in which human brains process, store, and retrieve information. Memories of activities are stored as images; our images of an activity affect the actions we take about that activity. When we did the activity about baseball, we demonstrated how people store information and showed that we could predict their actions. Those who declared themselves baseball fans had positive images of baseball and their actions (watching games, following statistics, playing the game, and so on) showed them to be fans. Those who said that they did not like baseball reported negative images of baseball and their actions reinforced the fact that they were not fans.

Mind-sets are the result of information and behavior. The more a person takes in consistent information about a topic and the more that person takes consistent action, the more he or she forms a mind-set.

Organizations, like individuals, have mind-sets that affect how they act. Shared mind-sets in an organization lead to a cohesive sense of purpose, and employees work together toward common goals. Ideally employees, customers, and suppliers all will share the same mind-set.

What is shared and *where* the mind-set is shared are key factors in the success of an organization. An understanding of both the means and the ends, internally and externally, means that there is a common vision of what the organization is trying to accomplish and how it intends to go about doing that. The interactions of these factors result in a shared mind-set that is unique to a particular organization. This uniqueness is a fundamental element in competitive advantage.

---

[4] The idea of shared mind-set is based on *Organizational Capability: Competing from the Inside Out*, by Dave Ulrich and Dale Lake, copyright © 1990 by John Wiley & Sons, Inc. Used with permission of John Wiley & Sons, Inc. *Organizational Capability* is available from Pfeiffer & Company, 8517 Production Avenue, San Diego, California 92121. (619) 578-5900.

		WHERE THE MIND-SET IS SHARED	
		Internal	External
WHAT MIND-SET IS SHARED	Means (Processes, Routines)	Type II	Type IV
	Ends (Goals, Outcomes)	Type I	Type III

Figure 1. Shared Organizational Mind-Sets

Reference

Ulrich, D., & Lake, D. (1990). *Organizational capability: Competing from the inside out.* New York: John Wiley & Sons.

506. INTERNATIONAL EQUITY CLAIMS DEPARTMENT: DESIGNING WORK

Goals

I. To introduce the participants to the basic elements of work design and the application of these elements.

II. To explore the value of work design that takes into account the needs of those who do the work as well as the needs of the customer and what needs to be done.

III. To encourage the participants to focus on a work process that is driven by customer and employee needs, a vision for the work design, and measurable work-process goals.

Group Size

Fifteen to thirty-five participants in subgroups of five to seven members each.

Time Required

Approximately two to three hours.

Materials

I. A copy of the International Equity Claims Department Case-Study Sheet for each participant.

II. A copy of the International Equity Claims Department Work Sheet for each participant.

III. A copy of the International Equity Claims Department Guidelines for Work Design for each participant.

IV. A newsprint flip chart and a felt-tipped marker for each subgroup.

V. Masking tape for posting newsprint.

Physical Setting

A large room in which the subgroups can work without disturbing one another. Movable chairs should be provided.

Process

I. The facilitator announces that the participants will be working on a case study involving the redesigning of work and then asks them to assemble into subgroups of five to seven members each. Each subgroup is given a newsprint flip chart and a felt-tipped marker.

II. Each participant is given (1) a copy of the case-study sheet, (2) a copy of the work sheet, and (3) a copy of the guidelines for work design and is asked to read these three handouts in that order. After the participants have finished reading, the facilitator elicits and answers questions about the case, the task, and the guidelines. The facilitator also may offer examples of how the guidelines can be put into practice. (Fifteen minutes.)

III. After stipulating that each subgroup has one hour and fifteen minutes to develop a design and to prepare its presentation, the facilitator asks the subgroups to begin. While the subgroup members work, the facilitator provides consultation as necessary and announces the remaining time at regular intervals. (One hour and fifteen minutes.)

IV. At the conclusion of the working period, the facilitator calls time and reconvenes the total group. The subgroups are asked to take turns making their presentations. (Fifteen minutes to one hour and ten minutes, depending on the number of subgroups and the length of the presentations.)

V. The facilitator concludes the activity with a discussion that focuses on the following questions:

1. What is your reaction to the work-design proposals that you have just heard? What changes do you think will be most beneficial to the work process?

2. What things need to be kept in mind when redesigning work?

3. What generalizations can you make about the benefits of a work design that considers not only the work to be done and the needs of the customer but also the needs of those who do the work?

4. How could you apply the concepts of work design to your own work environment?

Variations

I. During the course of the activity, the participants may be asked to develop a vision statement for the Claims Department.

II. The activity may be used as part of a workshop on self-managed teams.

III. The activity may be used with an intact work group, a steering committee, or a design team as a warm-up to an actual work-design effort.

IV. Between Steps IV and V the facilitator may encourage examination and discussion of the viability of the proposals presented.

Submitted by Homer H. Johnson and Karen S. Tschanz.

Homer H. Johnson, Ph.D., *is the Director of the Center for Organization Development and the Master's Program in Organization Development at Loyola University of Chicago, where he teaches courses on total quality, work redesign, and strategic planning. He is a member of Pfeiffer & Company's Advisory Board for Theories and Models in Applied Behavioral Science.*

Karen S. Tschanz *is a candidate for a Master's degree in Organization Development, Loyola University of Chicago. She has consulting experience in strategic planning, analysis of business processes, and introduction and assessment of automated technology. Her professional interests include organizational learning, high-involvement systems, and work design.*

INTERNATIONAL EQUITY CLAIMS DEPARTMENT
CASE-STUDY SHEET

The Claims Department of International Equity Life Insurance Company processes death-benefit claims on the deaths of policyholders. The procedure includes ensuring that the policy is in effect, checking the eligibility of the beneficiaries, processing the necessary paperwork, and authorizing the payment of the death benefits in accordance with the terms of the policy.

The department staff includes one manager (at a salary of $42,000 per year), three assistant managers (at $27,500 each per year), eighteen claim representatives (at $21,000 each per year), and five clerk-typists (at $17,000 each per year). The manager is responsible for the overall operation of the department. The assistant managers not only supervise and train the claim representatives and the clerk-typists but also work with the staff to resolve problem claims. All authorizations for payment of benefits must be checked and approved by an assistant manager. In addition to typing, the clerk-typists' responsibilities include distributing and filing paperwork. Organized as a "pool," they work on a "first-come, first-served" basis.

As claim inquiries or materials related to a claim are received, they are put in the in-basket of one of the claim representatives. This is done in such a way that the representatives have equal work loads.

For each claim the representative first checks to see whether a file has been started. If so, the representative writes a work order asking a clerk to retrieve the file from a central file room. If no file has been started on the claim, the representative obtains a file number from an assistant manager and starts a file.

Then the representative takes whatever claim action is necessary, such as checking eligibility, adding completed claim forms to the file, and so on. Once the representative decides what needs to be done and fills out any necessary paperwork by hand, the file of materials is given to a clerk-typist so that the handwritten paperwork can be typed. After all handwritten paperwork has been typed, the file is returned to the representative for proofreading and signing. The representative then gives the file to the clerk-typist to mail typed materials as necessary and to return the file to the central file room. (No files are kept at the representative's work station.)

This process is repeated for each new action that has to be taken on that claim. Each action requires that the file be retrieved from and returned to the central file room.

The claim representative has the key role in this process. He or she determines whether the deceased person has a valid policy; verifies the details of the policy, including payment amounts; identifies the paperwork that is to be sent to beneficiaries; and checks returned paperwork and has it filed. When the papers are in order, the representative prepares a request for payment and sends it to Financial Disbursement. A variety of problems can arise during this process, such as death of one or more beneficiaries; and the claim representative must handle such problems.

Each week two claim representatives are designated as "on call," which means that they handle phone inquiries. While they are on call, their work on mail inquiries is reduced. "On-call" assignments are rotated weekly among the eighteen claim representatives.

Last year the department processed 13,000 claims, a 10-percent increase over the number processed in the previous year. Each claim takes an average of forty-three days to process from the time of initial inquiry to the date that payment is authorized.

Management concern about the operations of the Claims Department has been increasing. This concern centers around three areas:

1. Over the past two years, customer complaints have increased. Customers say that claims take too long to process; some claims get "lost" or do not receive follow-up; and too many mistakes are made on routine claims. A recent study found that there were approximately 1.2 "errors" per claim. These errors included misplaced files, lost forms, and mistakes in recording.

2. Employee turnover is 35 percent per year. This is felt to be too high and too expensive in view of the fact that claim representatives must be trained extensively in claims procedures and insurance-policy language. Although management feels that the work is interesting and challenging, exit interviews indicate that this opinion is not shared by the workers.

3. The average salary cost for processing a claim—$45—is too high. This cost has to be passed on to the customer.

INTERNATIONAL EQUITY CLAIMS DEPARTMENT
WORK SHEET

You are a team of managers from International Equity Life Insurance Company. Your superiors in top management have asked your team to redesign the work of the Claims Department. They are hopeful that you will find a way to serve customers better, which means that the claims will be processed faster, without error, and at a lower cost. They are also hopeful that the expensive turnover in personnel will be lowered significantly.

In your discussions with top management you have been assured that (1) adequate funds will be made available for new equipment, if needed; and (2) comparable jobs will be found in the company for any employee who is replaced or who chooses to leave the Claims Department because of this reorganization.

Your team will be given a designated period of time to redesign the Claims Department and to prepare a five-to-ten-minute presentation of the new design for the total group. Consider choosing one person to record the salient points of the design and to make the presentation. In your presentation you should accomplish the following:

1. Describe the organizational structure of the new design. Be specific about the number of employees, their roles, and the supervisory relationships that will be necessary.

2. Describe the work flow—the steps to be taken with a claim from initial inquiry to final payment.

3. Describe how the new design will reduce employee turnover. (How will it be more motivating to employees? How will it lead to a better quality of work life?)

4. Compare the new design with the current design using the table that appears below. The data for the current design is taken from the case-study sheet. You will have to *estimate* the data for some measurements in your new design.

	Current Work Design	New Work Design
Total Number of Employees	27	
Annual Payroll Cost	$587,500	
Average Time to Process a Claim	43 days	
Average Number of Errors per Claim	1.2	
Annual Employee Turnover	35 percent	
Salary Cost per Claim	$45	

Pfeiffer & Company

INTERNATIONAL EQUITY CLAIMS DEPARTMENT
GUIDELINES FOR WORK DESIGN

1. Invent the process from the customer's perspective.

2. Determine key process measurements, such as number of errors and average time to process a claim. Set ambitious goals for these elements under the new process.

3. Determine what internal stakeholders (employees and management) need and want with regard to the work and the work environment. Here are some examples:

   - Interaction with others;
   - Identifiable, complete pieces of work;
   - Autonomy;
   - Variety;
   - Task significance; and
   - Feedback from others and from the work itself.

4. Design the whole work system, not just individual jobs. Have people do more than one task.

5. Reduce or eliminate activities that do not contribute directly to what customers need and want. (For example, consider tasks such as checking the work and transferring files.)

6. Add or reconfigure technology, such as automation, procedures, tools, equipment, and facilities.

507. COLOR ME: GETTING ACQUAINTED

Goals

I. To introduce the participants to one another.

II. To offer the participants an opportunity to become acquainted in a way that allows them to reveal as much or as little about themselves as they wish.

Group Size

As many as twenty participants.

Time Required

Approximately forty-five minutes with twenty participants.

Materials

I. A copy of the Color Me Information Sheet for each participant.

II. A newsprint flip chart and a felt-tipped marker.

III. Masking tape for posting newsprint.

Physical Setting

A room with movable chairs arranged in a circle.

Process

I. The facilitator welcomes the participants and announces that the upcoming activity will give them a chance to become acquainted with one another.

II. Each participant is given a copy of the Color Me Information Sheet and is asked to read the sheet and to be prepared to introduce himself or herself on the basis of a color discussed on the sheet. The facilitator gives the following instructions for choosing a color and making an introduction:

1. The color choice may be based either on how the participant presently characterizes himself or herself or on how the participant would like to be perceived. The choice should not be based on a color preference but rather on the characteristics associated with a particular color.

2. The participant may share as little or as much personal information as he or she wishes.

3. The introduction is to be stated in these terms: "My name is _____ and you can color me _____ because _____."

The facilitator writes the introduction phraseology on newsprint and posts the newsprint so that the participants can refer to it during the introduction process. (Ten minutes.)

III. The facilitator asks the participants to take turns introducing themselves. (Approximately one minute per participant.)

IV. The facilitator leads a brief concluding discussion by asking questions such as these:

1. What went through your mind in choosing a color to represent yourself? How did you feel when introducing yourself?

2. What similarities did you notice in the introductions? What differences did you notice? How do you account for those similarities and differences?

3. What did you learn about introducing yourself to a group of new people? What can be generalized about first meetings?

4. When you meet people for the first time on the job or are responsible for assisting others in meeting people, how can you use what you have learned?

Variations

I. If the activity is used to begin diversity-awareness training, the facilitator may add this question to Step IV, number 2: How might race, ethnicity, creed, background, or other affiliations have affected the similarities or differences in choices of color or in introductions?

II. If there are more than twenty participants, the facilitator may assemble subgroups for Step III.

III. The facilitator may provide swatches of fabric in the information-sheet colors and ask each participant to choose the appropriate color of swatch and to wear that swatch attached to his or her name tag. The fabric device serves as a conversation starter between or among participants from different subgroups.

IV. The participants may be asked to circulate around the room, introducing themselves one on one.

V. Participants who choose the same color may be instructed to meet and discuss their reasons for choosing that color. Spokespersons from the color subgroups should summarize reasons for the total group.

Submitted by Jacque Chapman.

Jacque Chapman *is the director of the Leadership Lamar Institute, Office of Student Development, at Lamar University in Beaumont, Texas. Previously she was the director of the Setzer Student Center and the Panhellenic advisor. Her work at Lamar has concentrated in the areas of team building, social-skill development, and leadership development.*

COLOR ME
INFORMATION SHEET[1]

Instructions: You will be asked to introduce yourself to the group by selecting one of the colors described below, based on the *characteristics* of that color rather than your preference for that color. When you introduce yourself, state how these characteristics apply to you.

Red is the color of extroversion, of people with desire, appetite, and a will to live life fully. Those who identify with this color have great interest in the world rather than in themselves and are somewhat aggressive, impulsive, and perhaps athletic. They tend to exaggerate and are quick to let others know their feelings and emotions. "Red" people form opinions rapidly, express them boldly, and choose sides quickly but may be swayed easily from one viewpoint to another.

Orange connotes people who are extroverted but are less aggressive and intense than those who choose red. Orange is the color of expectation and optimism. "Orange" people are able to make friends readily; they have a remarkable talent for small talk. They are generally good natured, likable, and social. Those who select orange care profoundly for people and are natural-born politicians.

Yellow is a radiant color associated with a high intellect and is preferred by those who have great expectations and who diligently seek self-fulfillment. "Yellows" are well aware of contemporary happenings, have superior minds, and enjoy using their minds. They may tend to be aloof, though not shy. They are often liked and admired for their orderly minds.

Green is preferred by those who exhibit a balance between introversion and extroversion. They are constant, persevering, sensible, and respectable, while being social with many friends. They are also ambitious but not unduly aggressive. Of top importance to "green" people are social standing, financial position, and reputation.

Blue represents people who prefer a calm life—neat and orderly, with peace and tranquility. They are introverts, often deliberate and introspective but not too intellectual. "Blue" people are steady, diligent, hard working, and with the persistence to become successful and make a lot of money. They are admired and respected for their sensitivity to others and their secure hold on their emotions. "Blues" know how to concentrate and how to accept responsibilities and obligations.

Purple is for those who are introspective, probably temperamental, and creative. They have a deep understanding and observe subtle things that go unnoticed by the average person. "Purples" have grand ideas about how the world should be; they have things to do that are meaningful and to which they are passionately devoted. They are versatile in the arts, are seekers of culture, and admire artists.

Brown is preferred by those who are steady in their ways, persistent and tenacious, rational, and sensible. "Brown" people tend to indulge themselves; they have an ageless quality and never seem to change. They are able to think things through and assume responsibilities. They never seem to make promises that they do not intend to carry out, and they are conscientious in all they undertake.

White is totality, the blend of all colors, sometimes thought of as impersonal. Those with a preference for white cherish innocence, purity, and chastity.

Black represents a number of things to different people. Although it is associated with mourning, in other situations it represents sophistication, wit, savoir-faire, poise, discretion, and sagacity. Those preferring black choose to look life coolly in the eye and bravely challenge it. They mind their own business and want others to do the same.

508. ZODIAC FOR TRAINERS: DETERMINING COMPETENCIES

Goals

I. To assist the participants in identifying attitudes and skills that they feel are essential to being an effective human resource development (HRD) trainer.

II. To provide the participants with an opportunity to assess their levels of competence in various trainer attitudes and skills.

III. To offer the participants an opportunity to discuss ways to capitalize on their strengths as trainers and ways to address their areas for improvement as trainers.

Group Size

Twenty-four to forty-five participants. This activity is designed for use with practicing and prospective HRD trainers as participants.

Time Required

One hour and forty minutes to two hours.

Materials

I. One copy of each of the Zodiac for Trainers Horoscope Sheets for each participant. (Each participant receives only one of these sheets, the one that represents his or her birthday. However, by preparing a copy of each of the sheets for each participant, the facilitator ensures that enough copies of the horoscope sheets will be available.)

II. A copy of the Zodiac for Trainers Theory Sheet for each participant.

III. A copy of the Zodiac for Trainers Assessment Sheet for each participant.

IV. Blank paper and a pencil for each participant.

V. A clipboard or other portable writing surface for each participant.

VI. Twelve newsprint posters prepared in advance. The facilitator writes one of the following Zodiac signs and its corresponding dates at the top of each poster:

1. Aries (March 21-April 20)

2. Taurus (April 21-May 21)

3. Gemini (May 22-June 21)

4. Cancer (June 22-July 23)

5. Leo (July 24-August 23)

6. Virgo (August 24-September 23)

7. Libra (September 24-October 23)

8. Scorpio (October 24-November 22)

9. Sagittarius (November 23-December 21)

10. Capricorn (December 22-January 20)

11. Aquarius (January 21-February 19)

12. Pisces (February 20-March 20)

If the facilitator wishes, he or she may tape a copy of the appropriate Zodiac for Trainers Horoscope Sheet under the sign and dates on each poster.

VII. A newsprint flip chart and a felt-tipped marker.

VIII. Masking tape for posting newsprint.

Physical Setting

A large room in which the twelve subgroups can work without disturbing one another. Each of the subgroups meets next to one of the twelve posters of Zodiac signs described in the Materials section. (Prior to conducting the activity, the facilitator tapes the twelve posters to the walls, thereby creating twelve stations for subgroups.)

Movable, lightweight chairs should be provided. Before the activity the facilitator places the chairs in the center of the room; when the participants are asked to assemble into subgroups and then to reconvene as a total group, they take their chairs with them.

Process

I. The facilitator states that during the upcoming activity the participants will identify the specific attitudes and skills that a human resource development (HRD) trainer must have in order to work effectively with groups.

II. The facilitator points out the twelve Zodiac signs on the walls and asks each participant to go to the sign that represents his or her birthday. The facilitator mentions that some of the signs may not be represented.

III. The facilitator gives each participant a copy of the appropriate Zodiac for Trainers Horoscope Sheet, a pencil, and a clipboard or other portable writing surface. The members of each subgroup are asked to spend ten minutes reading and discussing the horoscopes and then choosing *two attitudes and/or skills* represented in those horoscopes that they feel are essential to being an effective HRD trainer. The facilitator stipulates that once each subgroup has made its choices, one member should mark these choices or jot them down on his or her handout and should be prepared to announce them to the total group. (Ten to fifteen minutes.)

IV. After ten minutes the facilitator calls time, reconvenes the total group, and asks representatives from the Zodiac subgroups to take turns announcing the subgroup choices. As these choices are announced, the facilitator records them on newsprint. (Ten minutes.)

V. The facilitator leads a discussion about the listed items, helping the participants to clarify meanings; to check for attitudes and skills; and to reach a decision about items they want to retain, combine, delete, or add. This discussion continues until the participants are satisfied with their selections. The resulting items are recorded on newsprint. (Fifteen minutes.)

VI. The participants are given copies of the Zodiac for Trainers Theory Sheet and are asked to read this sheet. (Five minutes.)

VII. The facilitator assists the participants in drawing connections between the items on their list and the content of the theory sheet. If the participants decide to amend their list, the facilitator records their changes. (Ten minutes.)

VIII. The facilitator distributes copies of the Zodiac for Trainers Assessment Sheet and states that as the items on the participants' list are read aloud, the participants are to write them in the left column of their assessment sheets. (Five to ten minutes.)

IX. Each participant is instructed to review each item written on the assessment sheet; to determine his or her competence level in that attitude or skill; and to record the number from 1 to 10 that represents that competence level. The facilitator adds that after all items have been assessed in this way, each participant is to identify his or her three greatest strengths and the three areas in which he or she most needs to improve; the strengths are to be marked with the letter "S" (for "strength"), and the areas for improvement are to be marked with the letter "I" (for "improvement"). (Ten minutes.)

X. The facilitator assembles subgroups of four or five participants each, distributes blank paper, and asks the members of each subgroup to discuss ways in which they use their strengths as well as ways to improve. The participants are encouraged to make notes about any ideas that they find useful. (Fifteen to twenty minutes.)

XI. The facilitator leads a final discussion by asking the following questions:

1. What reactions do you have to the attitudes and skills that appear on the assessment sheet?

2. What similarities do you see in the attitudes and skills listed on the assessment sheet? What differences do you see?

3. What have you learned about your own competence in the attitudes and skills listed on the assessment sheet?

4. What does the list of attitudes and skills tell you about HRD training competencies in general?

5. What approaches or techniques were mentioned in your subgroup work on strengths and areas for improvement? Which of these approaches or techniques do you plan to try in future training experiences? How will you apply them?

(Fifteen to twenty minutes.)

XII. The facilitator encourages the participants to keep their assessment sheets and their theory sheets and to add information to them from time to time as they gain experience in training.

Variations

I. The theory sheet may be omitted.

II. In Step III each Zodiac subgroup may be asked to choose only one attitude or skill. In this case the participants' final list for the assessment sheet would be shorter. Similarly, in Step IX each participant may be asked to select one strength and one area for improvement (instead of three of each).

Submitted by Bonnie Jameson.

Bonnie Jameson is a private consultant who works as a designer, trainer, and facilitator in human resource development. Her focus is on the development of the individual, the group, and the organization. As the lead trainer of the MANAGE program for the United Way of America in the San Francisco area, she trains in all aspects of not-for-profit management, including planning, change, and problem solving. Ms. Jameson also administers and interprets the Myers-Briggs Type Indicator and provides organizations with training in psychological type theory.

ZODIAC FOR TRAINERS HOROSCOPE SHEET

Aries (March 21-April 20)

1. Assess political atmosphere in the workplace and tailor your behavior accordingly. Lend an understanding ear to a distressed friend. Happy hours can be beneficial to your career as well as your social life.

2. Put aside your egotistic tendencies and discover what is really meaningful to you. Financial gain may be yours if you take the initiative and follow your instincts.

3. Don't be too quick to judge others; find out all the facts first. You will be given additional responsibilities at work. Avoid "stressing out" through strenuous daily workouts and rigorous attention to nutrition.

4. Organization is the key to completing assignments quickly and efficiently. Strong passions will play a significant role at home and at work. Clear up misunderstandings as soon as they occur, but hold your ground.

5. Conflicting demands begin to overwhelm you; be assertive and say no with confidence. Also, learn to ask for and accept help when needed. A team effort will make the job more fun and increase the potential for success.

6. Distance yourself from a difficult situation to be objective and make the right choices. Obstinate attitude will not work. Choose a path toward self-improvement; a weekend getaway is a good start.

7. New job opportunity involves relocating; commitments are tested. Talk over your concerns with a friend. Try an inventive approach to a recurring dilemma. Get a good night's rest.

8. Emphasis is on eliminating chaos; make a list of things to do in order of importance. Your ambition and loyalty are attracting attention; continue to establish this reputation. Rainy day provides opportunity for reflection.

9. Follow the advice of your colleagues and avoid being overly sensitive to criticism. Time for a reality check—review your short- and long-term goals; make sure you are doing what you really want. You will feel good if you do a favor for a friend.

10. Concentrate on repairing broken appliances and reinforcing unstable fixtures. Stop striving for perfection and accept your best effort. Outdoor adventure proves challenging and stimulating.

Aries

ZODIAC FOR TRAINERS HOROSCOPE SHEET

Taurus (April 21-May 21)

1. Be proud of your individuality. You can boost your income by finding an outlet for your creative interests. Take a leadership role in your areas of expertise. Forecast features an increase in social obligations.

2. Heavy workload is stimulating and reassuring, but deal with one task at a time. Try an original approach to an old problem. A team effort might be the answer. Revelation will cause you to reconsider your views on a controversial subject.

3. Ability to communicate on many levels comes in handy. Take advantage of opportunities for change; don't let your insecurities hold you back. Keeping up with your many friendships is demanding; be sure to find time for yourself.

4. A close call will renew your vigor for life and pursuing interests outside of work. Focus on communicating with family and friends. Ask for help or suggestions if you are in a rut at work.

5. Sudden changes at work will cause you some uneasiness; be flexible and patient. It is a good time to review your financial situation and make long-term plans. Treat yourself to a facial or a massage.

6. Investigate sound financial investments; don't be hasty. Advise a friend about the importance of keeping a budget. A strong, confident appearance during difficult times will be reassuring to others.

7. Resolve to revamp your appearance: A new suit and a trip to a hair salon will do you wonders. Explore your heritage; consider planning a family reunion. Avoid overextending yourself; emphasize moderation in order to fulfill your many pursuits.

8. Leisure activities take a back seat while you concentrate on completing a critical project. You will soon be in a terrific position to bargain for your interests. A new discovery is on the horizon; keep your senses alert.

9. You will be the center of attention for the next few days; don't shy away, make the most of it. Put your own problems on hold and spend time assisting a loved one. Remember that the healing process is slow; just take things one day at a time.

10. Someone new in your life will make you a tempting offer; consider all the implications. Maintaining an old correspondence has its rewards. Your dwelling is due for a spring cleaning; roll up your sleeves and get started.

Taurus

ZODIAC FOR TRAINERS HOROSCOPE SHEET

Gemini (May 22-June 21)

1. Be patient while explaining ideas to co-workers; try demonstrating to get your point across. Boss will acknowledge your skills as a writer. An uncomfortable situation will require your wit and imagination.

2. Heed your instincts and be cautious about financial investments; require written documentation once a decision has been made. Follow through on projects before starting something new.

3. Stop going in circles; try someone else's idea. A good sense of humor will turn a bad day into a positive one. Avoid commitment right now; leave your options open.

4. Accent goodwill toward others; consider making a charity donation or spending time as a volunteer. Your past experiences will shed new light on an old problem; trivial knowledge will also come in handy.

5. Stick with your resolution to be independent; try making a fresh start. Visualize yourself as you want to be. Having a wide range of acquaintances will be beneficial.

6. Time spent creating an efficient distribution system pays off; colleagues show their appreciation. Confront a so-called friend who has been spreading rumors and betraying your confidence. New relationship has its challenges; don't give up on it yet.

7. Being a high-profile person means your absences are duly noted; focus on punctuality. Puzzles and games are excellent mental exercises and provide a break from routine work. Overlook a colleague's minor error.

8. Address problems of irresponsibility at home and at work; you are doing more than your fair share. It is time to consider going back to school to further your education or to change your career. Loved ones will support you.

9. Team efforts are successful; stick with a good thing. Resist temptation and avoid large purchases. You will feel more secure if you continue putting money aside for a rainy day.

10. Anger and aggression need to be confronted and resolved. In the meantime use extra caution in delicate situations; your intuition isn't up to par. An unannounced visitor will prove to be an excellent sounding block.

$$\textrm{II}$$

Gemini

ZODIAC FOR TRAINERS HOROSCOPE SHEET

Cancer (June 22-July 23)

1. Take care of routine tasks and details quickly and accurately. Find time to spend with friends and relatives. Focus on present problems rather than long-range plans.

2. Unconventional procedure proves successful; your confidence is boosted. Eliminate potential hazards and use caution. Be sensitive of others; avoid gossip.

3. Surprise a co-worker with a special gift. Your knack for remembering names will come in handy at a social function. Don't let your sentimental nature cloud your judgment; outline several alternatives.

4. Turmoil on the home front is causing distress; talk it out with a friend to get a fresh perspective. Draw on your emotional reserves to avoid slippage at work. A hot bath will do you good.

5. Others look to you during an unexpected crisis at work; utilize your imaginative powers. Someone who cares will treat you to lunch. Mentally rehearse an upcoming interview.

6. Your reserved nature might be holding you back; open up so others will feel more comfortable around you. An important relationship is teetering on the edge; don't let minor quirks ruin a good thing.

7. Let others take control for a change; just sit back and enjoy. Spend time playing with children. Highly productive week cements your position as vital to the company. A donation to a charity has many rewards.

8. Make the most of your commute time; listen to an inspirational tape or learn a new language. Jealous co-workers may try to cause problems; ignore them and stay positive. Go to a garage sale this weekend.

9. Take time to personalize your work area at a new job with family pictures and plants. Ventilate your frustrations to confidant after a day of troubleshooting, but be sure to review positive aspects first.

10. Shrewd instincts draw praise from your colleagues. Maybe it's time to say yes to a persistent admirer. Overcome your fear of failure; take a risk. Watch the sunset tonight.

Cancer

Pfeiffer & Company

ZODIAC FOR TRAINERS HOROSCOPE SHEET

Leo (July 24-August 23)

1. Transform roadblocks into tools for getting ahead. Past experience sheds new light on a business dilemma; focus on logical solutions. Slow down; save energy for other endeavors.

2. Take the lead and deal with problems as soon as they arise. Hard work will pay off in the near future. Others flock to you for inspiration and motivation. Let your roommates know if you are expecting guests.

3. Give yourself a pat on the back for your hard work even if others don't. A past mistake haunts you; take time to correct it. Unexpected disruptions cause a change in plans; accent flexibility and a sense of adventure.

4. Put a tighter rein on your extravagant tastes; unforeseen expenses might arise. Highlight humor in the workplace to ease tensions. A good friend will call on you in an emergency.

5. Find a balance between your need for independence and a budding relationship. Focus on clear communication when proposing a new idea. While waiting for a response, polish your skills and increase knowledge.

6. A chance encounter in a stuck elevator has long-term consequences. Breakdown causes inconvenience; be patient and accept fate. Search for quality products rather than cheap imitations.

7. A friend begins to take your good nature for granted; gently put your foot down to unreasonable requests. Joining a health club might be just the thing to get you back in shape. The pressure is on at work; strive to meet deadlines.

8. Energy drain is making you grumpy; bring a toy to work or read the comics to revitalize. A large bouquet of flowers will make someone's day. Tonight is a good time to polish your listening skills.

9. While filling in for a vacationing supervisor, allude to your authority and make the necessary decisions. Employees respond favorably to praise and recognition of their hard work. Don't let the rainy weather get you down; wear a bright color to work.

10. Curiosity is high; experiment with new techniques. It is up to you to build bridges between disgruntled workers and get the project rolling. Discourage no-win, negative attitudes.

Ω

Leo

ZODIAC FOR TRAINERS HOROSCOPE SHEET

Virgo (August 24-September 23)

1. Praise and acknowledge your peers' successes through written communication. However, don't pander to their insecurities. Spend time working on a hobby this weekend.

2. Have faith in your abilities; someone will seek you out for a special project. Focus on resolving conflicts. Good news is cause for celebration; make an exception and indulge.

3. Share a new discovery with friends. Jump in and lend a hand with routine drudge work. Pay attention to details, but don't let your need for perfection impede progress. Let others have a say in final decisions.

4. Passion is strong, but hang on to your sensibility; avoid hasty decisions. Focus on getting your health back on track so that you can clear your head and be objective. Hold your instinct to criticize in check.

5. Seek out bargains to reduce expenditures. A co-worker will ask for your help in organizing files. Scientific research will answer questions about health. A productive week will leave time for exploring new interests.

6. Don't accept game playing in relationships; an ultimatum may be necessary. You are taking the lead at work, and colleagues are coming to you for recommendations; clarify your position.

7. Start the day off by having breakfast with a friend. Double-check the facts before drawing conclusions. Avoid the trap of perfectionism; search for shortcuts to save time and money.

8. A large sum of money will fall into your hands; think before you spend. A forthright approach will impress a new co-worker. Role play upcoming situations that are making you nervous.

9. Constant worrying lately is taking its toll; take time off to renew your energy. Strive for harmony and spiritual growth. This is not a good time to be dieting; instead emphasize moderation.

10. Your phone will be ringing nonstop; get out for a walk during lunch. New acquaintance makes a strong impression. Expect a lot of work in the next week; get plenty of rest.

Virgo

Pfeiffer & Company

ZODIAC FOR TRAINERS HOROSCOPE SHEET

Libra (September 24-October 23)

1. Co-workers in conflict will turn to you for an empathetic ear. Strive for harmony, but maintain a professional attitude when office politics get stormy. You will be asked to attend many social functions; do not feel obligated if other responsibilities are more pressing.

2. A new art exhibit will inspire you. Learn from your failures; accent versatility and optimism. Seek out budget entertainment this weekend. A brush with the past causes old feelings to surface; don't let them hinder your progress.

3. Take advantage of an opportunity to clear up misunderstandings; a direct approach should work best, but remain diplomatic. Resist the temptation to make an expensive purchase right now; concentrate on saving money.

4. A sense of humor will lighten a tense situation. Use caution when dabbling in areas less familiar to you. Punctuality is rewarded; you will be included on an exciting new project. Relax and enjoy an excellent meal.

5. Reserve some time for career networking this weekend. Advice from an unlikely source could prove rewarding. Your power of concentration is acute right now; volunteer for time-consuming research project.

6. Your sense of justice will compel you to action during a controversy; be careful not to jeopardize your position. Accept reality and get on with your life. Avoid rushing a new relationship.

7. Concentrate on self-control this weekend; sweet treats will be tempting. Additional job benefits are accrued; get details in writing. A loved one needs special care tonight.

8. Stop taking responsibility for other peoples' problems; get on with your own life. A new job offer leaves you on the spot; do you want to take a risk or stick with security? A quiet evening will give you time for reflection.

9. Don't delay taking charge of your career; get those resumes out. Share a good laugh with a friend; it will do you both good. Seek alliances with those who can help you achieve your goals.

10. A heart-to-heart talk will alleviate unwarranted fears; however, it's up to you to make the first move. You will be asked to help plan a wedding. Organization will get you through the next couple of weeks.

Libra

ZODIAC FOR TRAINERS HOROSCOPE SHEET

Scorpio (October 24-November 22)

1. A new clothing purchase will enhance pride in your appearance. Be prepared for some unpleasant times ahead; determination and purpose will steer you through. Review practicality of an old partnership.

2. Let down your guard; confiding in someone will establish the basis of a new friendship. Find peace through inner explorations; start a personal journal to examine feelings and explore dreams.

3. Imagination and ambition are instrumental to career advancement; extra effort will not go unnoticed. Travel plans are confirmed; make preparations now. Look up an old friend.

4. Follow through on all projects that you begin; be especially aware of details. Pat yourself on the back for your accomplishments, and remember that money isn't the only measure of success. A dream will be fulfilled unexpectedly.

5. Friend offers support and encouragement through uncertain times; remember to show your appreciation when things are more stable. Push to excel beyond expectations; you may surprise yourself.

6. You will be unusually accident prone this week; use extra caution. A surprising confession will throw you for a loop; strive for an honest response. Take your phone off the hook and focus on self-improvement this weekend.

7. Anxiety over uncertain relationship subsides; position is clarified. Solicit help on large projects; fresh input can get those projects rolling again. Little one can teach you how to have fun.

8. You may need to play the waiting game today; remain patient and calm. Rely on your common sense to guide you through uncharted territory. A new movie will make a big impression on you.

9. Confront your differences with partner; a compromise will satisfy both of you. It is best to keep quiet about a tip on a financial investment. Your zest for work is at an all-time high; put in some extra hours at the office.

10. Complications are developing, and co-workers are engaging in mind-games; be alert and avoid getting caught up in messy politics. Sources that you thought were stable are proving fallible; it's time to search for alternatives.

Scorpio

ZODIAC FOR TRAINERS HOROSCOPE SHEET

Sagittarius (November 23-December 21)

1. Attention revolves around you today; make the most of it and take the initiative. Scrupulous attention to detail involving a money matter pays off. Take your dog for a long walk.

2. Act as a liaison for those who cannot communicate nor work cooperatively. Realize that not everyone holds the same ideals as you; however, you still need to learn to work with everyone. Follow an inspiration and take a short trip.

3. Avoid prejudging other people's abilities. Find new ways to boost your energy during the day—perhaps a five-minute break to read the comics. Daily routine is disrupted unexpectedly; be flexible and enjoy the change of pace.

4. You will be asked to fill in for someone who is not up to par; take advantage of this opportunity to show off your abilities. Financial picture is looking good; investigate ownership possibilities.

5. Concentrate on the positive aspects of your job; search for creative ways to make a tedious task interesting. Go along with an unexpected change in plans; a surprise may be in store for you. Relieve unnecessary worries; get a checkup.

6. A cheerful demeanor will reassure troubled mate. Take advantage of your latest success and ask for a long-overdue raise. Resolve to be well read in your field so that you can stay up-to-date on innovations and changes.

7. A lull in the work load is a perfect opportunity for you to spend time on a special-interest venture. Low-budget entertainment is available right in your neighborhood; check the local paper.

8. It is high time you began setting limits; your credit cards are "maxed out." An article about a new scientific development fascinates you; find out more. Invite a friend over for dinner and a video.

9. A good joke will alleviate a tense situation; others will be grateful for your quick thinking. An action-packed weekend requires that you get plenty of rest; you won't want to miss out on anything.

10. This week responsibilities will put a rein on your freedom; reschedule previously made plans. An emotional acquaintance needs frank and sincere advice. Ask for thorough explanations before granting favors.

Sagittarius

ZODIAC FOR TRAINERS HOROSCOPE SHEET

Capricorn (December 22-January 20)

1. Spotlight is on public relations skills; schedule interviews and meetings. Thoroughness pays off; keep your options open. Consolidate your financial responsibilities.

2. Lighten the mood at work with a cookie/ice-cream break. Continue to follow your chosen path and success will be yours. Your supervisor recognizes a job well done.

3. Brace yourself for criticism of an earlier mistake; do not take it to heart. You have anonymous admirers. Pay attention to your health; make necessary appointments.

4. If you can't be there in person, a phone call is the next best thing. Channel your energies into completing projects and you will be rewarded with a leadership role.

5. What seems like a golden opportunity may have a few invisible strings attached; read the fine print. Take time to brighten your work environment. Avoid steadfast commitment to established routines.

6. Your timing is slightly off as of late; however, don't lose faith. A friend will offer to support your latest business venture; cover all your bases and have a backup plan. Delve into a good book tonight.

7. Focus on paying off debts incurred from previous indulgences. Feelings of nostalgia are aroused; spend time perusing family photo albums. You will be interviewed by a reporter about your opinion on a local controversy.

8. Refrain from being embarrassed about an unforeseeable mishap; others will admire your professionalism. An upcoming presentation has you feeling nervous; careful preparation and a good night's rest will calm you.

9. Well-chosen words brighten a co-worker's day. Original approach augments popularity and success. Family members complain that you are being stingy; persist in an economical approach, and they will be grateful later.

10. Good fortune comes your way; but, beware, prestige causes you to temporarily neglect friends and responsibilities. Regain your senses and make the necessary apologies. A long walk will invigorate you mentally and physically.

Capricorn

Pfeiffer & Company

ZODIAC FOR TRAINERS HOROSCOPE SHEET

Aquarius (January 21-February 19)

1. Your nurturing instincts can be put to good use through volunteer work. Long-deserved recognition is finally achieved. The go-ahead is given on political ambitions.

2. Numerous requests and tasks each day require organization and commitment. Encourage teamwork when overlap and conflict begin to arise. It is best to put any new ideas in writing.

3. Give your self-esteem a boost; take a class and focus on exercise and nutrition. Bonus money is best spent in a savings account. A friend in need will call on you for support.

4. Beware of trivial disputes; remain sensible and be willing to give in. Subtle gestures are duly appreciated. If necessary, distance yourself to achieve stability.

5. A peculiar problem requires your analysis. False accusations will stir up your ire; an emergency meeting may be necessary to straighten out the facts. A new appliance will alleviate overload.

6. Keep your cool while others fly off the handle; calm manner will be regarded most favorably. Spend the day taking care of errands that have been put off. An eccentric relative with colorful stories to tell shows up on your doorstep.

7. Hard work has paid off; it is time for you to take a leadership role. Mend a long-bygone quarrel with a family member. A lifelong dream once thought unreachable now has definite possibilities.

8. Is it possible to combine an outside interest with career skills into a lucrative business? You can finally be your own boss. Re-examine your vision of the future. A strained relationship demands attention.

9. You've outgrown your rebellious nature; consider joining the family business. Plan a high-energy weekend to burn off some calories. A gentle approach is needed with temperamental associates.

10. Seek out a mentor who can show you the ropes and help you find your strengths. Confront fears that are holding you back from advancing in your career. A light meal at lunch will keep you from feeling drowsy.

Aquarius

ZODIAC FOR TRAINERS HOROSCOPE SHEET

Pisces (February 20-March 20)

1. Taking a chance on a risky opportunity could pay off nicely; however, research legal limitations. Those who have been skeptical will now be firm believers. Contribute to a worthy cause.

2. Hold out for job offers that meet your skill and financial requirements. Focus on fulfilling resolutions at home and at work. Invite some friends over for socializing.

3. Forgive minor bad habits; they aren't worth the worry. Seek help if you find you've dug too deep a hole. A distant relationship proves beneficial.

4. A positive attitude and a bright smile will keep you going. Your boss will back your ideas. Comparison shopping is time consuming but can save you money; resist sales pitches.

5. Untapped resources will come in handy during recession. Past mistakes can be drawn on in an upcoming decision. Spend your weekends fulfilling outside interests.

6. You will overcome your shyness and voice your opinions during a social gathering. A worthy cause deserves your attention and input. Try meditating to find inner peace, calm, and strength.

7. New acquaintance is acting wishy-washy; don't pursue a commitment right now. Timely payment of debts will ensure excellent credit down the road. Clear up misunderstanding with a co-worker; you both will feel better.

8. You will be in the right place at the right time for an exciting new job opportunity. Finding time to spend with a senior will make you all the wiser. Brush off intimidation attacks and stand by your beliefs.

9. Start the day by visualizing yourself as successful and positive. A weekend getaway has added benefits: you will cross paths with influential people. Subtle gesture begets lasting impression; a single rose is all it takes.

10. Immerse yourself in work to avoid brooding over past mistakes. A counselor may help you identify pent-up feelings. Add your own personal twist to an old family recipe.

Pisces

ZODIAC FOR TRAINERS
THEORY SHEET

Human resource development trainers need to develop certain attitudes and skills that will help them to influence and motivate participants to learn and apply new knowledge. Although each trainer has a unique style, these attitudes and skills transcend style and combine to form a *facilitator presence*—an authenticity that allows a trainer to command personal power with almost any type of group.

The foundation for facilitator presence is self-confidence—knowing and liking oneself enough to have faith in one's spontaneous actions. There is a point at which a trainer is so competent at particular attitudes and skills that he or she is no longer conscious of using them. The paragraphs that follow describe the attitudes and skills that need to be mastered to the point at which they can be used without conscious effort:

1. *Listening.*[1] To listen effectively, a trainer must pay close attention not only to the words being spoken but also to the nonverbal cues that clarify meaning, to the degree of consistency in verbal and nonverbal messages, and to the feelings and intentions behind the words. The trainer can encourage a speaking participant by maintaining eye contact, nodding, and smiling. Another critical aspect of listening is to hear the entire message before evaluating what is said, and one way to obtain the entire message is to ask questions in a nonaccusing way so that the speaker does not feel judged. Finally, to avoid misinterpretation, the trainer may paraphrase the participant's message and ascertain whether the paraphrasing reflects what was meant.

2. *Nondefensiveness.* To act nondefensively, a trainer must like himself or herself and must feel confident about the behaviors that he or she chooses to use in front of a group. Feedback from the group—whether verbal, nonverbal, or written—will show whether those behaviors are ones that the participants like; ones that energize them; and ones that allow them to learn, to grow, and to take risks. Nondefensive behavior requires personal awareness and commitment to one's own growth. The more awareness of personal behavior that a trainer commits to—and the more feedback he or she is willing to receive and process—the better he or she becomes at developing nondefensiveness.

3. *A thirst for knowledge.* A broad base of knowledge is gained by having a lifelong thirst to know, particularly in the fields of psychology, organization development, philosophy, metaphysics, anthropology, history, and all kinds of literature. Self-directed learning builds on itself; as more and more knowledge is gained, connections and patterns are noticed and put to use in creative ways. Trainers who continually learn are increasingly able to apply what they have learned to the training setting, developing spontaneous and intuitive designs and processes for working with groups.

---

[1] The information on listening is adapted from "Poor Listening Habits: Effective Listening Sheet" by J. Seltzer and L.W. Howe, in J.W. Pfeiffer (Ed.), *The 1987 Annual: Developing Human Resources* (p. 30), San Diego, CA: Pfeiffer & Company.

4. *A democratic spirit.* The best trainer attitudes are developed from the idea of the democratic spirit—in the sense of wanting all participants to succeed and to be enthusiastic about participating, sharing, and achieving in the group. When the trainer approaches the group with a democratic spirit and the group becomes infused with that spirit, then consensus, win-win solutions, and synergy are a natural by-product.

5. *Problem-solving and strategic-planning skills.* Group-process skills that are essential in a trainer's repertoire are problem solving and strategic planning. Facilitating problem solving means helping a group to define a problem, to analyze the problem by collecting and assessing accurate information, to set problem objectives, to generate alternatives and the criteria with which to choose alternatives, to select the best alternative, to implement it, and to evaluate results. Each of these phases, if led by a trainer who exhibits nondefensive behavior and a democratic spirit, can be exciting, energizing, and productive for a work group. The same is true of the strategic-planning process. Developing a mission based on values and ethics, clear policy statements reflected in long-range goals, and specific and measurable objectives for implementing goals can be an exciting experience for a group. Additional group benefits include a sense of teamwork and a respect for group processes, both of which are transferable to and useful in other settings.

ZODIAC FOR TRAINERS
ASSESSMENT SHEET

Trainer Attitudes and Skills (The Group's List)	Your Competence Level on a Scale of 1 to 10

INTRODUCTION TO THE
INSTRUMENTATION SECTION

The contents of the Instrumentation section are provided for training and developmental purposes. These instruments are not intended for in-depth personal growth, psychodiagnostic, or therapeutic work. Instead, they are intended for use in training groups; for demonstration purposes; to generate data for training or organization development sessions; and for other group applications in which the trainer, consultant, or facilitator helps respondents to use the data generated by an instrument for achieving some form of progress.

One of the principal benefits of using instrumentation in human resource development (HRD) is that instruments typically provide respondents with nonpejorative words to describe behavior. With such a new vocabulary, one can begin to describe another person's behavior in ways that enhance communication.

In addition to helping respondents to identify behavior, the comparison of scores from an instrument provides respondents with a convenient and comparatively safe way to exchange interpersonal feedback. The involvement with their own scores helps participants to understand the theory on which the instrument is based—a typical reason for using an instrument in training. Therefore, there are strong, positive reasons for using instruments in training and development work.

The trainer, consultant, or facilitator must recognize that the scores obtained by individuals on any instrument are the results of their answers to a series of verbal questions at one point in time and that those scores should not be treated with reverence. Such responses typically change over time, for a variety of reasons. The individual's interpretation of a single question the next time may affect his or her answer; a variety of experiences may change the person's self-perception; and so on. Professionals in HRD are encouraged to use instruments simply as one additional means of obtaining data about individuals, with all the risks and potential payoffs that any other data source would yield.

There are four instruments in this year's *Annual*. The first, the "Consulting-Style Inventory," is based on the eight consulting roles identified by Gordon Lippitt and Ronald Lippitt (1986) in their book titled *The Consulting Process in Action*. The instrument allows consultants and others in the helping professions to examine their styles and their abilities to shift styles to adjust to changing client needs.

The second instrument, the "Cultural-Context Inventory," is based on the cultural framework of high/low context developed by anthropologist Edward Hall (1959, 1969, 1976, 1983). The inventory was developed as a tool for increasing understanding of one's own culturally based behavior at work as well as the behaviors of others. As a training device, it not only helps trainees to identify ways in which they are similar to or different from others but also points out the need to develop effective ways of managing interpersonal differences.

The third instrument, the "Empowerment-Readiness Survey," offers an opportunity to discover an organization's propensity toward empowerment principles and the degree to which a foundation for empowerment exists. The survey focuses on the following dimensions of empowering organizations: communication, value of people, ambiguity, concepts about power, information, and learning. This survey can be used for two purposes: (1) to determine the status of the organization prior to implementing empowerment strategies and (2) to guide the initiation of organizational change.

The final instrument, "Strategic Leadership Styles Instrument," uses Lawrence M. Miller's (1989) theory of corporate life cycles and the leadership styles that dominate each of the stages of organizational life. After completing the instrument, the respondents graph their comparative style preferences. An interpretation sheet provides brief descriptions of the eight strategic leadership styles and suggestions for working with both managers and subordinates who exhibit these styles.

Readers of earlier *Annuals* will note that the theory necessary for understanding, presenting, and using each instrument now is included with the instrument itself. This eliminates the necessity of referring to several sections of the *Annual* in order to develop a program based on any of the instruments. All interpretive information, scales or inventory forms, and scoring sheets are also provided for each instrument. In addition, Pfeiffer & Company publishes all of the reliability and validity data contributed by the authors of instruments; if readers want additional information on reliability and validity, they are encouraged to contact instrument authors directly. (Authors' addresses and phone numbers are provided in the Contributors list that follows the Professional Development section.)

REFERENCES

Hall, E. (1959). *The silent language*. New York: Doubleday.

Hall, E. (1969). *The hidden dimension*. New York: Doubleday.

Hall, E. (1976). *Beyond culture*. New York: Doubleday.

Hall, E. (1983). *The dance of life*. New York: Doubleday.

Lippitt, G., & Lippitt, R. (1986). *The consulting process in action* (rev. ed.). San Diego, CA: Pfeiffer & Company.

Miller, L.M. (1989). *Barbarians to bureaucrats: Corporate life cycle strategies—lessons from the rise and fall of civilizations*. New York: Clarkson N. Potter.

CONSULTING-STYLE INVENTORY: A TOOL FOR CONSULTANTS AND OTHERS IN HELPING ROLES

Timothy M. Nolan

The process of serving as an effective consultant or helper to a person, a group, or an organization is a demanding one. It requires providing needed assistance to an appropriate degree and in a manner that is likely to be useful to the client.

The effective consultant must be flexible, able to adapt to changing client needs. Therefore, he or she must have a repertoire of behaviors as well as the willingness to shift behaviors to adjust to the needs of each client. Most people in the consulting/helping professions have styles or patterns of doing their work. However, when a particular consulting style becomes so pervasive that it excludes the use of certain behaviors, it limits the consultant's effectiveness.

Gordon Lippitt and Ronald Lippitt (1986) addressed this problem in their book *The Consulting Process in Action*. They developed a model that identifies eight roles that may be considered as consulting styles:[1]

1. *Objective Observer.* This role consists of several activities that are intended to stimulate the client toward insights into growth, more effective methods, long-range change, and greater independence. This is the most nondirective of the eight roles. The consultant does not express personal beliefs or ideas and does not assume responsibility for the work or the result of that work. Instead, the consultant observes the client's behavior and provides feedback; the client alone is responsible for the direction that is ultimately chosen.

One important function of the objective observer is to ask questions that help the client to clarify and confront a problem and to make decisions. The consultant also may paraphrase the client's comments and may be empathic, sharing the client's experience of the blocks that led to the problem.

2. *Process Counselor.* This role consists of observing the client's problem-solving processes and offering suggestions for improvement. The consultant and the client jointly diagnose the client's process, and the consultant assists the client in acquiring whatever skills are necessary to continue diagnosing the process.

The focus of this role is on the interpersonal and intergroup dynamics that affect the problem-solving process. The consultant observes people in action, interviews management personnel to obtain facts, and reports the data to the client in order to improve relationships and processes.

---

[1] The following paragraphs have been adapted from Lippitt & Lippitt (1986).

3. *Fact Finder.* In this role the consultant serves as a researcher, collecting and interpreting information in areas of importance to the client. This function includes developing criteria and guidelines for collecting, analyzing, and synthesizing data.

The process of collecting can be accomplished through any of five methods: (1) interviewing, (2) administering a questionnaire, (3) observing, (4) analyzing records and documents, and (5) administering and analyzing appropriate tests or surveys. Fact finding enables the consultant to develop an understanding of the client's processes and performance; as a result of the insights gained, the consultant and the client can evaluate the effectiveness of a change process in terms of solving the client's problem.

4. *Identifier of Alternatives and Linker to Resources.* The consultant identifies alternative solutions to a problem; establishes criteria for evaluating each alternative; determines the likely consequences of each alternative; and then links the client with resources that may be able to help in solving the problem. However, the consultant does not assist in selecting the final solution.

5. *Joint Problem Solver.* The consultant works actively with the client to identify and solve the problem at hand, often taking a major role in defining the results. This function consists of stimulating interpretations of the problem, helping to maintain objectivity, isolating the causes of the problem, generating alternative solutions, evaluating alternatives, choosing a solution, and developing an action plan. The consultant also may function as a third-party mediator when conflict arises during the problem-solving process.

6. *Trainer/Educator.* The consultant provides instruction, information, or other kinds of directed learning opportunities for the client. The ability to train and educate is necessary in many helping situations, particularly when a specific learning process is essential if the client is to develop competence in certain areas. As a trainer/educator, the consultant must be able to assess training needs, write learning objectives, design learning experiences and educational events, employ a range of educational techniques and media, and function as a group facilitator.

7. *Information Specialist.* The consultant serves as content expert for the client, often defining "right" and "wrong" approaches to a problem. The client is primarily responsible for defining the problem and the objectives of the consultation, and the consultant plays a directive role until the client is comfortable with the approach that has been recommended. Although the needs of both the consultant and the client may encourage this consulting role, the consultant should not adhere to this behavior pattern exclusively. The client may become increasingly and inappropriately dependent on the consultant; also, the dependence may lead to poor problem solving because of limited consideration of alternatives.

8. *Advocate.* The consultant consciously strives to have the client move in a direction desired by the consultant. In the most directive of the eight roles, the consultant uses power and influence to impose his or her ideas and values about either content or process issues. As a content advocate, the consultant tries to influence the client's choice of goals and means; as a process advocate, the

consultant tries to influence the methodology underlying the client's problem-solving behavior.

As a consultant moves from Objective Observer to Advocate, the locus for decision making moves from client centered to consultant centered. The author's work also makes it clear that each of the eight roles is appropriate if it meets the following conditions:

1. It is negotiated with the client and agreed to by the client; and

2. It is needed in the current situation that the consultant and the client share.

THE INSTRUMENT

The Consulting-Style Inventory was created to provide a tool that consultants and others in the helping professions could use to examine their styles as well as their ability to shift styles to adjust to changing client needs. It is based on the Lippitt and Lippitt (1986) model of consultant roles.

The inventory may be completed independently by a single person working alone or in a group setting by a number of people who wish to compare and discuss their styles. As a component of a training session, the inventory is useful for consultants, counselors, group facilitators, and others in professional helping roles.

Reliability and Validity

There are no reliability and validity data for the Consulting-Style Inventory. However, when the inventory is used to encourage introspection, discussion, and a focus on professional development, it has high face validity with a range of people in helping roles.

Administration

The process for administering the inventory is as follows:

1. Using the instructions printed on the instrument form, the consultant completes the Consulting-Style Inventory (either alone or in a group setting).

2. Using the Consulting-Style Inventory Scoring Sheet, the consultant scores the inventory and makes vertical bar-graph entries for each of the total scores from a through h.

3. The consultant reads the Consulting-Style Inventory Interpretation Sheet. For each role that represents a growth area, the consultant creates an action plan designed to help him or her to acquire the skills necessary for functioning in that role comfortably.

If the instrument is being used with a group, the facilitator leads a discussion designed to surface what has been observed and learned as well as some of the action plans for acquiring desired skills. Before the total-group discussion, the facilitator may ask the respondents to form triads to consult with one another about proposed plans.

REFERENCE

Lippitt, G., & Lippitt, R. (1986). *The consulting process in action* (2nd ed.). San Diego, CA: Pfeiffer & Company.

Timothy M. Nolan, Ph.D., is the president of Innovative Outcomes, Inc., in Milwaukee, Wisconsin. He is also the president of the Applied Strategic Planning Institute, an organization committed to making strategic-management technology broadly available. His consulting practice is devoted to the related areas of strategy development and innovation. Dr. Nolan's clients range from new businesses to the largest corporations and include for-profit, not-for-profit, and governmental organizations. With Leonard D. Goodstein and J. William Pfeiffer, he is the co-author of Pfeiffer & Company's popular series of products on applied strategic planning. He recently served as the primary author of one of these products, Applied Strategic Planning: The Consultant's Kit.

CONSULTING-STYLE INVENTORY[2]

Timothy M. Nolan

Instructions: In this inventory there are seven situations, each of which offers eight courses of action for a consultant to the group in question. For each of these situations, number the eight alternative actions from the one that you would *most likely take (8)* to the one that you would *least likely take (1)*. To maximize the value of this inventory, respond on the basis of what you *typically* would do. Do not try to search for "correct" answers or assign numbers according to what you think you should do. Instead, read the statement and imagine what you *typically* would do as a consultant to the group in question.

Situation 1

You are working with a strategic planning team whose members are in the process of creating a vision of their ideal organization.

Number the eight following alternative actions from the one that you would *most likely take (8)* to the one that you would *least likely take (1)*:

_____ f   Do a training session on how to develop a vision.

_____ h   Present them with an organizational vision that you find very useful.

_____ b   Observe their process and make interventions when you feel that these might help the team.

_____ d   Identify resource people who have developed organizational visions.

_____ e   Work with them actively to develop a deep, meaningful vision.

_____ g   Lay out the six necessary components for an organizational vision.

_____ a   Watch their progress as a team and provide feedback at the end of the session or when they ask for it.

_____ c   Do an analysis of the organization and its marketplace and present the analysis to them.

---

[2] This instrument first appeared as the "Making Choices Inventory" in *Applied Strategic Planning: The Consultant's Kit* (pp. 64-67) by T.M. Nolan, L.D. Goodstein, and J.W. Pfeiffer, 1992, San Diego, CA: Pfeiffer & Company. *The Consultant's Kit* offers seventy-nine activities and numerous instruments that are useful in leading a planning team through the process of applied strategic planning.

Situation 2

You are working with a group whose members are attempting to define their values.

Number the eight following alternative actions from the one that you would *most likely take (8)* to the one that you would *least likely take (1):*

_____ g Provide them with two major alternative approaches that can be used to clarify values.

_____ a Watch their discussion closely, making notes to support a quality debriefing of the meeting.

_____ c Gather data by interviewing them about their values and preferences; then present them with these data.

_____ e Work with them to develop a group values statement.

_____ f Do a training session on values and appropriate approaches to values clarification.

_____ h Push them to adopt a values-clarification structure that you know will work well for them.

_____ b Observe them and intervene when doing so will improve interaction and clarity.

_____ d Help them to identify and make contact with an expert on values clarification.

Situation 3

You are working with a strategic planning team whose members are exploring how to respond to the competition that their organization is facing.

Number the eight following alternative actions from the one that you would *most likely take (8)* to the one that you would *least likely take (1):*

_____ h Present them with a complete set of tactics to meet the competition.

_____ b Focus on and observe group process; intervene when you feel that it would be helpful.

_____ d Help them to identify written or other resources on competitive environments.

_____ f Do a training session on sources of competition and how to meet these challenges.

_____ g Provide them with a clear framework that you have developed to enable them to define and respond to the competitive forces they face.

_____ a Observe them and give them feedback on their process when asked.

_____ c Do a competitor analysis and present the data to them.

_____ e Work directly with them to identify each competitive force and to develop responses to each.

Pfeiffer & Company

Situation 4

You are working with a group whose members are preparing to make a presentation to top management.

Number the eight following alternative actions from the one that you would *most likely take (8)* to the one that you would *least likely take (1):*

_____ a Observe their efforts and give feedback as requested.

_____ c Gather information about the interests of the top managers in the organization and present them with this information.

_____ e Work with them to develop a top-quality presentation.

_____ g Personally provide the presentation-skills expertise that they need.

_____ h Ensure their success by advocating a particular mix of media and activities.

_____ b Observe their group process and make interventions when doing so appears helpful to them.

_____ d Match them up with a specialist on presentation skills.

_____ f Do a brief input session on the major components of a quality presentation.

Situation 5

You are working with a group whose members are developing a customer-service program for their organization.

Number the eight following alternative actions from the one that you would *most likely take (8)* to the one that you would *least likely take (1):*

_____ b Observe their group dynamics and intervene when appropriate.

_____ d Provide them with a quality videotape and good written materials on customer service.

_____ f Conduct a session for them on the major components of good customer service.

_____ h Redirect them from thinking about customer service; have them approach the topic from the standpoint of customer satisfaction.

_____ a Allow them to proceed on their own; give them feedback on their process when they ask for it.

_____ c Do an analysis of quality customer-service programs that they could use.

_____ e Work with them to develop the best customer-service program that you and they can come up with.

_____ g Share with them your insights regarding successful customer-service programs.

Situation 6

You are working with a group on the redesign of a major work process that will greatly reduce the time involved from the beginning to the completion of the work cycle.

Number the eight following alternative actions from the one that you would *most likely take (8)* to the one that you would *least likely take (1):*

_____ c Complete an analysis of the current work flow and present it to them.

_____ e Work with them to develop a greatly improved work flow.

_____ g Share with them two major ways of organizing work flow.

_____ a Do not interrupt them; observe and discuss your observations if asked.

_____ b Observe them and make suggestions about group process when appropriate.

_____ d Provide prework in the form of readings on work-flow design; identify an outside expert as a potential resource.

_____ f Do a training session on work-flow design and cycle time.

_____ h Encourage them to adopt a work-flow design that you believe will enable them to meet their goals.

Situation 7

You are working with a group whose members have been assigned the task of resolving recurrent problems with the quality of a line of products provided by their organization.

Number the eight following alternative actions from the one that you would *most likely take (8)* to the one that you would *least likely take (1):*

_____ d Match them up with the best resources available regarding quality products of this type.

_____ f Do a carefully designed training session on quality.

_____ h Convince them that to be successful they should approach this task from the customer's point of view.

_____ b Concentrate on group process; make suggestions for improvement as they do their work.

_____ c Gather data on the current level of quality in this product line and give this information to them.

_____ e Work with them to develop the best possible approach to resolving lapses in quality.

_____ g Introduce them to a process that you have used successfully in the past to resolve comparable quality problems.

_____ a Observe how they approach this problem; if they ask for feedback on their group process, give it to them.

CONSULTING-STYLE INVENTORY
SCORING SHEET

Instructions: Each of the eight alternative actions for each situation in the Consulting-Style Inventory has a lowercase letter next to it. For each situation, record the number you assigned to the "a" alternative, the number you assigned to the "b" alternative, the number you assigned to the "c" alternative, and so on. Then add the numbers in the vertical columns and record the totals where indicated.

	a	b	c	d	e	f	g	h
Situation 1	___	___	___	___	___	___	___	___
Situation 2	___	___	___	___	___	___	___	___
Situation 3	___	___	___	___	___	___	___	___
Situation 4	___	___	___	___	___	___	___	___
Situation 5	___	___	___	___	___	___	___	___
Situation 6	___	___	___	___	___	___	___	___
Situation 7	___	___	___	___	___	___	___	___
Totals	___	___	___	___	___	___	___	___

```
60 |
50 |
40 |
30 |
20 |
10 |
   |_____
     a    b    c    d    e    f    g    h
```

Consulting-Styles Profile

CONSULTING-STYLE INVENTORY
INTERPRETATION SHEET

The Consulting-Style Inventory employs the eight consulting roles discussed by Gordon Lippitt and Ronald Lippitt in their book titled *The Consulting Process in Action*. The chart on the following page, which appears in their book, explains these roles in terms of how directive or nondirective the consultant is in his or her relationship with the client. In other words, the consultant roles on the left of the chart reflect a heavy involvement of the client, whereas those on the right reflect a heavy involvement of the consultant.

The eight roles, as represented in the Consulting-Style Inventory, are as follows:

a. Objective Observer

b. Process Counselor (or Process Consultant)

c. Fact Finder

d. Resource Identifier or Linker

e. Joint Problem Solver

f. Trainer/Educator

g. Information Specialist (or Content Expert)

h. Advocate

To be able to function effectively as a consultant, you want to achieve comfort in each of these roles. Think about how you would answer the following questions:

1. Is your style more client centered or consultant centered?

2. How flexible are you in your use of consulting roles? Do you move easily from one to another as the situation demands?

3. Are there any roles that are particularly dominant for you? How do they serve your clients?

4. Are there any roles that you underutilize? How could the increased use of these roles benefit your clients?

5. What could you do to lessen your reliance on favorite roles and/or to utilize all of the options with equal ease?

MULTIPLE ROLES OF THE CONSULTANT

CLIENT   CONSULTANT

Objective Observer	Process Counselor	Fact Finder	Identifier of Alternatives and Linker to Resources	Joint Problem Solver	Trainer/Educator	Information Specialist	Advocate
Raises questions for reflection	Observes problem-solving process and raises issues mirroring feedback	Gathers data and stimulates thinking	Identifies alternatives and resources for client and helps assess consequences	Offers alternatives and participates in decisions	Trains client	Regards, links, and provides policy or practice decisions	Proposes guidelines, persuades, or directs in the problem-solving process

LEVEL OF CONSULTANT ACTIVITY IN PROBLEM SOLVING

Nondirective   Directive

From *The Consulting Process in Action* (2nd ed.) (p. 61) by G. Lippitt and R. Lippitt, 1986, San Diego, CA: Pfeiffer & Company.

CULTURAL-CONTEXT INVENTORY: THE EFFECTS OF CULTURE ON BEHAVIOR AND WORK STYLE

Claire B. Halverson

INTRODUCTION: THE THEORY OF CULTURAL CONTEXT

Culture, as defined by anthropologist Edward Hall (1959, pp. 16, 20), is "The way of life of a people. The sum of their learned behavior patterns, attitudes and material things.... It is not innate, but learned; the various facets of a culture are interrelated." Although people often equate culture with nationality, the concept of culture is actually much broader. In almost any country there are separate cultural groups based on such differences as race, ethnicity, religion, region, and gender. Each of these cultural groups has enough significant differences from the dominant society to have its own distinct way of life. Hall (1959, 1969, 1976, 1983) has developed a concept that is useful in understanding the differences among cultural groups. He places cultures on a continuum from high to low context. The term "context" refers to the interrelated conditions in which something exists—the social and cultural conditions that surround and influence the life of an individual, an organization, or a community.

In a high-context culture, the surrounding circumstances of an interaction are taken into account; in a low-context culture, these circumstances are filtered out. It is important to note that no value is assigned to either high or low context.

In high-context cultures, much attention is paid to the surrounding circumstances of an event. In an interpersonal communication, for example, the parties involved use such factors as paraphrasing, tone of voice, gesture, posture, social status, history, and social setting to interpret the spoken words. High-context communication requires time; factors such as trust, relationships between friends and family members, personal needs and difficulties, weather, and holidays must be considered. An example of this kind of communication in organizations is the Japanese practice of long hours of socializing after work.

In low-context cultures, the circumstances surrounding an event do not warrant attention; instead, the parties involved focus on objective facts that are conveyed. Consequently, interactions in low-context cultures are characterized by speed and efficiency. The best-seller *The One-Minute Manager* (Blanchard & Johnson, 1987) promotes a managerial approach based on low-context communication: The book describes how a manager can motivate employees with one-minute statements focusing on positive or corrective feedback and goal setting.

Hall has identified a number of dimensions of human activity, five of which are crucial to understanding cultural differences in organizations:

1. Association (relationships with others);

2. Interaction (verbal and nonverbal communication with others);

3. Territoriality (use of space);

4. Temporality (time, orientation); and

5. Learning (what knowledge and skills are developed and how they are transmitted).

The Cultural-Context Inventory Characteristics Sheet, a handout that follows the instrument and the scoring sheet, compares high and low context on these five dimensions.

Patterns of High and Low Context in Groups

Hall has identified patterns of high/low context in nationality groups (1959, 1969) and in urban/rural groups (personal communication, August 19, 1992). Additional research and literature, as cited in the following paragraphs, document the applicability of the same framework to gender groups. It should be noted that these patterns, which are depicted in Figure 1, reflect cultural tendencies rather than stereotypes; they do not apply to all members of a group.

High	Medium	Medium-Low	Low
Latin America	Greece	United States	Scandinavia
Asia	France		Germany
Africa	Italy		
	Spain		
	Middle East		
Women			Men
Rural			Urban

Figure 1. Patterns of High/Low Context in Various Cultures

As mentioned previously, within a country there may be a number of "micro cultures." In Switzerland, for example, the German, Italian, and French ethnic groups have distinct cultures; in Canada the same is true of the French and English. In the United States, assimilation has traditionally been necessary in order to gain economic power and middle-class status. Members of groups that are economically separate from the dominant society, such as people of color and white women, either have retained some cultural differences or have become bicultural—able to function in the mode of the dominant culture as well as in that of their own micro cultures. The current trend toward honoring diversity may mean that members of micro cultures will assimilate to a lesser degree than they previously did.

Studies conducted by African Americans (Foster, 1971; Hillard, 1976; Lewis, 1975) and by Mexican Americans (Castenada, Herold, & Ramirez, 1974), on those respective cultural groups, describe high-context characteristics. Some of the characteristics they note that are different from the dominant United States culture are an emphasis on collectivism rather than individualism, the importance of process and relationships in completing a task, greater use of the message as an art form than as a simple means of communication, the perception that everything has its own time, and an emphasis on learning by practicing what is modeled rather than by experimenting.

Women tend to be more high context than men. Many studies by U.S. women (Bem, 1977; Gilligan, 1982; Sargent, 1981; Schaef, 1981; Tannen, 1990) describe the high-context behaviors of women in the United States. For example, U.S. women have a greater concern for process (how things are accomplished and the interpersonal relationships with people in a work team) than for task; their orientation is that a task should not be accomplished at the expense of process and relationships. They heavily personalize disagreements, tending to avoid them or needing to solve them before work can progress; however, if they avoid conflict, they tend to have difficulty continuing in the work relationship. In contrast, women tend to have egalitarian social structures, a low-context characteristic. Feminist organizations, for instance, frequently have flat organizational structures and tend to avoid designating a leader.

Lewis (1975) has noted differences between Euro-American and African-American women. Euro-American women tend to avoid direct conflict, whereas African-American women are more assertive. However, in both groups, disagreement is personalized and emotions are involved.

Rural people have a tendency toward high-context behavior, which may be attributable to the need to consider time as a process that belongs to nature. Urban people are more free to schedule their time. In Japan rural agricultural people had to exercise a high-context behavior, working collectively, in order to manage irrigation and the water supply. In the United States, in contrast, the individual farmer historically has managed his or her own land (Ouchi, 1982).

Biculturalism

The high-/low-context framework can be used to conceptualize patterns of informal behavior for cultural groups. However, it is important to re-emphasize that the framework should not be seen as a set of boxes in which to place individual people. Every person is a member of a variety of micro-cultural groups, each one of which may be on a different point on the high-/low-context continuum. In addition to membership in various micro-cultural groups, numerous factors affect one's socialization and, therefore, one's orientation toward high context or low context: amount of time spent living with different cultural groups, geographic proximity to different cultures, language, birth order in the family, education, professional status, and visible identity. Groups with high visible identity are those who are easily identified as not being of the dominant culture. In the United States, for example, people of color and women are easily identified as not being of the dominant white-male culture. Factors like visible identity can accentuate differences.

Many people have lived in more than one dominant culture. A person who enters a new dominant culture exhibits one or more of the following three responses:

1. *Assimilation,* which means assuming the behaviors of the dominant culture;

2. *Maintenance,* which refers to maintaining one's own cultural identity; and

3. *Biculturalism,* which means behaving differently according to the situation in which one finds oneself.

The literature on cultural adaptation discusses the concept of culture shock experienced by people who recently have moved to a different culture. The first two behavioral responses, assimilation and maintenance, are more typical for the earlier stages of adjustment, whereas the third behavioral response, biculturalism, is not always reached. For example, when members of racial, ethnic, and gender groups enter a new dominant culture, they typically undergo a process of assimilation, differentiation from the dominant group, and then integration of aspects of their own cultures with those of the dominant culture (Halverson, 1982). After integration they are able to be bicultural.

MANAGING CULTURAL DIFFERENCES

People's cultural tendencies lead to vastly different approaches to life activities. This fact has important implications for the workplace. Kogod (1991) offers a helpful explanation of these implications for organizations:

> Difficulties inevitably arise when there is a great deal of diversity within an organization. Most of us have limited information about other people's world views. Frustration often occurs when two people with different world views interact; frequently, neither person feels valued or understood. Often one or the other practices ethnocentric thinking, experiencing his or her unique sense of time, use of language, and beliefs about work styles as comprising the one appropriate way to behave. When ethnocentric thinking pervades an organizational culture, the result can be exclusion of some, favoritism toward others, and intragroup conflict. (p. 8)

There are two methods of managing cultural differences in the workplace: (1) conformity and (2) synergy.

Conformity

Conformity consists of requiring members of nondominant cultures to adopt the norms, policies, and practices that characterize or favor the dominant group. (In the case of the United States, the dominant group is generally considered to be Euro-American male and low context.) Conformity generally limits the potential of nondominant groups, as they are forced to adjust. In the United States, for example, it has the disadvantage of limiting the contributions that women, people of color, and foreign-born nationals may bring to the workplace. If people from nondominant cultures are not allowed to express their diversity, the organizational culture loses the benefit of new ideas and approaches that would lead to a greater number of alternatives in solving problems.

Sometimes, though, there are norms, policies, or practices reflecting the standards of the dominant group that the team manager feels must be maintained. In these cases the following steps should be followed to minimize the impact on nondominant groups:

1. Identify the impact on the nondominant group(s).

2. Identify the advantages and disadvantages of maintaining the norm, policy, or practice in question.

3. Provide training or coaching for members of nondominant groups to clarify the norm, policy, or practice so that they understand what is expected and why.

Synergy

Synergy consists of developing norms, policies, and practices that are acceptable to both high- and low-context people; it enables full participation of all groups. Although synergy may initially be more time consuming and confusing as new methods are devised, it has the potential of producing benefits resulting from "gifts" brought by members of nondominant cultures—different communication patterns, decision-making styles, and conflict-resolution methods, for instance. The steps involved in the synergistic approach, developed by Adler (1986), are as follows:

1. Meet with people from all cultural groups involved to identify the norm, policy, or practice that is causing difficulty. Have members of all groups describe the situation from their own cultural perspectives.

2. Identify the cultural assumptions that explain the behaviors of those involved.

3. Pinpoint the cultural similarities and differences in the behaviors.

4. Create new alternatives based on, but not limited to, the cultures involved.

5. Select an alternative that will enable the full participation of all.

6. Implement the solution.

7. Assess the impact of the solution from the viewpoints of all cultural groups involved. Refine the solution if necessary.

THE INSTRUMENT

The Cultural-Context Inventory is based on the cultural framework of high/low context developed by Edward Hall (1959, 1969, 1976, 1983). The inventory was developed as a tool for increasing understanding of one's own culturally based behavior at work as well as the behaviors of others. As a training device, it not only helps trainees to identify ways in which they are similar to or different from others but also points out the need to develop effective ways of managing interpersonal differences. Although the inventory does not address culture-specific differences, it is useful in developing understanding of the broad dimensions of cultural differences.

Objectives

The specific objectives of using the instrument are as follows:

1. To increase respondents' awareness of the cultural dimensions that affect interpersonal interactions and organizational behavior;

2. To enhance respondents' understanding of their own work-style preferences and how these preferences relate to their individual cultural identities;

3. To assist respondents in comparing their own work styles with those of others;

4. To point out the need to develop effective ways of managing differences in work style; and

5. To encourage respondents to use a synergistic approach to managing differences in work style.

Validity and Reliability

No validity or reliability data are available on the Cultural-Context Inventory, but it does have face validity.

Administration and Interpretation

The following steps offer a process for administering the Cultural-Context Inventory and conducting subsequent training in cultural context:

1. The Cultural-Context Inventory is introduced as an instrument that will help respondents to gain a better understanding of their own culture-related work styles and how their styles differ from those of others. The trainer emphasizes that the best way to complete the instrument is to focus on one's preferences or what makes one most comfortable.

2. After all respondents have completed and scored the inventory, the trainer distributes copies of the characteristics sheet and delivers a lecturette on high/low context, using the information presented in that sheet and elsewhere in this article (adding, if desired, supplementary material from Hall's books, as referenced in this article). The following are some important aspects of high/low context that should be covered in the lecturette:

- The terms "high context" and "low context" refer only to the extent to which one either includes various elements of context or screens out such elements. No value is assigned to either high or low context. In fact, in an organizational setting, both are needed to create an effective team.

- Although there are patterns of high or low context for cultural groups, one's cultural identity is influenced by membership in many different micro-cultural groups as well as by individual forces and experiences.

- The inventory may enhance understanding of one's work-style preferences, but it should be broadly interpreted. Establishing one's numerical score is less important than identifying items that indicate strong preferences, which could cause difficulty in interactions with others who have strong preferences in the opposite direction.

- Previous experience with the inventory indicates that a person whose High Context and Low Context scores differ by 11 or more might have difficulty interacting with another person whose scores differ by 11 or more in the opposite direction (one person's scores favoring High Context and the other person's scores favoring Low Context).

3. The trainer forms three groups: (1) those whose HC scores are considerably higher than their LC scores, (2) those whose LC scores are considerably higher than their HC scores, and (3) those whose HC scores and LC scores are close or approximately equal. (In order to avoid labeling, the trainer gives no specific numerical scores for determining how to assemble into groups. Instead, the trainer divides the group into thirds based on their scores, ensuring that each group has enough members to facilitate a useful discussion.) The trainer asks the members of each group to discuss their responses to questions such as these:

- How do your inventory responses help you to understand your behavior in relation to the high-/low-context framework?

- How has membership in various cultural groups influenced your behavior?

- How do you feel and behave with someone from a different culture?

- What are the drawbacks of your own high- or low-context orientation? What are the advantages?

- What are some challenges that you face in working with those whose scores are very different from your own? How might you meet some of those challenges?

- What are some benefits of working with those whose scores are very different from your own? How might you capitalize on those benefits?

4. Representatives from the three groups are asked to share their responses to the questions. The trainer forms mixed groups, each of which has

members representing all three of the groups formed during the previous step. Each new group is asked to choose a challenging behavioral difference based on contextual orientation and to develop a role play for a work setting that will demonstrate how this challenge might be met. The members of each group then use a problem-solving process to develop a synergistic method of managing the difference. These role plays are performed for the total group, and the results are discussed.[1] *Option:* If the inventory is used as part of a team-building session, the team members may be asked to identify one or more areas of difference that are challenges for them and to develop a synergistic method of managing the difference(s).

REFERENCES AND BIBLIOGRAPHY

Adler, N.J. (1986). *International dimensions of organizational behavior.* Boston: Kent.

Bem, S. (1977). *Psychological androgyny.* St. Paul, MN: West.

Blanchard, K., & Johnson, S. (1987). *The one-minute manager.* New York: Berkley.

Castenada, A., Herold, L., & Ramirez, J. (1974). *New approaches to bilingual, bicultural education.* Austin, TX: The Dissemination and Assessment Center for Bilingual Education.

Foster, B. (1971). Toward a definition of black referents. In V. Dixon & B. Foster (Eds.), *Beyond black or white* (pp. 7-22). Boston: Little, Brown.

Gilligan, C. (1982). *In a different voice.* Cambridge, MA: Harvard University Press.

Hall, E. (1959). *The silent language.* New York: Doubleday.

Hall, E. (1969). *The hidden dimension.* New York: Doubleday.

Hall, E. (1976). *Beyond culture.* New York: Doubleday.

Hall, E. (1983). *The dance of life.* New York: Doubleday.

Hall, E. (1989). *Understanding cultural differences.* Yarmouth, ME: Intercultural Press.

Halverson, C.B. (1982). Training and stages of consciousness of racism and sexism in the world of work. In *Breakthroughs: Creating a world that works: Presenters' papers.* Proceedings of the OD Network Conference, Lake Geneva, WI.

Hillard, A. (1976). *Alternatives to IQ testing: An approach to the identification of gifted minority children.* California State Dept. of Education, Frederick Burk Foundation for Education.

Hofstede, G. (1980). *Culture's consequences: International differences in work related values.* Beverly Hills, CA: Sage.

Kluckholn, F., & Strodtbeck, F. (1961). *Variations in value orientations.* Evanston, IL: Row, Peterson.

Kogod, S.K. (1991). *A workshop for managing diversity in the workplace.* San Diego, CA: Pfeiffer & Company.

Lewis, D. (1975). The black family: Socialization and sex roles. *Phylon, 36(3),* 221-237.

---

[1] The simulation *Bafá Bafá* is useful for identifying dimensions or cultures that are similar to high/low context. Participation in this simulation also enhances people's understanding of how they might feel and behave when visiting a dominant culture that is different from the ones in which they have been socialized. This simulation can be obtained from Simulation Training Systems, Inc., 218 12th Street, P.O. Box 910, Del Mar, California, 92014, phone 619-755-0272.

Ouchi, W.G. (1982). *Theory Z: How American business can meet the Japanese challenge.* New York: Avon.

Sargent, A. (1981). *The androgynous manager.* New York: AMACOM.

Schaef, A.W. (1981). *Women's reality.* Minneapolis, MN: Winston.

Tannen, D. (1990). *You just don't understand: Women and men in conversation.* New York: William Morrow.

Claire B. Halverson, Ph.D., *is a professor of organizational behavior in the Master's program of intercultural management, School for International Training, in Brattleboro, Vermont. She consults in the areas of diversity and multicultural team buildng, working with a variety of organizations in the public, profit, and not-for-profit sectors. She has been director of the Southeastern Wisconsin Sex-Equity Training Institute and of the Southeastern Wisconsin Race-Desegregation Training Institute. She is a member of the NTL Institute.*

CULTURAL-CONTEXT INVENTORY
Claire B. Halverson

Instructions: For each of the following twenty items, circle 1, 2, 3, 4, or 5 to indicate your tendencies and preferences *in a work situation.*

	Hardly Ever		Sometimes		Almost Always
1. When communicating, I tend to use a lot of facial expressions, hand gestures, and body movements rather than to rely mostly on words.	1	2	3	4	5
2. I pay more attention to the context of a conversation— who said what and under what circumstances—than I do to the words.	1	2	3	4	5
3. When communicating, I tend to spell things out quickly and directly rather than talk around and add to the point.	1	2	3	4	5
4. In an interpersonal disagreement, I tend to be more emotional than logical and rational.	1	2	3	4	5
5. I tend to have a small, close circle of friends rather than a large, but less close, circle of friends.	1	2	3	4	5
6. When working with others, I prefer to get the job done first and socialize afterward rather than socialize first and then tackle the job.	1	2	3	4	5
7. I would rather work in a group than by myself.	1	2	3	4	5
8. I believe rewards should be given for individual accomplishments rather than for group accomplishments.	1	2	3	4	5

Pfeiffer & Company

	Hardly Ever	**Sometimes**	**Almost Always**

9. I describe myself in terms of my accomplishments rather than in terms of my family and relationships.
    1   2   3   4   5

10. I prefer sharing space with others to having my own private space.
    1   2   3   4   5

11. I would rather work for someone who maintains authority and functions for the good of the group than work for someone who allows a lot of autonomy and individual decision making.
    1   2   3   4   5

12. I believe it is more important to be on time than to let other concerns take priority.
    1   2   3   4   5

13. I prefer working on one thing at a time to working on a variety of things at once.
    1   2   3   4   5

14. I generally set a time schedule and keep to it rather than leave things unscheduled and go with the flow.
    1   2   3   4   5

15. I find it easier to work with someone who is fast and wants to see immediate results than to work with someone who is slow and wants to consider all the facts.
    1   2   3   4   5

16. In order to learn about something, I tend to consult many sources of information rather than go to the one best authority.
    1   2   3   4   5

17. In figuring out problems, I prefer focusing on the whole situation to focusing on specific parts or taking one step at a time.
    1   2   3   4   5

	Hardly Ever		Sometimes		Almost Always
18. When tackling a new task, I would rather figure it out on my own by experimentation than follow someone else's example or demonstration.	1	2	3	4	5
19. When making decisions, I consider my likes and dislikes, not just the facts.	1	2	3	4	5
20. I prefer having tasks and procedures explicitly defined to having a general idea of what has to be done.	1	2	3	4	5

Pfeiffer & Company

CULTURAL-CONTEXT INVENTORY
SCORING SHEET

Instructions: Transfer the circled numbers to the appropriate blanks provided below. Then add the numbers in each column to obtain your scores for High Context and Low Context.

High Context (HC)	Low Context (LC)
1. _____	3. _____
2. _____	6. _____
4. _____	8. _____
5. _____	9. _____
7. _____	12. _____
10. _____	13. _____
11. _____	14. _____
16. _____	15. _____
17. _____	18. _____
19. _____	20. _____
Total _____	Total _____

Put a check mark in the appropriate blank below to indicate which score is larger:

_____ High Context

_____ Low Context

Subtract your smaller score from your larger score. Record the difference in the blank below:

_____ Difference

CULTURAL-CONTEXT INVENTORY CHARACTERISTICS SHEET[2]

HIGH CONTEXT (HC)	LOW CONTEXT (LC)

Association

- Relationships depend on trust, build up slowly, are stable. One distinguishes between people inside and people outside one's circle.

- Relationships begin and end quickly. Many people can be inside one's circle; circle's boundary is not clear.

- How things get done depends on relationships with people and attention to group process.

- Things get done by following procedures and paying attention to a goal.

- One's identity is rooted in groups (family, culture, work).

- One's identity is rooted in oneself and one's accomplishments.

- Social structure and authority are centralized; responsibility is at top. Person at top works for good of group.

- Social structure is decentralized; responsibility goes further down (is not concentrated at the top).

Interaction

- High use of nonverbal elements; voice tone, facial expression, gestures, eye movement carry significant parts of conversation.

- Low use of nonverbal elements. Message is carried more by words than by nonverbal means.

- Verbal message is implicit; context (situation, people, nonverbal elements) is more important than words.

- Verbal message is explicit. Context is less important than words.

- Verbal message is indirect; one talks around the point and embellishes it.

- Verbal message is direct; one spells things out exactly.

- Communication is seen as art form —a way of engaging someone.

- Communication is seen as a way of exchanging information, ideas, opinions.

- Disagreement is personalized. One is sensitive to conflict expressed in another's nonverbal communication. Conflict either must be solved before work can progress or must be avoided because it is personally threatening.

- Disagreement is depersonalized. One withdraws from conflict with another and gets on with the task. Focus is on rational solutions, not personal ones. One can be explicit about another's bothersome behavior.

---

[2] The content of this sheet is based on the following works of anthropologist Edward Hall, all of which were published in New York by Doubleday: *The Silent Language* (1959), *The Hidden Dimension* (1969), *Beyond Culture* (1976), and *The Dance of Life* (1983).

HIGH CONTEXT (HC)	LOW CONTEXT (LC)

Territoriality

- Space is communal: People stand close to each other, share the same space.
- Space is compartmentalized and privately owned: Privacy is important, so people are farther apart.

Temporality

- Everything has its own time. Time is not easily scheduled; needs of people may interfere with keeping to a set time. What is important is that activity gets done.
- Things are scheduled to be done at particular times, one thing at a time. What is important is that activity is done efficiently.

- Change is slow. Things are rooted in the past, slow to change and stable.
- Change is fast. One can make change and see immediate results.

- Time is a process; it belongs to others and to nature.
- Time is a commodity to be spent or saved. One's time is one's own.

Learning

- Knowledge is imbedded in the situation; things are connected, synthesized, and global. Multiple sources of information are used. Thinking is deductive, proceeds from general to specific.
- Reality is fragmented and compartmentalized. One source of information is used to develop knowledge. Thinking is inductive, proceeds from specific to general. Focus is on detail.

- Learning occurs by first observing others as they model or demonstrate and then practicing.
- Learning occurs by following explicit directions and explanations of others.

- Groups are preferred for learning and problem solving.
- An individual orientation is preferred for learning and problem solving.

- Accuracy is valued. How well something is learned is important.
- Speed is valued. How efficiently something is learned is important.

EMPOWERMENT-READINESS SURVEY: FOUNDATIONS FOR TOTAL QUALITY MANAGEMENT

April G. Henkel, Cheryl Repp-Bégin, and Judith F. Vogt

INTRODUCTION AND THEORETICAL FRAMEWORK

Empowerment

In *The Silent Language,* Edward T. Hall (1959) notes that culture is a complex series of interrelated activities that largely govern how we act. Values, norms, and behaviors are taught without awareness in each society and in organizational settings; these translate into the ways in which things are done. Participative organizations focus on those behaviors, norms, and values that are empowering and that ensure movement toward effective change.

Empowered organizations, as described by Vogt and Murrell (1990), are characterized by participatory decision making. Members have a sense of responsibility for a shared mission and a belief in mutual values. Teamwork is fostered by the accessibility to and sharing of information and a high level of trust among employees and management. Empowered organizations value human resources and commit time and money to education, training, benefits, and recognition. The structure of empowered organizations spreads authority laterally rather than concentrating decision-making power at one level in the traditional, vertical line of authority. Organizational benefits of empowerment include innovative problem solving and an improved ability to anticipate, facilitate, and manage change in response to internal and external influences (Vogt & Murrell, 1990).

Change also is a key ingredient in empowered environments. To become empowered, an individual or organization must be willing to change; in empowered organizations, change is embraced rather than avoided or delayed. But change can be a painful experience—much like the feeling of loss—as old ways and patterns are replaced with new ways and patterns (Fossum, 1989; Scott & Jaffe, 1989). Resistance to change in organizations can take the form of mild skepticism, reluctance to contribute time or other resources to the process, and other behaviors that tend to delay or postpone involvement (Kanter, 1983). This resistance can be reduced through the exchange of information and feedback about the change, open and honest communication, understanding of the purpose for change, and a trusting and accepting environment (Vogt & Murrell, 1990).

To create and sustain an empowering environment in an organization, members of the organization must be committed to the change process and have a general propensity toward fundamental empowerment principles. Exploring the degree to which certain characteristics exist among an organization's members can help to determine the organization's overall level of readiness for empowerment. An assessment of organizational readiness can identify the existence of the characteristics that support the empowerment process and of those that hinder it.

Application to Total Quality Management

Total quality management (TQM) is a broad term that describes an organizational approach to implementing quality improvement, particularly of products and services. In TQM, the emphases are on planning, the development of innovative work teams, process improvement, measurement, relationships with customers and suppliers, and continuous improvement in all areas.

The focus on the tools, concepts, and philosophies of quality improvement was expanded when changes in organizational culture were recognized as fundamental to achieving quality (Jablonski, 1991). Any organization that is thinking about initiating TQM needs to establish an empowered culture beforehand, or the important TQM attributes of participation and employee contributions toward continuous improvement will not be realized. An organizational culture that encourages members to freely contribute ideas and become actively involved in problem solving and decision making promotes TQM and forms the foundation for integrating the cultural and technical dimensions of TQM (Atkinson, 1990; Jablonski, 1991).

EMPOWERMENT-READINESS SURVEY

The Empowerment-Readiness Survey can be used to discover an organization's propensity toward empowerment principles and the degree to which a foundation for empowerment exists. This survey can be used for two purposes: (1) to determine the status of the organization prior to implementing empowerment strategies (where are we now?), and (2) to guide the initiation of organizational change (where do we go from here and what are the steps we need to take?). The survey focuses on the following dimensions of empowering organizations: communication, value of people, ambiguity, concepts about power, information, and learning.

Description of the Instrument

The Empowerment-Readiness Survey gathers descriptive information about an organization, organizational subunit, or individual in terms of existing support for empowerment. It helps to determine how much preparatory training is needed to build an empowering environment.

The survey consists of seventeen statements that address six dimensions of empowerment:

- Communication (nine questions: 2, 4, 6, 10, 11, 12, 13, 14, 16);

- Value of people (thirteen questions: 2, 3, 5, 6, 7, 8, 9, 10, 11, 13, 14, 15, 16);

- Ambiguity (four questions: 2, 12, 16, 17);

- Concepts about power (eight questions: 1, 4, 6, 7, 8, 9, 10, 13);

- Information (eight questions: 2, 6, 11, 13, 14, 15, 16, 17); and

- Learning (eight questions: 3, 5, 7, 11, 12, 14, 15, 17).

Respondents are asked to read each of the seventeen statements and to indicate their degree of agreement or disagreement with each, using a seven-point Likert scale. The scale uses letters rather than numbers to allow for both supportive and nonsupportive phrasing of the statements and to simplify scoring. For supportive statements, the letters run from A to G; for nonsupportive statements, they run from G to A.

Application (Suggested Uses)

Although this survey was developed for use by internal or external consultants to explore the overall empowerment readiness of organizations, it has multiple applications.

1. The instrument can be used solely as an information-gathering tool for an organization that is considering or planning an empowerment program.

2. The instrument can be used as part of an organizational or group training program on empowerment.

3. Because the instrument is participant-driven, individual results (overall percentage scores) can be aggregated for interpretation at several levels. The survey can be used to explore the empowerment readiness of the entire organization; of subunits such as divisions, departments, or work teams; of individuals; or of functional groups or particular positions (for example, first-line supervisors or vice presidents) within the organization.

4. The individual, group, or organizational score for each of the six dimensions can be determined.

5. Another source of data is an item analysis (for example, for training purposes).

It should be noted that, although surveys can be returned to individual respondents for personal development and learning purposes, the survey was not designed to identify specific members of an organization or group for punitive purposes.

ADMINISTERING THE INSTRUMENT

When it is to be used to explore overall organizational readiness, the survey should be made available to all members of the organization (or subunit). The actual administration of the instrument can be accomplished in various ways.

Introduction

If the administration of the instrument is not to be done in a training or large-group setting, with everyone taking the instrument at the same time, employees can be given the instrument, asked to complete it within a specified period of time, and told how to return it. If this is the case, a brief cover letter of explanation from the chief executive officer (or subunit equivalent) should accompany the instrument. This letter should include the following kinds of information:

1. The purpose of the survey;

2. The time required (the survey should take respondents no longer than fifteen minutes to complete);

3. The fact that survey responses will be confidential (if this is true);

4. The date that completed surveys are due and how surveys will be collected; and

5. When and how results will be shared.

If the instrument is to be administered with employees *in situ*, the previous points can be conveyed by cover letter and also announced by the senior manager present or by the administrator/facilitator.

Participants have a right to know how their data will be used. It is a good idea to make a distinction between confidentiality (no responses will be revealed, and no one except the scorers will see the responses) and anonymity (some responses may be revealed, but the respondents will remain anonymous). The stated purpose of the survey should include why the survey is being administered (for instance, what the organization hopes/needs to know) and how the results will be used (for informational purposes, to plan organizational changes, to plan training, and so on).

After the survey has been distributed, participants should be given clear, sequential instructions about how to respond to it.

Theory Input

If the instrument is administered as part of a training program, when everyone has finished responding to it, the administrator/facilitator should give the respondents theoretical background about the instrument (for example, the concept of empowerment, its purposes, and the six dimensions of empowerment).

Prediction

In a training design, it is a powerful intervention to ask participants to predict their individual scores and the group scores. This helps open up the group for a subsequent discussion of the members' views on empowerment. For the purposes of an organizational-survey, prediction provides another view of how things really are; that is, do the members of the organization believe that they are "ready," "somewhat ready," or "not ready" for empowerment?

Scoring

In a training program, individual respondents may score their own instruments in order to receive immediate information on which to build discussion and learning. In this case, scoring sheets must be distributed and instructions for scoring given clearly and sequentially.

If the instrument is to be used as an organizational survey, it may be scored by respondents and then turned in so that organizational scores can be derived, or the scoring may be done by a central person or functional unit. To obtain information about the entire organization, score each individual survey before combining results to obtain a total organizational score.

In an organizational (nontraining) context, if the instrument is to be used for individual feedback purposes, each respondent should be provided with a survey form, scoring instructions, and an opportunity to meet with an internal or external consultant to interpret the results.

If desired, the following additional scoring procedures can be followed:

- Scores can be examined across functional groups.

- An item analysis can be done if more specific data are required.

- Bar graphs can be created to display pertinent data.

Interpretation

The interpretation information that accompanies the Empowerment-Readiness Survey determines the respondent's degree of readiness for empowerment by percentage of Level A scores. The instrument administrator/facilitator will help the respondents to interpret their scores. Interpretative categories are "ready," "somewhat ready," and "not ready."

In a training design, actual scores are compared with predictions at this stage. After individual scores are examined, the group's overall readiness profile can be determined.

Scores can be examined across the six dimensions of empowering organizations (communication, value of people, ambiguity, concepts about power, information, and learning). The information that is derived from this study can help to determine which areas are in need of further development and training and which are not. For example, scores may be high in communication, value of people, and learning, but low in ambiguity, concepts about power, and information.

Scores also can be checked across functional groups to find out which are supportive of empowerment and which are not. For example, top managers may be resistant to empowerment because they might perceive it as threatening to their traditional authority and power.

Processing

Discussion of the instrument in a training program can be focused in several ways, depending on the purpose of the session. Participants can examine their various views of the issue of empowerment. They then can discuss the overall organization's readiness for empowerment. If there is wide discrepancy between the scores of individuals or functional/positional groups, examination of the reasons for the differences may be appropriate. This could be followed by a discussion of organizational implications. A further extension of the discussion might be the suggestion of actions that could be taken to equalize and enhance the organization's overall readiness.

VALIDITY AND RELIABILITY

The Empowerment-Readiness Survey has face validity in that the seventeen statements ask members of the organization to report their agreement or disagreement with fundamental empowerment principles stated in organizational and/or managerial terms. The statements are representative of empowerment dimensions that are key ingredients in creating and sustaining a supportive environment for total quality management. The final version of the survey is the result of feedback from a four-member review panel and field tests in two organizational settings.

REFERENCES

Atkinson, P.E. (1990). *Creating culture change: The key to successful total quality management.* United Kingdom: IFS Limited.

Fossum, L. (1989). *Understanding organizational change: Converting theory to practice.* Los Altos, CA: Crisp Publications.

Hall, E.T. (1959). *The silent language.* New York: Doubleday.

Jablonski, J.R. (1991). *Implementing total quality management: An overview.* San Diego, CA: Pfeiffer & Company.

Kanter, R. (1983). *The change masters.* New York: Simon & Schuster.

Scott, C.D., & Jaffe, D.T. (1989). *Managing organizational change: A practical guide for managers.* Los Altos, CA: Crisp Publications.

Vogt, J., & Murrell, K. (1990). *Empowerment in organizations: How to spark exceptional performance.* San Diego, CA: Pfeiffer & Company.

April G. Henkel *is the director of program development for the Tallahassee consulting firm of Margaret Lynn Duggar & Associates, Inc. In this capacity she works with individuals, organizations, and businesses on creating products and services for an aging society. She also conducts training workshops and coordinates the annual Aging Network Conference. Ms. Henkel has worked as a professional in the field of aging for over ten years as case manager, government analyst, and executive director for the Senior Society Planning Council. She is the author of numerous grant proposals and co-author of an article on empowerment in organizations.*

Cheryl Repp-Bégin *is a total quality leadership (TQL) management specialist in the Department of Management Services, Florida, providing consultation, internally and to other state agencies, on implementation strategies of TQL. She also designs, develops, and presents training for team leaders and members on interpersonal and communication skills. Ms. Repp-Bégin specializes in cultural change and leadership/management development.*

Judith F. Vogt, Ph.D., *is an associate professor of organizational communication at Florida State University. She provides a cornerstone involvement in F.S.U.'s Total Quality and Continuous Improvement Certificate program. Her areas of expertise include team building, facilitation, empowerment, and assessing organizational readiness for Total Quality and Continuous Improvement transformation. Other relevant areas of competence include change theory and practice (organizational and personal), training design and implementation, leadership, and organizational learning and development. She is co-author of the books* Empowerment in Organizations: How to Spark Exceptional Performance *and* Retaining Professional Nurses: A Planned Process *as well as numerous articles on empowerment and consultant ethics and values. Currently, she is writing a book on team building and empowerment.*

EMPOWERMENT-READINESS SURVEY
April G. Henkel, Cheryl L. Repp-Bégin, and Judith F. Vogt

Instructions: For each of the following statements, please indicate the degree to which you, as an individual, agree or disagree with the statement by circling one of the letters on the continuum line below the statement. If you strongly agree with the statement, circle the letter to the left of the continuum under "Strongly Agree." If you feel neutral about the statement, circle the "D" in the middle. If you strongly disagree, circle the letter to the right of the continuum under "Strongly Disagree."

1. Decision-making authority in an organization can be spread effectively to all levels.

Strongly   Strongly
Agree   Disagree

A	B	C	D	E	F	G

2. Employees should be kept up-to-date about all organizational changes and decisions.

Strongly   Strongly
Agree   Disagree

A	B	C	D	E	F	G

3. People are an organization's most valuable resource.

Strongly   Strongly
Agree   Disagree

A	B	C	D	E	F	G

4. Decisions should be made by people who have the highest positions in the organization.

Strongly   Strongly
Agree   Disagree

G	F	E	D	C	B	A

Pfeiffer & Company

5. The "bottom line" should be given the greatest priority in organizational decision making.

Strongly
Agree

Strongly
Disagree

G	F	E	D	C	B	A

6. Input from front-line employees is valuable in organizational planning and decision making.

Strongly
Agree

Strongly
Disagree

A	B	C	D	E	F	G

7. The best way to increase productivity is to supervise employees closely.

Strongly
Agree

Strongly
Disagree

G	F	E	D	C	B	A

8. Decision making that involves employees is time consuming but results in better decisions.

Strongly
Agree

Strongly
Disagree

A	B	C	D	E	F	G

9. Only certain levels of employees should be given authority.

Strongly
Agree

Strongly
Disagree

G	F	E	D	C	B	A

10. If a decision is in the best interests of the organization, it probably is not in the best interests of the employees.

Strongly
Agree

Strongly
Disagree

G	F	E	D	C	B	A

11. A manager's time is best spent supporting employees by providing information and feedback that help employees to get the job done.

Strongly
Agree

Strongly
Disagree

A	B	C	D	E	F	G

12. When informed about organizational changes (for example, opening a new office or adding a new product or service), managers should let employees know as quickly as possible and give them an opportunity to ask questions.

Strongly
Agree

Strongly
Disagree

A	B	C	D	E	F	G

13. Decisions that directly affect employees should not be made without employee input.

Strongly
Agree

Strongly
Disagree

A	B	C	D	E	F	G

14. It is as important for an employee to understand the purpose/mission of the organization as it is to understand how to perform his or her specific job duties.

Strongly
Agree

Strongly
Disagree

A	B	C	D	E	F	G

15. Organizations should support employee participation in personal-growth opportunities, such as continuing education or fitness programs, by allowing flexible work schedules or other means.

Strongly   Strongly
Agree   Disagree

A	B	C	D	E	F	G

16. Organizations have a responsibility to consider the impacts of their decisions on the community (for example, expanding or relocating a production facility).

Strongly   Strongly
Agree   Disagree

A	B	C	D	E	F	G

17. It is better to continue as is, as long as the job gets done, than it is to make changes.

Strongly   Strongly
Agree   Disagree

G	F	E	D	C	B	A

EMPOWERMENT-READINESS SURVEY
SCORING SHEET

Instructions: For individual feedback purposes, complete steps one through three below; for group or organizational purposes, complete steps one through five.

Step One

For each individual survey, count the number of "A" and "B" answers circled (these letters indicate the two highest levels of agreement in support of empowerment principles).

Step Two

Use the following guide to determine the readiness level of the respondent:

- **Level A:** If the number of A and B responses equals 14 or more, the respondent generally is committed to empowerment principles, and there appears to be a foundation to support total quality management.
- **Level B:** If the number of A and B responses equals 10 to 13, the respondent needs more information about empowerment and the opportunity to discuss and to learn about empowerment principles before becoming involved in total quality management.
- **Level C:** If the number of A and B responses equals 9 or fewer, the respondent demonstrates lack of belief in and commitment to the empowerment principles necessary to effectively fuel the TQM process.

Step Three

Write the letter indicating the level of readiness (A, B, or C) in the upper right-hand corner of the first page of each individual survey for ease in counting the number of respondents at each level. Then organize the surveys by readiness level.

Step Four

Count the number of respondents at each readiness level and write the results on the appropriate lines below. Then total these numbers and write the result on the "total number participating in survey line."

Level A _____

Level B _____

Level C _____

TOTAL NUMBER PARTICIPATING IN SURVEY: _____

Step Five

Compute the percentage of respondents at each readiness level (number at each level divided by total in survey):

Number of Level A Responses: = [   ] (percentage of Level **A**'s)
    Total Number:

Number of Level B Responses: = [   ] (percentage of Level **B**'s)
    Total Number:

Number of Level C Responses: = [   ] (percentage of Level **C**'s)
    Total Number:

EMPOWERMENT-READINESS SURVEY
INTERPRETATION SHEET

Determine the degree to which the organization is ready for organizational empowerment by comparing the actual percentage of Level A scores with the percentages below:

- **Ready** *(percentage of Level A scores equals 80 percent or more):* The organization is generally committed to empowerment principles, and there appears to be a foundation to support total quality management.

- **Somewhat Ready** *(percentage of Level A scores equals 60 to 79 percent):* Organizational members need more information and the opportunity to discuss empowerment principles before going further with the TQM process.

- **Not Ready** *(percentage of Level A scores equals 59 percent or less):* Organizational members appear to lack the belief in and commitment to empowerment principles necessary to effectively fuel the TQM process. The organization's leadership needs more extensive preparation before deciding whether or not to initiate TQM throughout the organization. Preparation should include training about empowerment principles versus traditional management practices, the changed role of managers, and information about TQM in other organizations.

STRATEGIC LEADERSHIP STYLES INSTRUMENT[1]

Gaylord Reagan

Leadership styles are not static. They can be changed to serve the needs of an individual, group, or organization. A small investment of time and energy to identify and then to consider the significance of a strategic leadership style can return big dividends. Productive individuals, groups, and organizations who willingly make this investment and accept responsibility for shaping their own futures refuse to go on "doing what comes naturally."

THE INSTRUMENT

Theoretical Framework

Consultant Lawrence M. Miller (1989, p. 1) writes that "All living things...exhibit patterns or cycles of development, moving from periods of vitality and growth, to periods of decay and disintegration. The pattern of business growth and decline—and the behavior of leaders—follows this same course.... It is natural for leaders in every stage to rely on responses they find most comfortable and to fail when they do not adopt innovative responses.... [The history] of corporations demonstrates this relationship, between the behavior of leaders and the cycle of growth and decline."

Based on this observation, Miller constructs "a theory of corporate life cycles," which explains the natural stages of evolution experienced by organizations and the people who lead them as they confront day-to-day challenges. Miller also identifies a series of leadership styles that dominate each of the six stages of organizational life.

In designing the Strategic Leadership Styles Instrument, the author separated Miller's Builder and Explorer styles, added the Synergist style, and sequenced the resulting styles as follows:

1. *Prophet:* A visionary who creates breakthroughs and has the human energy to pursue them. The Prophet adheres to a set of values and has high standards. In pursuing goals, the Prophet tends to rely on the support of a small circle of true believers.

2. *Barbarian:* A conqueror who commands the organization and pursues rapid growth. The Barbarian takes the Prophet's vision and begins implementing it in a direct, pragmatic, action-oriented, and forceful

---

[1] This instrument is based on *Barbarians to Bureaucrats: Corporate Life Cycle Strategies—Lessons from the Rise and Fall of Civilizations* by Lawrence M. Miller (1989). New York: Clarkson N. Potter.

manner. Adherents of this style are self-confident and personally involved, and they demand complete loyalty from others.

3. *Builder:* A developer of structures required for successful organizational growth. Builders increase the efficiency of the Barbarian's early efforts. They focus on expansion, quantity, quality, and diversification, and they initiate the shift from command to collaboration.   .

4. *Explorer:* A developer of skills required for successful organizational growth. Explorers increase the efficiency of the Barbarian's early efforts. They focus on expansion, quantity, quality, diversification, and competition.

5. *Synergist:* A leader who helps the organization successfully balance expansion and the structures required to sustain that growth.

6. *Administrator:* An integrator of systems and structures to help organizations successfully shift their focus from expansion to safe and routine operation. The Administrator stresses perfecting financial and management practices but does not become involved with production operations.

7. *Bureaucrat:* An imposer of tight controls. Unlike the Prophet, the Bureaucrat has no interest in creativity; and unlike the Barbarian, no interest in growth. To improve performance the Bureaucrat relies on strategic planning, cost cutting, and acquiring (not inventing) new products or services.

8. *Aristocrat:* An alienated inheritor of others' results. Aristocrats do no work and produce only organizational disintegration. They also tend to be autocratic. They communicate poorly, tolerate warfare among internal fiefdoms, seek to acquire symbols of power, and avoid making decisions.

Reliability and Validity

The Strategic Leadership Styles Instrument is designed to be used as an action-research tool rather than as a rigorous data-gathering instrument. Applied in this manner, the instrument has demonstrated a high level of face validity when administered to groups ranging from executive managers to nonmanagement personnel.

Administration

The following suggestions will be helpful to the facilitator who administers the instrument:

1. Before respondents complete the instrument, discuss briefly the concept of organizational life cycles. Miller describes a process whereby all living things, including organizations, move through a series of developmental cycles. These cycles begin with vitality and growth but can end

with decay and disintegration. Miller's model also describes the challenges confronted by leaders as their organizations pass through these cycles. Miller contends that by breaking this cyclical pattern, leaders can help their organizations grow and develop.

2. Distribute copies of the Strategic Leadership Styles Instrument and read the instructions aloud as the respondents follow.

3. Instruct the respondents to read all eight phrases in a group before assigning ranking numbers. Make sure they understand that assigning "8" indicates that the phrase most accurately describes the respondent's behavior or beliefs and that "1" indicates the least accurate phrase. Respondents should select their "8" phrase first, then their "1" phrase, then assign the intermediate rankings ("2" through "7") to the remaining phrases.

4. Ask respondents to wait to score the instrument until everyone has completed the rankings.

Scoring

Each respondent should be given a copy of the Strategic Leadership Styles Instrument Scoring Sheet. Each respondent should complete the scoring sheet by transferring the ranking numbers from the instrument to the corresponding blanks on the scoring sheet. Then the five numbers in each category should be totaled.

Respondents should then proceed to their scoring grids. Each respondent circles the appropriate score below each of the eight styles. A line should then be drawn on the grid to connect the circled numbers.

Interpretation and Processing

The scoring grid offers respondents a means for assessing the strength of their relative preferences for the eight styles. The descriptors across the bottom of the grid help respondents assess the impact of their styles on their organizations; that is, they indicate whether their preferred styles fall into the command, collaboration, or disintegration area or some combination of those areas. Respondents should try to determine how their preferences match the current and future needs of their organizations.

It is sometimes useful for the facilitator to prepare a large copy of the scoring grid on newsprint. In this case, the facilitator polls the individual respondents and posts their individual scores for each of the eight styles, drawing a line to connect each individual's scores. The various patterns can form the basis for a discussion. It may also be useful to compute average scores for each of the eight styles and provide the respondents with group norms.

The facilitator distributes the Strategic Leadership Styles Interpretation Sheet, which gives brief descriptions of the eight leadership styles. It also offers suggestions to respondents whose supervisors exemplify the different styles and to supervisors whose employees demonstrate preferences for the various styles.

The facilitator divides the respondents into small groups (four or five members in each group). If intact work groups are present, the small groups should be comprised of the work groups. The Strategic Leadership Styles Instrument Discussion Guide is distributed, and the facilitator instructs the groups to use the guide to stimulate discussion and then to prepare individual action plans.

Uses of the Instrument

The Strategic Leadership Styles Instrument is designed to accomplish the following objectives:

1. To help individual respondents to examine their relative preferences for strategic leadership styles associated with Miller's developmental cycles;

2. To help respondents to differentiate the impact of the eight leadership styles on their organizations;

3. To facilitate discussion by members of intact work groups about their collective style pattern;

4. To initiate discussions about the appropriateness of individual or group leadership style preferences within the context of an organization's short- and long-term viability; and

5. To stimulate planning designed to increase individual and group use of appropriate leadership styles.

SELECTED BIBLIOGRAPHY AND REFERENCES

Clifford, D.K., Jr. (1985). *The winning performance: How America's high-growth midsize companies succeed.* New York: Bantam.

Collins, E.G.C. (Ed.). (1983). *Executive success: Making it in management.* New York: John Wiley.

Hickman, C.R., & Silva, M.A. (1984). *Creating excellence: Managing corporate culture, strategy, and change in the new age.* New York: New American Library.

Kilmann, R.H. (1989). *Managing beyond the quick fix: A completely integrated program for creating and maintaining organizational success.* San Francisco: Jossey-Bass.

Kouzes, J.M., & Posner, B.Z. (1989). *The leadership challenge: How to get extraordinary things done in organizations.* San Francisco: Jossey-Bass.

Maccoby, M. (1988). *Why work: Leading the new generation.* New York: Simon & Schuster.

Manz, C.C., & Sims, H.P., Jr. (1989). *Super leadership: Leading others to lead themselves.* New York: Prentice-Hall Press.

Miller, L.M. (1989). *Barbarians to bureaucrats: Corporate life cycle strategies—lessons from the rise and fall of civilizations.* New York: Clarkson N. Potter.

Steers, R.M. (1977). *Organizational effectiveness: A behavioral view.* Santa Monica, CA: Goodyear.

Tichy, N.M., & Devanna, M.A. (1986). *The transformational leader.* New York: John Wiley.

Waterman, R.H., Jr. (1987). *The renewal factor: How the best get and keep the competitive edge.* New York: Bantam.

Gaylord Reagan, Ph.D., *is an independent consultant specializing in total quality management, executive team building, organization development, and management training. He has conducted programs for managers in corporations, government, health care, and publishing. In addition to having served various organizations as director of management development, director of training, employee development manager, and human resource manager, Dr. Reagan has been a faculty member at several universities. He is a member of various professional organizations, including the American Management Association, Academy of Management, and the Society for Human Resource Management. Dr. Reagan is also included in the* International Directory of Distinguished Leadership, International Leaders in Achievement, Who's Who in America, Who's Who in American Education, *and* Who's Who in the Midwest.

STRATEGIC LEADERSHIP STYLES INSTRUMENT

Gaylord Reagan

Instructions: Within each of the five groups of statements (Group A through Group E), read all eight statements; then write the number "8" in the space preceding the statement that most accurately describes you, your behavior, or your beliefs with regard to your organization. Next, write the number "1" in the space preceding the statement that least accurately describes you or your behavior or beliefs. Finally, use the numbers "2" through "7" to indicate the best intermediate rankings for the remaining statements. Then proceed to the next group and repeat the operation. Rank all statements (leave none blank), and use each ranking number only once within each group of statements.

Group A

_____ 1. My ideas are long range and visionary.

_____ 2. My top priority is survival, and my mission is clear and urgent.

_____ 3. I enjoy actually making products or delivering services.

_____ 4. I am a convincing and enthusiastic communicator.

_____ 5. I seek to balance opposing forces.

_____ 6. Thus far, my career has taken place mainly in staff areas rather than production areas.

_____ 7. In meetings, my remarks review what has already happened.

_____ 8. I have not personally developed a new product or service in a long time.

Group B

_____ 9. I am willing to make sacrifices to see my ideas realized.

_____ 10. I do not like analyzing numbers and trends prior to acting.

_____ 11. I like measuring the results of my work.

_____ 12. Sometimes I feel as though I work for my customers or clients rather than for this organization.

_____ 13. I openly discuss the philosophy and values behind my decisions.

_____ 14. I consider myself to be an expert at procedures, processes, and systems.

_____ 15. I do not see my job as including the development of new products or services.

_____ 16. I concentrate on strategic planning rather than actually producing products or services.

Group C

_____ 17. I tend to withdraw for long periods to think about ideas.

_____ 18. I am in charge and am very comfortable making decisions.

_____ 19. I make decisions quickly, take action, and see the results.

_____ 20. I like to keep score and am competitive by nature.

_____ 21. I am hard on performance but soft on people.

_____ 22. Order, consistency, and smooth operations are high priorities for me.

_____ 23. Views of the organization are more important than those of its customers.

_____ 24. A person in my position has a right to enjoy exclusive perks.

Group D

_____ 25. Other people see me as being a bit different.

_____ 26. Other people say I am authoritarian and do not consult them on decisions.

_____ 27. I am not a visionary and do not devote a lot of time to dreaming.

_____ 28. I believe this organization should place a greater emphasis on expansion.

_____ 29. I stress teamwork and constant improvement of products and services.

_____ 30. I focus more on the present than on the future.

_____ 31. I believe that tighter controls will solve many of the organization's problems.

_____ 32. Only I and a few others really understand the organization's strategy.

Group E

_____ 33. I am neither well organized nor overly interested in details.

_____ 34. I am action oriented and do not like careful planning.

_____ 35. I do not like wasting time doing things through committees.

_____ 36. I feel that the organization gets bogged down in paperwork.

_____ 37. I believe in the value of organizational flexibility.

_____ 38. I place heavy emphasis on control and discipline.

_____ 39. I spend more time with staff personnel than production personnel.

_____ 40. Many times I cannot trust people to do what is right.

STRATEGIC LEADERSHIP STYLES INSTRUMENT
SCORING SHEET

Instructions: Transfer the number you assigned to each statement in the Strategic Leadership Styles Instrument to the corresponding blank on this sheet. Then add the numbers under each category and write the total in the blank provided.

1. Prophet Category:

Statement 1. _____

Statement 9. _____

Statement 17. _____

Statement 25. _____

Statement 33. _____

Total = _____

This is your **Prophet** score. Prophets are visionaries who create breakthroughs and the human energy needed to propel organizations forward.

2. Barbarian Category:

Statement 2. _____

Statement 10. _____

Statement 18. _____

Statement 26. _____

Statement 34. _____

Total = _____

This is your **Barbarian** score. Barbarians are leaders who thrive on crisis and conquest, who command organizations during periods of rapid change.

3. Builder Category:

Statement 3. _____

Statement 11. _____

Statement 19. _____

Statement 27. _____

Statement 35. _____

Total = _____

This is your **Builder** score. Builders are developers of the specialized structures required for successful change and growth. They *initiate* the shift from command to collaboration.

Pfeiffer & Company

4. Explorer Category:

Statement 4. _____

Statement 12. _____

Statement 20. _____

Statement 28. _____

Statement 36. _____

Total = _____

This is your **Explorer** score. Explorers are developers of the specialized skills required for successful change and growth. They *complete* the shift from command to collaboration.

5. Synergist Category:

Statement 5. _____

Statement 13. _____

Statement 21. _____

Statement 29. _____

Statement 37. _____

Total = _____

This is your **Synergist** score. Synergists are leaders who maintain a balance and continue the forward motion of a growing and complex organization by unifying and appreciating the diverse contributions of Prophets, Barbarians, Builders, Explorers, and Administrators.

6. Administrator Category:

Statement 6. _____

Statement 14. _____

Statement 22. _____

Statement 30. _____

Statement 38. _____

Total = _____

This is your **Administrator** score. Administrators create integrating systems and structures, and they shift the organization's focus from expansion toward security.

7. Bureaucrat Category:

  Statement 7. _____

  Statement 15. _____

  Statement 23. _____

  Statement 31. _____

  Statement 39. _____

  Total = _____

This is your **Bureaucrat** score. Bureaucrats impose tight controls that inhibit the creativity of Prophets and the risk-taking habits of Barbarians.

8. Aristocrat Category:

  Statement 8. _____

  Statement 16. _____

  Statement 24. _____

  Statement 32. _____

  Statement 40. _____

  Total = _____

This is your **Aristocrat** score. Aristocrats are those who inherit success and are alienated from those who do the actual work. They often cause rebellion and disintegration.

STRATEGIC LEADERSHIP STYLES INSTRUMENT
SCORING GRID

Instructions: On the grid below, circle your scores for each of the eight leadership styles shown at the top. Then connect the circles with a line to form a graph of your comparative style preferences.

Prophet	Barbarian	Builder	Explorer	Synergist	Adminis-trator	Bureau-crat	Aristocrat
40	40	40	40	40	40	40	40
39	39	39	39	39	39	39	39
38	38	38	38	38	38	38	38
37	37	37	37	37	37	37	37
36	36	36	36	36	36	36	36
35	35	35	35	35	35	35	35
34	34	34	34	34	34	34	34
33	33	33	33	33	33	33	33
32	32	32	32	32	32	32	32
31	31	31	31	31	31	31	31
30	30	30	30	30	30	30	30
29	29	29	29	29	29	29	29
28	28	28	28	28	28	28	28
27	27	27	27	27	27	27	27
26	26	26	26	26	26	26	26
25	25	25	25	25	25	25	25
24	24	24	24	24	24	24	24
23	23	23	23	23	23	23	23
22	22	22	22	22	22	22	22
21	21	21	21	21	21	21	21
20	20	20	20	20	20	20	20
19	19	19	19	19	19	19	19
18	18	18	18	18	18	18	18
17	17	17	17	17	17	17	17
16	16	16	16	16	16	16	16
15	15	15	15	15	15	15	15
14	14	14	14	14	14	14	14
13	13	13	13	13	13	13	13
12	12	12	12	12	12	12	12
11	11	11	11	11	11	11	11
10	10	10	10	10	10	10	10
9	9	9	9	9	9	9	9
8	8	8	8	8	8	8	8
7	7	7	7	7	7	7	7
6	6	6	6	6	6	6	6
5	5	5	5	5	5	5	5

└── COMMAND──┘└────── COLLABORATION──────┘└─ DISINTEGRATION─┘

STRATEGIC LEADERSHIP STYLES INSTRUMENT
INTERPRETATION SHEET

This interpretation sheet gives a brief description of the eight strategic leadership styles. Now that you have determined which leadership style or styles you generally use, you should be able to recognize the styles used by others in your organization. Under each description listed below, you will find some suggestions about how to work with both managers and subordinates who exhibit that style. You may find it useful to share the suggestions under your own leadership style with your manager and your subordinates.

1. **Prophets** are at their best when organizations are getting started or are entering a period of major restructuring and renewal. Prophets hold—and engender in others—a strong belief in new products and services. They have high standards and do not believe in the abilities of people outside their own small group. They make decisions by themselves; and although they may listen to others, they are not likely to make effective use of participative decision making. They tend to have many ideas that can confuse other people, because they have little use for either structure or systems. They tend to change on a whim.

If you work for a Prophet:

- Do not expect him or her to provide specific objectives or instructions. Ask to discuss your objectives and then write your own, based on your discussion.

- Do not expect him or her to follow up on details of your work. Discuss the larger goals toward which your are working.

- Seek out him or her for advice and ideas.

- Be tolerant of his or her latest ideas, even if they seem illogical and inconsistent. Do not confront Prophets about their apparent lack of direction; instead, ask leading questions that will help them shape their brainstorms into practical courses of action.

- Realize that Prophets do not expect you to share their characteristics. In fact, they often appreciate having people around who organize and accomplish their ideas for them.

If Prophets work for you:

- Recognize them for their creative abilities, and reinforce and encourage those talents. Do not demand that they be well organized or conform to standard procedures.

- Listen to them. They need to know that their visionary ideas are important to you. Let them know that within your organization there is room and opportunity for the implementation of their ideas.

- Help Prophets distinguish between their regular jobs and their creative activities. Prophets may need to justify their salaries with mundane work.

- Protect them from Bureaucrats. Remember that in mature organizations Prophets are all too often ignored or eliminated.

- Have patience. Prophets work not for this quarter's results, but for the impact they can have over the long run. Their view is very long-range. Insisting on immediate results destroys their creativity.

2. **Barbarians** excel when organizations are struggling to survive or to broaden their base or attempting to diversify. Barbarians see themselves as being in life-or-death struggles to accomplish the Prophet's objectives. High control and direct action appeal to Barbarians, who like to personally lead the troops into battle. They want others to join the team or move out of the way. Barbarians prefer to establish a few simple systems and structures while stressing a high degree of task flexibility.

If you work for a Barbarian:

- Be prepared for action. Barbarians expect you to act quickly and not to engage in lengthy or detailed planning exercises. Go to the heart of the matter and take action.

- Do not expect to be involved in long meetings or consensus decision making. Barbarians will make the decisions and you will carry them out.

- When Barbarians ask for your input, be completely honest and direct. Do not beat around the bush or give lengthy explanations.

- Go to Barbarians; do not wait for them to come to you. If you want a Barbarian to give you a promotion or different job or if you have an idea, you must seek out him or her and discuss your needs in a straightforward manner.

If Barbarians work for you:

- Be sure that their assignments are appropriate for command and single-minded action.

- Leave no confusion about Barbarians' areas of responsibility and what you expect of them. If you do not establish limits for them, they may run down the road so fast that you will have trouble getting things back under control.

- Take advantage of Barbarians' greatest talents: working in turnaround situations and managing organization units that are growing fast and need quick decisions. If your organization is in decline and needs a revolution, Barbarians—if put in charge—can inject excitement and urgency and can renew the vision.

- Help Barbarians make the transition to the next management stage by encouraging them to involve their people more, to delegate more, and to consider longer-range factors and outcomes.

3. **Builders** are most valuable when successful organizations are confronted by many opportunities for growth and diversification. Builders believe in their organization's products and services. They are interested in the means of production,

although they focus their energies on making those means more efficient. They are detail oriented and are concerned with short-range numbers. They initiate their organization's leadership shift from "command" to "collaboration."

If you work for a Builder:

- Offer clear, specific, written objectives. Builders hate surprises and believe that you should have a blueprint for your activities.

- Realize that Builders are not the world's greatest communicators. You can help them by initiating needed communication. Do not expect them to do so.

- Do not expect a great deal of positive reinforcement. Builders take satisfaction from the quality and volume of the products that go out the door, and they expect that you will, too.

- Realize that Builders appreciate creativity within bounds. They want better ways to get things accomplished. Builders are more interested in "how" than in "what" or "why."

If Builders work for you:

- Be sure that your measurement and feedback is not based entirely on the short term. Builders already tend toward that direction. You need to help them learn to think in the long term.

- Help them to understand the need for involving people below them in decision making.

- Remember that Builders respond to rewards for improving processes ("how") more than for results ("what").

- Do not burden Builders with too much central-staff help. They like to run their own operations with the greatest possible degree of autonomy. Hold Builders accountable for improvements. Offer help but do not impose it.

4. **Explorers** are similar to Builders, but Explorers place their emphasis on increasing the efficiency of the *skills* used to produce the organization's products and services. They are the organizational members most in touch with customers. They are highly competitive and enjoy keeping score. Interpersonal relationships are important to Explorers, and they are enthusiastic and intuitive. On the other hand, they hate paperwork and do little or no managing.

If you work for an Explorer:

- You will win points for producing results and gaining new business—things Explorers understand most.

- Tell him or her about your plans. Explorers want to know that their employees have high objectives and expectations.

- Do not tell him or her what cannot be done or what should have been done. Keep your level of enthusiasm high, and frame your comments in a positive context.

If Explorers work for you:

- Remember that they appear to need your approval more than others do, because they are "out in the wilderness" most of the time. When they come back to the office they need your praise. Let them have it.
- When they seem overly optimistic about their own performance, do not shoot them down. Instead, help them develop more realistic expectations and projections.
- When they want you to spend more time in the field with customers than you can afford, work with them on making the best use of their time.
- When they do not have the best relations with those whose support they need in production, help them understand the importance of these members of their team. Explorers often have difficulty along this line.

5. **Synergists** do not favor a single leadership style. Instead, they incorporate the different styles of leadership required to succeed throughout an organization's life cycle. Synergists seek social unity, balance, teamwork, and continuous improvement of products and services (total quality management). To achieve these goals and foster development of the production process, they emphasize positive behavioral reinforcement by using symbols, participative decision making, interpersonal skills, and high levels of technical competence.

If you work for a Synergist:

- Be sensitive to his or her need to blend and balance the characteristics of Prophets, Barbarians, Builders, Explorers, and Administrators.
- Do not expect consistency. Demonstrate flexibility in your own approach to problems.
- Demonstrate ability in teamwork, participation, delegation, and constant improvement of products and services.
- Appreciate the Synergist's need for emphasizing both the material and spiritual aspects of the organization.

If Synergists work for you:

- Reward them for achieving a balance between the preservation of creativity and the need for order.
- Realize that Synergists may want you to increase the amount of time that you spend with personnel in production areas instead of staff areas. Although this is generally a good idea, there is still a need to take care of the administrative aspects of the organization.

6. **Administrators** contribute most when organizations have entered a secure stage, are financially successful, are developing broader markets for their products and services, and are developing more complex internal structure. Administrators believe in efficiency and in maximizing the financial side of the organization. To this end, they stress perfecting management control systems and tend to take the organization's products and services for granted. They are not effective in dealing

with people. They make decisions based on data and spend lots of time seeking "correct" answers. Under Administrators, line managers lose power while staff gains it.

If you work for an Administrator:

- Realize that he or she is more likely to reward you for conforming than for creating.

- Understand his or her essential need for administrative control and discipline. When that control becomes stifling, you must help the Administrator to recognize your situation.

- Recognize who you are and what your ambitions are. If you always work for an Administrator, you can develop the same characteristics, which may or may not be the best for you.

If Administrators work for you:

- Remember that Administrators are good at taking care of details; reward them for that. Also help them to see the larger picture, direction, trends, and reasons. Keep them in touch with what is important to the organization.

- Help Administrators to see their jobs as serving those whose performance should be enhanced by their systems: the Builders and Explorers.

7. **Bureaucrats** are most visible in diversified organizations, where primary products and services are viewed as being mature "cash cows." For Bureaucrats, growth occurs through acquiring younger organizations and cost cutting. Bureaucrats confront no problems that cannot be overcome through sound financial management and controls. They place little emphasis on creativity and are more concerned with numbers than people. Bureaucrats like written reports, and they cultivate the flow of paper. They seek to increase autocratic command throughout their organizations, often resulting in overorganization, overspecialization, and a lack of trust between levels.

If you work for a Bureaucrat:

- Remember that the Bureaucrat tends to focus on performance that fits the system, without asking whether it is the right performance. Help him or her by asking questions that will lead to a consideration of more creative responses.

- Since Bureaucrats need order and conformity, do not make them nervous by being "weird." It is difficult to work for a nervous boss, particularly if you are the one who makes the boss nervous.

- Serve as a buffer for your subordinates. Manage them to produce creative responses without interference from your Bureaucratic supervisor. Do not make your own problem your subordinates' problem.

If Bureaucrats work for you:

- Remember that Bureaucrats are better in staff jobs, not line jobs.

- Make sure that they do not spin a web of stifling systems and structure around others.
- Since Bureaucrats constantly complain about others who are violating the sanctity of their systems, learn to ask, "So what?"
- Reward them for developing and managing the most efficient administrative processes. Define efficient as meaning the fewest possible staff requiring the least amount of time from line managers.

8. **Aristocrats** are generally most evident when the organization's primary products and services are declining because of a lack of attention, investment, and creativity; when organizational components are being eliminated and divested; and when cash is desperately needed. At these times cynicism permeates all parts and levels of the organization. Aristocrats increasingly surround themselves with expensive tokens of their positions ("perks") and view their primary mission as preventing further organizational erosion. They have an aloof management style and do not like making decisions. If forced to do so, they generally use a highly autocratic style. Their organizations are burdened with excessive layers of management, poor communication, little clarity of mission, low motivation, lots of internal warfare, and ineffective formal structures.

If you work for an Aristocrat:

- Quit.
- If you cannot quit, consider the Aristocrat's objectives but create your own independently. Hope that the Aristocrat's successor appreciates your efforts.

If Aristocrats work for you:

- Encourage them to leave.
- If they will not quit, ask them specific questions about their efforts to improve the organization, the quality of their products and services, and their plans for creative developments. Let them know that their jobs depend on a change in behavior.

STRATEGIC LEADERSHIP STYLES INSTRUMENT
DISCUSSION GUIDE

Use the following questions to stimulate a discussion in your group.

1. Which of the eight leadership styles do your scores on the Strategic Leadership Styles Instrument suggest that you are most likely to use? Least likely to use? In what ways are these styles important to your work?

2. What are your key subordinates' leadership styles? What behaviors could you use to improve your relationships with those people? What behaviors should you avoid using?

3. What are your key peers' leadership styles? What behaviors could you use to improve your relationships with those people? What behaviors should you avoid using?

4. What is your supervisor's leadership style? What behaviors could you use to improve your relationship with that person? What behaviors should you avoid using?

5. What suggestions would you give to the following people about how to relate to you better and what to avoid doing?

   a. Your supervisor
   b. Your peers
   c. Your subordinates

6. Which leadership styles are most needed in your organization if it is to adapt successfully to its changing environment? Which behaviors may need to be de-emphasized?

7. To what extent do the behaviors of your leadership style fit with those most needed by your organization? In other words, is your leadership behavior part of the solution or part of the problem? In what ways?

INTRODUCTION TO THE
PROFESSIONAL DEVELOPMENT SECTION

This year marks the tenth anniversary of the *Annual's* Professional Development section, which was introduced in the 1984 *Annual* to encompass a variety of materials that would be useful to human resource development (HRD) practitioners in their personal and professional development. The Professional Development section includes contents such as those included in the Lecturette, Theory and Practice, and Resources sections of the first twelve *Annuals*. These materials provide information about such diverse topics as new directions and trends in HRD; new technologies (and new uses of old technologies); issues that affect HRD practitioners; new areas for application; and new processes, perspectives, outlooks, and theoretical developments.

Included in this section are articles that HRD practitioners can bring to the attention of management or use as handouts or lecturette content in a training session. Such articles often are useful in documenting or supporting a position or in explaining a complex or subtle point. In addition, these articles can be used to explain the HRD function or various HRD technologies to line managers and others within organizations.

This year's section consists of eight articles. The first, "The Dunn and Dunn Model of Learning Styles: Addressing Learner Diversity," presents a research-based model incorporating twenty-one elements that affect people's abilities to learn. These elements are divided into five categories: psychological, environmental, emotional, sociological, and physical. This fascinating article offers much food for thought in terms of how to expose people to new information or new projects.

The second article in the section, "How to Make New-Employee Orientation a Success," describes twelve key factors of successful orientation programs— the results of a survey of more than one hundred United States and Canadian companies during a six-year period. A bonus to this article is its comprehensive Orientation-Content Checklist, which should expedite the process of developing an orientation program in an organization.

The third article reflects the continuing interest in the issue of diversity in organizations. "Managing and Motivating the Culturally Diverse Work Force" offers seven steps to motivating in ways that are sensitive to cultural differences and helpful in maintaining harmony and productivity in the multicultural workplace. This article is rich in concrete examples of things to do and say.

"The Effective Use of Humor in Human Resource Development," the fourth article in the section, is as entertaining as it is informative. It describes the benefits of using humor, documents the link between fun and effectiveness in an organizational setting, and presents guidelines for using humor in a way that enhances communication.

The fifth piece, "The Initial Interview: Assessing Client Needs," offers twelve questions for an organization development consultant to ask a prospective client during their first meeting about a particular problem or issue. The initial client contact is crucial, and this article can help a consultant to structure that contact so that it sets the stage for an effective relationship and a successful intervention.

Many organizations today are experiencing growing pressure to find, develop, and keep the best employees. The sixth article, "Growing by Leaps and Bounds: Management Development Through Key Growth Experiences," addresses this important need. It describes a strategy for developing managers via an accelerated growth process that virtually any organization can adopt successfully.

Another article that addresses a timely issue is the seventh in the Professional Development section, "Sexual Differences in the Workplace: The Need for Training." This article thoroughly discusses the workplace implications of male-female differences, sexual discrimination and harassment, the impact of legislation, and the role of training in this complicated issue.

The eighth and final article presents a comprehensive training design. "Stress-Management Training for the Nineties" also offers information on the causes of stress, the symptoms of stress and its impact in the workplace, and current stress-management efforts. In addition, this article includes an appendix on the physiology of the stress response, which will be intriguing to participants with a technical orientation or a particular interest in the subject.

As is the case with every *Annual*, several topics are covered in this volume; not every article will appeal to every reader. Nevertheless, the range of articles presented should encourage a good deal of thought-provoking, serious discussion about the present and the future of HRD.

THE DUNN AND DUNN MODEL OF LEARNING STYLES: ADDRESSING LEARNER DIVERSITY

Joanne Ingham and Rita Dunn

INTRODUCTION

Research on learning styles explains why individuals within the same family or organization perform differently. It demonstrates the differences in style among individual members of the same class, culture, community, profession, or socioeconomic group, and simultaneously reveals the differences and similarities among groups.

Every adult possesses unique learning style preferences (Dunn, 1986; Smith, 1976) that determine how he or she approaches work and responds to selected educational programs. These preferences are consistent over time and task (Elliott, 1975). When learning style theory and its related practices are properly applied, the following significant outcomes can be expected (Dixon, 1982; K. Dunn, 1982; Freeley, 1984):

- Increased achievement success;
- More positive attitudes toward learning;
- Improved interpersonal communication;
- More effectively designed educational programs;
- More efficient time management; and
- Greater application of newly acquired information and skills in the work setting.

BACKGROUND OF THE DUNN AND DUNN MODEL OF LEARNING STYLES

In 1967, Rita Dunn undertook a project with the New York State Department of Education to design and to direct a program that would help educationally disadvantaged learners to increase their achievement levels. The conclusions that Rita and Kenneth Dunn reached through observation were corroborated by substantial educational and industrial literature concerning how people learn.

By 1972, the Dunns had identified twelve variables that significantly differentiated among learners; three years later they reported the existence of eighteen variables; by 1979, they had incorporated hemispheric preference and global/analytic inclinations into their framework. The resulting model, which traces its roots to cognitive theory and brain lateralization theory, includes twenty-one variables that significantly affect how individuals begin to concentrate on, process, absorb, and retain new and difficult information or skills.

Research on the Dunn and Dunn Model of Learning Styles has been extensive. As of 1991, experimentation had been conducted at more than seventy institutions of higher education, with diverse age groups (kindergarten through adult), and at every level of academic proficiency, including gifted, average, underachieving, at risk, dropout, special education, vocational education, adult education, and corporate employee training. Details of this research are provided in the *Annotated Bibliography* (Center for the Study of Learning and Teaching Styles, St. John's University, 1991). Furthermore, the experimental research in learning styles conducted at St. John's University, New York, has to date received one regional, twelve national, and two international awards and citations for its quality.

LEARNING STYLE: A DEFINITION

A person's learning style is the way in which he or she concentrates on, processes, and retains new and difficult information and engages in challenging tasks (Dunn, 1990). This interaction process is unique to each person. Identifying a person's learning style requires first examining that person's multidimensional characteristics. This examination identifies many key traits inherent in a person's natural processing style, including what most likely triggers concentration, how it is sustained, and the bases of long-term memory. To conduct a truly successful examination, it is necessary to use a comprehensive model of learning style. Only a comprehensive model fully appreciates that different people are affected by different elements of style. Each of these elements is capable of increasing academic achievement to some extent among those for whom it is important.

THE DUNN AND DUNN MODEL OF LEARNING STYLES

The Dunn and Dunn model includes twenty-one elements that, when classified, reveal that learners are affected by the following factors, illustrated in Figure 1:

- Psychological elements—global/analytic, hemispheric preference, and impulsive/reflective;

- Environmental elements—sound, light, temperature, and furniture/seating designs;

- Emotional elements—motivation, persistence, responsibility (conformity versus nonconformity), and the need for either externally imposed structure or the opportunity to do things their own way;

- Sociological elements—learning alone, in pairs, in a small group, as part of a team, with an authoritative or collegial adult, and wanting variety as opposed to patterns and routines; and

- Physical elements—perceptual strengths, time-of-day energy levels, and the need for intake or mobility while learning.

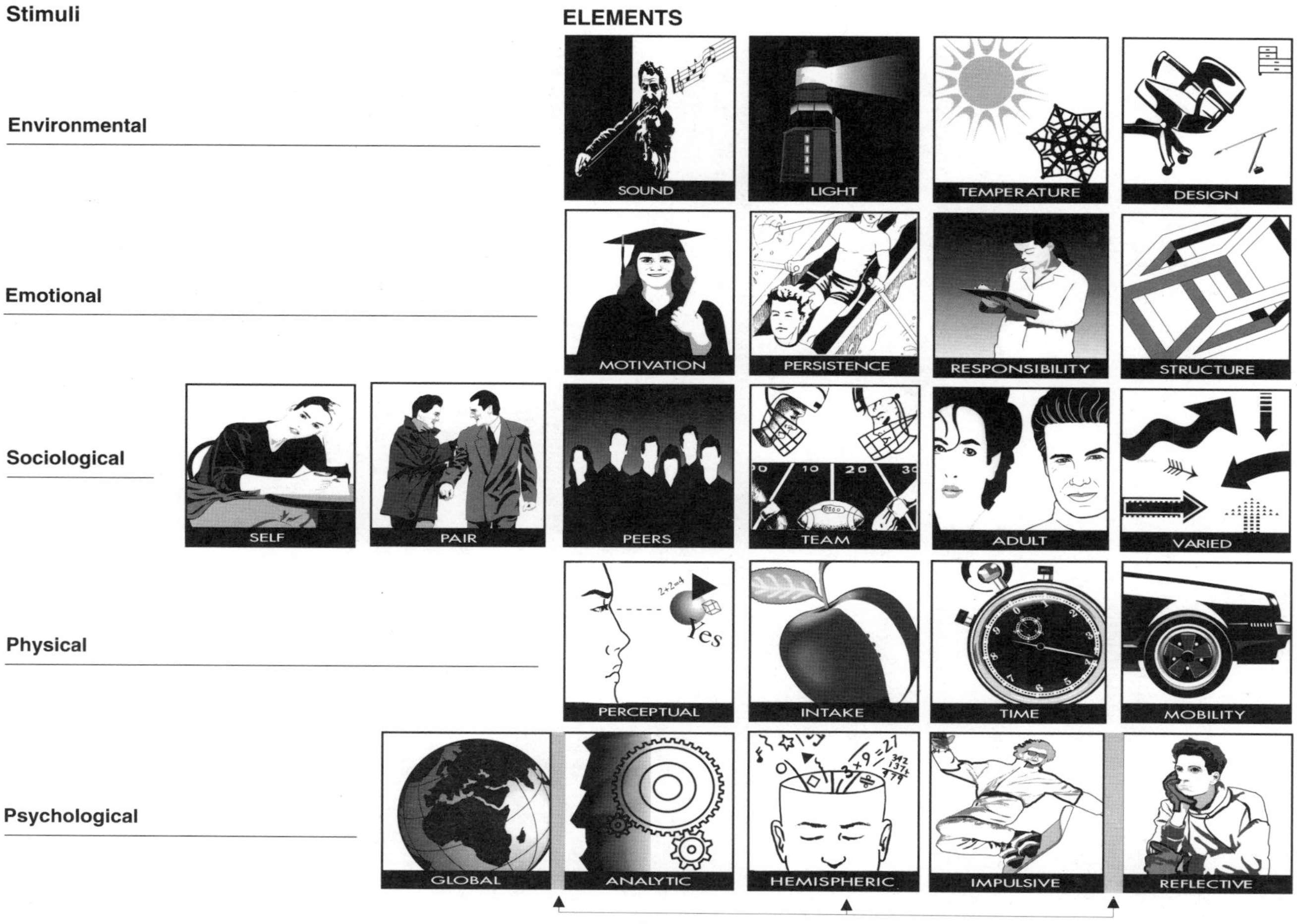

Stimuli

Environmental

Emotional

Sociological

Physical

Psychological

ELEMENTS

DESIGN STRUCTURE VARIED MOBILITY REFLECTIVE

TEMPERATURE RESPONSIBILITY ADULT TIME IMPULSIVE

LIGHT PERSISTENCE TEAM INTAKE HEMISPHERIC

SOUND MOTIVATION PEERS PERCEPTUAL ANALYTIC

PAIR

SELF

GLOBAL

Simultaneous or Successive Processing

Figure 1. The Dunn and Dunn Learning Styles Model

THE ELEMENTS OF LEARNING STYLE

Psychological Elements

Individuals process new and difficult information in fundamentally different ways. The terms analytic/global, hemispheric preference, sequential/simultaneous, and inductive/deductive have been used interchangeably in the literature. The descriptions of these variables tend to parallel one other.

Those who tend to be analytics learn more easily when information is presented step by step in a cumulative sequential pattern that builds toward a conceptual understanding. Conversely, those who tend to be globals learn more easily when they understand the concept first. After they see the "whole picture" they then can concentrate on details. Globals also enjoy being introduced to the information with a humorous short story replete with examples and graphics. Whether analytic or global, however, what is crucial to understanding brain functioning is that both types do reason, but by different strategies (Levy, 1979; Zenhausern, 1980). Each strategy is "a reflection of a trend toward optimalization of efficient use of neural space" (Levy, 1982, p. 224).

Thus whether adults are analytic or global, sequential or simultaneous, inductive or deductive, or have a certain hemispheric preference, they are capable of mastering identical information or skills and working productively if their processing styles are complemented. That conclusion has been documented at the high school and adult levels.

Analytic and global processors have different environmental and physiological needs (Cody, 1983; Dunn, Bruno, Sklar, & Beaudry, 1990; Dunn, Cavanaugh, Eberle, & Zenhausern, 1982). Many analytic preferents tend to opt for learning and working in a quiet, well-illuminated, formal setting; they often have a strong emotional need to complete the tasks they are working on; and they rarely eat, drink, smoke, chew or bite on objects while concentrating. Conversely, global preferents appear to work with what some describe as distractors: they concentrate best with sound (music or background talking), soft lighting, an informal seating arrangement, and some form of intake. In addition, globals take frequent breaks while concentrating and often stay with a task for a short amount of time, stop, do something else, and eventually return to the original task. Neither set of procedures is better or worse than the other; they merely are different. Many globals prefer learning with peers rather than alone or with an instructor or supervisor, and they also often prefer to structure tasks in their own way; they tend to dislike imposed directives.

The psychological element of impulsive/reflective is a function of individual verbal risk-taking behavior. Impulsives are quick to say what first comes to mind. Reflectives, however, need time to consider the question or problem and think through alternative solutions before verbalizing. Both response styles are beneficial. Instructors and managers should consider building buffer time into training discussions and office meetings to ensure the input of the reflectives is not compromised by pressure to move through the agenda.

Instructors and employers need to know how to guide and interact with both analytic and global processors whether on the job or in a learning environment. A necessary precondition to this management approach is understanding one's own learning style preferences. Understanding and capitalizing on an individual's preferred processing style clearly will enhance academic and job-related productivity.

Environmental Elements

How people physically react to the elements of sound, light, temperature, and design in the immediate environment is biologically based (Restak, 1979; Thies, 1979). Some individuals prefer absolute quiet while concentrating; others need background sound, such as a radio, to produce their best work. Light and temperature fall on a similar continuum. Some people prefer varying amounts of light, such as that provided by task lighting; some prefer a warm environment and others a cooler work area.

The study of the relationship between workers and their environment is called ergonomics. Studies have shown that such environmental factors as lighting, heating, furniture design, and noise affect individual employees differently. There is a direct correlation between those factors and the individual's productivity (Whitehouse, 1988). Accommodating an individual's unique preferences leads to an increase in productivity (Durante, 1988). Ergonomics takes a human-centered approach to addressing the requirements of workplace systems. Although people are adaptive, this adaptation effort creates a corresponding reduction in the individual's ability to devote energies and skills to job performance or learning. Excessive adaptation may lead to discomfort, fatigue, and in extreme cases a medical problem (Springer, 1988).

Similar differences are evidenced with varied seating arrangements. Some prefer concentrating in wooden, plastic, or steel chairs, but many others become so uncomfortable in conventional seats that they are prevented from engaging in productive thinking or learning. Few people are aware that when a person is seated in a hard chair, fully 75 percent of the total body weight is supported by four square inches of bone (Branton, 1966). The resulting stress on the tissues of the buttocks causes fatigue, discomfort, and frequent postural change. Only naturally well-padded people can tolerate conventional seating for long periods of time.

For those reasons, the physical layout and furnishings of offices, work spaces, and classrooms have profound effects on productivity levels. Flexibility in lighting intensity, type of seating, and quiet or sound (such as with portable stereos) will allow individuals to create personally productive work spaces. Employees' preferences in terms of environmental elements can guide organization decision makers in the selection and furnishing of facilities.

Emotional Elements

Emotional elements address the ways in which a person approaches a learning situation or undertakes a difficult project. A key emotional element is motivation (how driven one is, whether one is a self-starter, and whether one is willing to take risks). Highly motivated individuals require little supervision and learn new skills quickly; individuals with low motivation require frequent positive feedback and constant supervision, even in tasks they easily can accomplish. Another emotional element is persistence. Learners who tend to be nonpersistent prefer to work with many short-term projects. Those who tend to be persistent are more productive working on one project at a time. Both types will be equally productive despite the dissimilarity in approach.

Responsibility (the extent to which one takes direction versus a preference to personalize a task) is an indication of degree of conforming behavior. Those who are conforming by nature take direction and feel compelled to do what they "should"; nonconformists question authority and thrive on collegial relationships. The element of structure impacts whether one wants directions spelled out specifically or prefers reaching the goal with choices and options. A mismatch of responsibility or structure orientations can be a source of conflict or discomfort between manager/employee and instructor/learner. An awareness of these differences when working or learning is critical to establishing productive relationships.

Sociological Elements

Sociological elements influence one's preference for working independently; with a team, a mentor, or a colleague; or in a variety of groupings. The sociological preferences of an individual directly affect how successful small-group instructional techniques work as an instructional strategy or the degree to which one is perceived as a team player. Often a member of a quality circle or project team who prefers to work independently will work on specific portions of the project alone and then bring back to the group his or her finished product.

Physical Elements

Physical elements, which are also biologically based, include intake (the need to eat, drink, or chew); mobility (the need to move or stretch periodically); time of day (peak energy times); and perceptual preference (whether one learns best in an auditory, visual, tactual, or kinesthetic manner). Although some individuals need to eat, drink, or chew when they work, others prefer not to do so until they have completed their tasks. In terms of mobility, some individuals can sit at their desks for long periods of time when working on challenging tasks, whereas others need to get up frequently to take breaks, stretch, and move around.

The physical element of time of day has received substantial attention in terms of chronobiology, peak energy times for individuals, time management, and the implications for flextime. Task efficiency also is related to each person's temperature cycle (Biggers, 1980); thus it is related to when each person is likely to concentrate and/or learn best. Individuals have specific chronobiological cycles and times of day during which they can perform maximally. Performing challenging tasks or learning new information at the best time of day impacts the quality of the work produced. Furthermore, statistics show that information taught to an individual at his or her best time of day is more often used on the job than information taught at another time (Freeley, 1984).

Perceptual preference, or sensory modality, refers to the different paths through which people can absorb information (auditory, visual, tactual, or kinesthetic). Research has verified that when an adult is taught with instructional resources that complement his or her sensory strength, more is learned and the person experiences a more positive attitude toward basic learning itself (Buell & Buell, 1987; Farr, 1971; Ingham, 1989).

Perceptual preference tends to develop with physical maturation. The tactual/kinesthetic modes are strongest among young children; the visual mode takes over in approximately the second or third grade; and at the end of elementary school, the auditory mode predominates (Keefe, 1979; Price, 1980). According to Keefe (1979), adults tend to possess a preference for one modality or another. One cannot assume that individual adults will achieve optimal learning or concentration regardless of the instructional approach utilized. Based on tests of thousands of adults with the *Productivity Environmental Preference Survey (PEPS)*, Dunn, Dunn, and Price (1989) concluded that many possessed only one perceptual strength, whether tactual/kinesthetic, auditory, or visual. Approximately 40 percent were visually oriented, 30 percent were auditory, and 30 percent were tactual/kinesthetic (Dunn, 1986). In short, a majority of adults have perceptual learning preferences dominated by one modality.

Some people can remember approximately 75 percent of what they hear; those are considered auditory learners. Visual learners remember 75 percent of what they read or see. As people get older, they tend to be more visual. The legendary command of "put it in writing" may reflect a real need for some people. Approximately 40 percent of the population tends to possess a visual strength. Others learn through physical engagement; they learn by doing. A person with a kinesthetic strength needs to be actively involved in a task such as a site inspection or field trip, or learning by doing. An on-the-job training program is far more effective for those people than an office manual, text, or lecture. Those with a tactual strength are best able to remember new and difficult information when they use their hands during the learning process. Building models, drawing diagrams or pictures, and using manipulatives all enhance the concentration of tactual/kinesthetic individuals.

It is imperative that a person's first exposure to new information or a new project be through his or her strongest modality. Using all four modalities in sequence does not ensure that each person is introduced to difficult material correctly (that is, through his or her perceptual preference/strength). Using multiple stimuli is often counterproductive. For example, many highly auditory individuals listen better when they are not required to take notes; in effect, note taking interferes with their listening. These critical findings should guide instructors, employers, and individual learners to make wise decisions concerning selection of courses or training programs and strategies for accomplishing challenging tasks (Buell & Buell, 1987; Dunn, 1988, 1990; Ingham, 1990).

IMPORTANT RAMIFICATIONS

Both Restak (1979) and Thies (1979) ascertained that 60 percent of learning style is biological; the remainder, apart from persistence, develops through experience. Individual responses to sound, light, temperature, seating arrangements, perceptual strengths, intake, time of day, and mobility are biological. Sociological preferences, motivation, responsibility, and a need for structure versus a need for self-direction are thought to be developmental. The significant differences among the learning styles of individuals in diverse cultures tend to support this theory (Dunn, 1989; Dunn, Gemake, Jalali, Zenhausern, Quinn, & Spiridakis, 1990; Dunn, Gemake, & Zenhausern, 1989; Dunn & Griggs, 1990; Guzzo, 1987; Jacobs, 1987; Jalali, 1989; Lam-Phoon, 1986).

Every person has an individual learning style, and every person has learning style strengths. People tend to learn more when taught with their own strengths than when taught with the instructor's strengths. However, no learning style is better or worse than another. Each style encompasses similar intelligence ranges. People tend to learn, concentrate, remember, and enjoy learning and working to a significantly greater extent when they are taught through their learning style preferences.

Responding to individual learning style characteristics increases the rate and level of retention of those adults trying to concentrate and learn new or difficult information. The lessons for instructors, trainers, and supervisors are manifest. First, one must analyze a person's learning style strengths. That information can be applied on a personal, interpersonal, and organizational level to enhance productivity. Individual differences must be assessed and respected and that information must then be integrated into educational programs and work environments.

A driving goal of adult educators and human resource development professionals is to support adults' individual strengths so they learn in ways that maximize performance. Learning style theory and practice will provide the framework for successfully accomplishing that goal.

As early as 1973, Hess and Sperry (1973) made the following observations:

> The need to understand individual differences and how learners learn...is emerging as a number one concern for training directors.... While it is obvious that much more theory and research is needed in this area [learning styles], it is equally obvious that the educational planner and the trainer in an organizational setting must become more aware of the individual differences in the learners and how these differences affect the organization's productivity and moral. (p. 825)

Knowles (1978) emphasized that adults learn in unique ways that should be considered when developing educational programs. At the heart of andragogy (adult learning) lies a respect for the differences in individual adult learners and the impact those differences have in various instructional situations. To facilitate the learning process, those individual differences must be taken into account. Dixon (1982) further indicated the following:

> Information on learning styles is a relatively new consideration in the design of training programs.... By considering these [learning style] differences and taking them into account in designing training programs, greater gains can be made in learning.... Participants' reactions will be more positive and training time can be reduced. (p. 62)

Based on research conducted under a two-year, joint project of the American Society of Training and Development (ASTD) and the United States Department of Labor, Carnavale, Gainer,. and Meltzer (1988) drew the following conclusions:

> Trainers seeking to teach the skill of learning to learn should attempt to identify the type of sensory stimulus—whether visual, auditory, or tactile—that helps each employee learn best, and then design multiple-use training that addresses all preferences. (p. 6)

Human resource development professionals and educators of adults have been asked by government agencies and corporate leaders to seek solutions to the training challenges to the twenty-first century. Given the vast resources companies have committed—and must continue to commit to training programs—the development and implementation of training programs effective in reaching individual adult learners remains critical.

REFERENCES

Biggers, J.L. (1980). Body rhythms, the school day, and academic achievement. *Journal of Experimental Education, 49*(1), 45-47.

Branton, P. (1966). *The comfort of easy chairs (FIRA Technical Report No. 22).* Hertfordshire, England: Furniture Industry Research Association.

Brennan, P.K. (1984). An analysis of the relationships among hemispheric preference and analytic/global cognitive style, two elements of learning style, method of instruction, gender, and mathematics achievement of tenth-grade geometry students (Doctoral dissertation, St. John's University, 1984). *Dissertation Abstracts International, 45,* 3271A.

Bruno, J. (1988). An experimental investigation of the relationships between and among hemispheric processing, learning style preferences, instructional strategies, academic achievement, and attitudes of developmental mathematics students in an urban technical college. (Doctoral dissertation, St. John's University, 1988). *Dissertation Abstracts International, 48,* 1066A.

Buell, B.G., & Buell, N.A. (1987). Perceptual modality preference as a variable in the effectiveness of continuing education for professionals. (Doctoral dissertation, University of Southern California, 1987). *Dissertation Abstracts International, 48,* 283A.

Cafferty, E. (1980). An analysis of student performance based upon the degree of match between the educational cognitive style of the teachers and the educational cognitive style of the students (Doctoral dissertation, University of Nebraska, 1980). *Dissertation Abstracts International, 41,* 2908A.

Carnavale, A.P., Gainer, L.J., & Meltzer, A.S. (1988). *Workplace basics: The skills employers want.* Alexandria, VA: American Society for Training and Development.

Center for the Study of Learning and Teaching Styles, St. John's University. (1991). *Annotated Bibliography.* Jamaica, New York: Author.

Clark-Thayer, S. (1987). The relationship of the knowledge of student-perceived learning style preferences, and study habits and attitudes to achievement of college freshmen in a small urban university. (Doctoral dissertation, Boston University, 1987). *Dissertation Abstracts International, 48,* 872A.

Cody, C. (1983). Learning styles, including hemispheric dominance: A comparative study of average, gifted, and highly gifted students in grades five through twelve. (Doctoral dissertation, Temple University, 1983). *Dissertation Abstracts International, 44,* 1631A.

DeBello, T. (1990). Comparison of eleven major learning styles models: Variables, appropriate populations, validity of instrumentation and the research behind them. *Reading, Writing, and Learning Disabilities International, 6*(3), 203-222.

Dixon, N. (1982). Incorporating learning style into training design. *Training and Development Journal, 36*(7), 62-64.

Douglas, C.B. (1979). Making biology easier to understand. *The Biology Teacher, 41*(5), 277-299.

Dunn, K. (1982). Measuring the productivity preferences of adults. In J.W. Keefe (Ed.) *Student learning styles and brain behavior,* (pp. 136-141). Reston, VA: National Association of Secondary School Principals.

Dunn, R. (1986). Learning styles: Link between individual differences and effective instruction. *North Carolina Educational Leadership, 11*(1), 3-22.

Dunn, R. (1988). Capitalizing on students' perceptual strengths to ensure literacy while engaging in conventional lecture/discussion. *Reading Psychology: An International Quarterly, 9,* 431-453.

Dunn, R. (1989). Do students from different cultures have different learning styles? *Inter-Ed, 16*(50), 3-7.

Dunn, R. (1990). Understanding the Dunn and Dunn learning styles model and the need for individual diagnosis and prescription. *Reading, Writing, and Learning Disabilities International, 6,* 223-247.

Dunn, R., Bruno, J., Sklar, R., & Beaudry, J. (1990). The effects of matching and mismatching minority developmental college students' hemispheric preferences on mathematics test scores. *Journal of Educational Research, 83*(5), 283-288.

Dunn, R., Cavanaugh, D., Eberle, B., & Zenhausern, R. (1982). Hemispheric preference: The newest element of learning style. *The American Biology Teacher, 44*(5), 291-294.

Dunn, R., Deckinger, L., Withers, P., & Katzenstein, H. (1990). Should college students be taught how to do homework? *Illinois Research and Development Journal, 26*(2), 96-113.

Dunn, R., Dunn, K., & Price, G. (1985). *Productivity environmental preference survey (PEPS).* Lawrence, KS: Price Systems, Inc.

Dunn, R., Gemake, J., Jalali, F., Zenhausern, R., Quinn, P., & Spiridakis, J. (1990). Cross-cultural differences in the learning styles of fourth-, fifth-, and sixth-grade students of Afro, Chinese, Greek, and Mexican Heritage. *Journal of Multicultural Counseling and Development, 18*(2), 68-93.

Dunn, R., Gemake, J., & Zenhausern, R. (1989). Cross-cultural differences in learning styles. *Missouri Association for Supervision and Curriculum Development Journal, 1*(2), 10-17.

Durante, J. (1988). Companies find comfort can be cost effective. *Mid American Outlook, 11*(2), 8-9.

Elliott, P.H. (1975). *An exploratory study of adult learning styles.* Unpublished research report. (ERIC Document Reproduction Service No. ED 116 016).

Farr, B.J. (1971). Individual differences in learning: Predicting one's more effective learning modality (Doctoral dissertation, Catholic University of America, 1971). *Dissertation Abstracts International, 32,* 1332A.

Freeley, M.E. (1984). An investigation of the relationships among teachers' individual time preferences, inservice workshop schedules, and instructional techniques and the subsequent implementation of learning style strategies in participants' classrooms (Doctoral dissertation, St. John's University, 1984). *Dissertation Abstracts International, 46,* 403A.

Guzzo, R.S. (1987). *Dificuldades de apprenddizagem: Modalidade de atencao e analise de tarefas em materials didaticos.* Unpublished doctoral dissertation, University of San Paulo, Institute of Psychology, Brazil.

Hess, L., & Sperry, L. (1973). The psychology of the trainee as learner. *Personnel Journal, 52*(9), 781-785, 825.

Hermann, N. (1990). *The creative brain.* Lake Lure, NC: The Ned Hermann Group/Brain Books.

Ingham, J. (1991). Matching instruction with employee perceptual preference significantly increases training effectiveness. *Human Resource Development Quarterly, 2*(1), 53-64.

Jacobs, R.L. (1987). *An investigation of the learning style differences among Afro-American and Euro-American high, average, and low achievers.* Unpublished doctoral dissertation, Peabody University, Nashville, Tennessee.

Jalali, F. (1988). *A cross cultural comparative analysis of the learning styles and field dependence/independence characteristics of selected fourth-, fifth- and sixth-grade students of Afro, Chinese, Greek and Mexican heritage.* Unpublished doctoral dissertation, St. John's University, New York.

Keefe, J.W. (1979). Learning style: An overview. In J.W. Keefe (Ed.), *Student learning styles: Diagnosing and prescribing programs* (pp. 1-8). Reston, VA: National Association of Secondary School Principals.

Knowles, M. (1978). *The adult learner: A neglected species.* Houston, TX: Gulf Publishing Company.

Lam-Phoon, S. (1986). *A comparative study of the learning styles of southeast Asian and American Caucasian college students of two Seventh-Day Adventist campuses.* Unpublished doctoral dissertation, Andrews University, Berrien Springs, Michigan.

Levy, J. (1979). Human cognition and lateralization of cerebral functions. *Trends in Neuroscience,* 220-224.

Levy, J. (1982). What do brain scientists know about education? *Learning Styles Network Newsletter, 3*(3), 4.

Mickler, M.L., & Zippert, C.P. (1987). Teaching strategies based on learning styles of adult students. *Community/Junior College Quarterly, 11,* 33-37.

Price, G. (1980). Which learning style elements are stable and which tend to change? *Learning Style Network Newsletter, 1*(3), 1.

Restak, R. (1979). *The brain: The last frontier.* New York: Doubleday.

Smith, R.M. (1976). *Learning how to learn in adult education.* (Information Series No. 10, ERIC Clearinghouse in Career Education). DeKalb: Northern Illinois University, NIU Information Program. (ERIC Document Reproduction Service No. ED 132 245).

Springer, T.J. (1988). Ergonomics, productivity: Both are misunderstood. *The Office, 108*(4), 38-39, 44.

Tannenbaum, R. (1982) An investigation of the relationships between selected instructional techniques and identified field dependent and field independent cognitive styles as evidenced among high school students enrolled in studies of nutrition (Doctoral dissertation, St. John's University, 1982). *Dissertation Abstracts International, 43,* 68A.

Thies, A.P. (1979). A brain-behavior analysis of learning style. In J.W. Keefe (Ed.), *Student learning styles: Diagnosing and prescribing programs* (pp. 55-621). Reston, VA: National Association of Secondary School Principals.

Trautman, P. (1979). An investigation of the relationship between selected instructional techniques and identified cognitive style (Doctoral dissertation, St. John's University, 1979). *Dissertation Abstracts International, 40,* 1248A.

Whitehouse, D.L. (1988). Lighting's contribution to the well-run office. *The Office, 108*(6), 32, 41.

Zenhausern, R. (1980). Hemispheric dominance. *Learning Styles Network Newsletter, 1*(2), 3.

Joanne Ingham, Ed.D., *teaches graduate courses at both St. John's University and Queens College in learning style, innovative instruction, individualized instruction, and organizational behavior. She consults internationally for the Center for the Study of Learning and Teaching Styles with public school systems, universities, and business organizations. Dr. Ingham serves on the Board of Directors for the National Learning Styles Network. Her doctoral research, applying learning style to training effectiveness, was recognized as one of two national finalists by the ASTD Research Committee in 1989. The results of that research were published in* Human Resource Development Quarterly.

Rita Dunn, Ed.D., *is a professor in the Division of Administrative and Instructional Leadership and director of the Center for the Study of Learning and Teaching Styles, St. John's University, New York. Dr. Dunn has received numerous awards and honors including Education Press of America's national recognition for the best series published in an educational journal (1977), Association for Supervision and Curriculum Development's "Outstanding Consultant of the Year" (1982), and American Association of School Administrators' "Distinguished Lecturer" (1985). In conjunction with her husband, she has written numerous books on the topic of education. Their contributions to the field have been described by authors of many books and in popular publications such as* Redbook *(November, 1982) and* Readers' Digest *(1985).*

HOW TO MAKE NEW-EMPLOYEE ORIENTATION A SUCCESS[1]

Jean Barbazette

New-employee orientation (NEO) is a planned welcome to the organization that usually is shared by the human resource function or department and the new employee's supervisor. The Training Clinic of Seal Beach, California, surveyed more than one hundred United States and Canadian companies during a six-year period and subsequently identified twelve key factors of successful orientation programs. According to the survey results, successful orientation programs have the following characteristics:

1. *The orientation is conducted as an ongoing process, not just as a one-day program.* The orientation process, which usually begins with the hiring decision and continues well into the first year of employment, encompasses other programs that include performance reviews and skills training. When orientation is held over a period of time, overwhelming a new employee with information on the first day becomes unnecessary.

2. *Information is given to new employees in a timely manner, when it is needed.* For example, if an employee's health benefits vest thirty days from the start date, a benefits orientation is not needed during the first day or first week of employment. In fact, many companies separate benefits from other orientation information. If a benefits meeting is held in the evening, for instance, the spouses of new employees may attend and be provided with firsthand information about the choices available for a health plan. (See the checklist at the end of this paper for suggestions about the timing of specific orientation tasks.)

3. *The benefits of orientation are clear to both the new employee and the company.* The company might identify benefits such as reduced turnover or improved productivity. A new employee might note benefits such as feeling valued, "fitting in" easily and quickly, and being sufficiently relaxed to avoid making mistakes on the job.

4. *The organization's culture (its philosophy, mission, values, and norms) is clarified.* New employees need to be told the company norms, customs, and traditions. For

---

[1] An earlier version of this article appeared in "Designing a Successful Orientation Program" by J. Barbazette, 1991, in *Human Resources Policies and Practices,* New York: Warren Gorham Lamont. This article has been adapted by permission of Warren Gorham Lamont. A detailed presentation of the concepts in this article will appear in a book by Jean Barbazette, which will be published by Pfeiffer & Company sometime in 1993. Also available from Pfeiffer & Company is the *New Employee Orientation Presentation Organizer,* a slide program developed by The Training Clinic. This program helps an organization to prepare a customized orientation process.

example, if informality is a norm, the orientation should specify this fact so that a new employee knows that having coffee at his or her desk or leaving work on the desk overnight is acceptable. In contrast, if organizational rules are strictly enforced, the orientation must include not only this information but also specifics about such issues as dress code and the timing of breaks and lunch.

In some companies all employees are addressed by their first names. In other companies a strong sense of formality demands the use of surnames only. Sharing expectations and common definitions of "what is normal" contributes greatly to a successful orientation process.

5. *The employee's first day is a welcoming experience that helps the employee to feel useful and productive.* When a new employee arrives, his or her desk, chair, office space, phone, and supplies need to be ready. In addition, people in the organization need to be available to direct the new employee's activities and to teach the job to him or her. If the necessary supplies are not ready and/or people are inaccessible, a strong negative message is sent.

Several companies with successful orientation programs plan a welcome, an introduction process, and then a tour that ends in the new employee's work area. The new employee is then paired with an experienced "buddy" who teaches a specific task. In this way a new employee can perform a simple task that contributes immediately to the department's production.

6. *The supervisor's role in NEO is clear and well executed, with the human resource department or function providing assistance.* The supervisor and the human resource function share responsibility for the successful orientation of the new employee. It is important to determine which kinds of information and assistance ought to come from the supervisor and which need to come from the human resource department or function. Supervisors usually prefer to explain safety rules, reporting requirements, and job tasks, whereas the human resource department or function is usually better equipped to describe company policy, history, and benefits. The division of tasks must be negotiated between the supervisor and the human resource department or function if these tasks are to be shared successfully. (See the checklist at the end of this paper for a method to divide the tasks.)

7. *Orientation objectives are specific and measurable, and the timetable for achieving those objectives is reasonable.* The objectives must focus on the new employee's acquisition of specific knowledge, skills, and attitudes; and there must be some means of measuring the level of acquisition. The pacing of orientation—the rate at which a new employee is expected to acquire the necessary knowledge, skills, and attitudes—is also critical. Poor orientation programs often involve information overload that overwhelms new employees. Successful programs, on the other hand, are characterized by a balance of activity and pacing that makes orientation interesting, not overwhelming or boring.

8. *Adult-learning concepts guide the orientation.* If an organization wants its employees to use their initiative and exercise judgment, then a self-directed NEO is appropriate. Several successful NEO programs give a new employee a list of tasks to accomplish, a deadline, and the time and resources to complete the tasks. For

example, one manufacturing company gives each new hourly employee a checklist to be completed in five days; items on the checklist include completing forms and finding bulletin boards as well as safety and first-aid supplies. Another organization gives its new middle managers and staff people a list of key co-workers to interview along with a self-directed workbook that suggests interview questions such as these: What do you expect from me when we work together? What are your job and task goals, and how do they affect me?

Many unsuccessful NEOs spoon-feed all information to a new employee. This process says to the employee, "The organization will tell you everything you need to know; just wait for management to come to you." If an organization wants new employees to work independently, at least part of their orientation needs to be their responsibility.

9. *Guest speakers (live or on videotape) are used.* Many successful NEO programs use speakers who are well prepared, present only essential information with specific objectives, and employ good presentation techniques. In a number of cases, the personnel or human resource function coaches these speakers, outlines or scripts their talks, and provides professional-looking visual aids. When guest speakers are ill prepared, they may fail to meet their goals, digress from their subjects, or arrive late (or not at all).

10. *Audiovisual components of the orientation program lend emphasis to the program and provide a positive message.* In successful orientation programs, video or slide presentations frequently are used to describe the organization's culture, history, and philosophy. Guest speakers who deliver a consistent message and find it impossible to attend every session of NEO are good candidates for video.

Although the temptation is to put as much as possible on video, the content needs to be lasting. Information that changes often, such as information about benefits, is best presented "live." The organization chart, with the members of the current executive group named, is best provided in written form.

11. *The results of the NEO process are evaluated by participants, supervisors, and the human resource department or function.* Participants give their reactions to NEO and offer suggestions about the process and the timing of content delivery. Supervisors determine whether NEO information is used on the job and, as a result, to what degree the orientation program needs revision. A successful NEO process is also characterized by evaluation for bottom-line results. For example, by conducting a systematic NEO, one manufacturing organization was able to reduce turnover by 69 percent in the first three years. Similarly, a bank was able to reduce the time required for orientation and skills training for new tellers from six weeks to two weeks.

12. *Information is provided to the employee's family.* Providing information can include welcoming gestures, letters or company newsletters, and even more. Many companies welcome families at work one day each year. Others, as mentioned previously, schedule benefits orientations during the evening so that family members can attend. One organization even has a corporate "welcome wagon" that visits families of new employees.

These twelve characteristics suggest that NEO is a process that needs to be refined and customized for each organization. For example, in planning an orientation program, an organization ought to consider such issues as when orientation is first conducted and how many new employees are hired at one time.

The checklist that begins on the next page can be useful in identifying appropriate content and timing for the new-employee orientation process. This checklist has been designed to assist those who conduct NEO. It offers a comprehensive list of topics to help the new employee function productively. To avoid overwhelming the new employee on the first day, the person with primary responsibility for designing the orientation needs to identify the best timing for each item and follow the resulting schedule. It is important to remember that information is most beneficial when it is given to a new employee in a timely manner, closest to the time when it is to be used.

A critical step in the NEO process is to identify who is the best source of each kind of information to be provided. Some information is best learned and retained if the employee "discovers" it himself or herself; most standardized information is best delivered by the human resource department or function; and information that changes from one department to another is best given by the new employee's supervisor. To achieve consensus regarding the responsibility and timing of tasks, a discussion involving human resource personnel, supervisors, and new employees is advised.

Jean Barbazette is the president of The Training Clinic in Seal Beach, California, a training/consulting firm that she founded in 1977. Her company conducts needs assessments and designs training programs and self-paced learning packages. She is a specialist in new-employee orientation, the training of trainers, and enhancing the quality of training and instruction for major national and international clients. Previously, Ms. Barbazette worked for Blue Cross of California and the City of Long Beach; she also formerly taught at the University of California at Los Angeles.

ORIENTATION-CONTENT CHECKLIST[2]

Instructions: To designate *who* will be responsible for covering each item in the checklist, choose the appropriate letter from the following code and write it in the blank in the "Who" column next to each item:

$$E \quad = \quad \text{employee}$$
$$S \quad = \quad \text{new employee's supervisor}$$
$$HR \quad = \quad \text{human resource representative}$$

To designate *when* each item is to be done, choose the appropriate letter from the following code and write it in the blank in the "When" column:

$$D \quad = \quad \text{first day}$$
$$W \quad = \quad \text{first week}$$
$$M \quad = \quad \text{first month}$$
$$F \quad = \quad \text{follow-up after first month}$$

Who   **When**

ORGANIZATION

Who	When	Item
_____	_____	Our History
_____	_____	Company Philosophy
_____	_____	Company Objectives
_____	_____	Our Organization
_____	_____	Our Industry
_____	_____	Our Products and Services
_____	_____	Our Customers
_____	_____	Your Department
_____	_____	Facilities

COMPENSATION

Who	When	Item
_____	_____	Pay Schedule
_____	_____	Time Card
_____	_____	Salary Reviews
_____	_____	Overtime
_____	_____	Payroll Deductions
_____	_____	Forms, Forms, Forms
_____	_____	Charities
_____	_____	Workers' Compensation

---

[2] This checklist appeared in "Designing a Successful Orientation Program" by J. Barbazette, 1991, in *Human Resources Policies and Practices,* New York: Warren Gorham Lamont. It has been used here by permission and may not be reprinted or photocopied without prior written permission from Warren Gorham Lamont.

ORIENTATION-CONTENT CHECKLIST (continued)

Who   **When**

BENEFITS

Who	When	
_____	_____	Medical Plan
_____	_____	Dental Plan
_____	_____	Insurance
_____	_____	Pension Plan
_____	_____	Credit Union
_____	_____	Savings Plan
_____	_____	Incentive Programs
_____	_____	Service and Recognition Awards
_____	_____	Employee Purchases
_____	_____	Tuition Reimbursement
_____	_____	Training and Development Programs
_____	_____	Profit Sharing

ATTENDANCE

Who	When	
_____	_____	Work Hours
_____	_____	If You Are Late, Sick, or Absent

LEAVE AND HOLIDAYS

Who	When	
_____	_____	Holidays
_____	_____	Leave Policy
_____	_____	Vacation
_____	_____	Jury Duty

HEALTH AND SAFETY

Who	When	
_____	_____	Safety
_____	_____	Emergency Procedure
_____	_____	First Aid
_____	_____	If You Have an Accident
_____	_____	Childcare Program
_____	_____	Wellness Program
_____	_____	Employee-Assistance Program

Pfeiffer & Company

ORIENTATION-CONTENT CHECKLIST (continued)

Who   **When**

SECURITY

Who	When	
_____	_____	Security Procedures
_____	_____	Restricted Areas
_____	_____	Confidentiality
_____	_____	Name Badge
_____	_____	After-Hours Procedure
_____	_____	Keys
_____	_____	Fingerprinting
_____	_____	Loyalty Oath

INTERNAL COMMUNICATIONS

Who	When	
_____	_____	Company Newsletter
_____	_____	Company Bulletin Board
_____	_____	Employee Handbook

TRANSPORTATION

Who	When	
_____	_____	Carpool/Ridesharing
_____	_____	Parking
_____	_____	Travel Policies
_____	_____	Travel Expenses
_____	_____	Permits, Restricted Areas

YOUR COMFORT

Who	When	
_____	_____	Rest and Meal Breaks
_____	_____	Cafeteria/Break Facilities
_____	_____	Smoking Policy
_____	_____	Restroom Locations
_____	_____	Safeguarding Your Personal Belongings
_____	_____	Lunch the First Day

ORIENTATION-CONTENT CHECKLIST (continued)

Who   **When**

PERFORMANCE

Who	When	
_____	_____	What Is Expected of You
_____	_____	Quality
_____	_____	Ethical Standards
_____	_____	Conflict of Interest
_____	_____	Probationary Period
_____	_____	Dress Code
_____	_____	Telephone Procedures and Courtesy
_____	_____	Promotions
_____	_____	Performance Reviews
_____	_____	Discipline Process
_____	_____	Causes for Termination
_____	_____	Personal Calls and Visitors
_____	_____	Suggestions
_____	_____	Equal Opportunity
_____	_____	Sexual Harassment
_____	_____	Accepting Gifts
_____	_____	If You Have a Problem

Pfeiffer & Company

MANAGING AND MOTIVATING THE CULTURALLY DIVERSE WORK FORCE[1]

Sondra Thiederman

WORKPLACE DIVERSITY: AN OVERVIEW

The phrase "workplace diversity" describes a core characteristic of the work force of the United States. Managers as well as human resource development (HRD) professionals now realize that the days of the homogeneous workplace are over and that today's work force consists of people who are different from one another in terms of gender, age, ethnicity, sexual preference, race, and physical ability. In order to function effectively in today's diverse workplace, managers must gain the awareness, knowledge, and skills that are necessary to supervise and motivate employees whose values, perspectives, and needs might not match their own. And HRD practitioners must be prepared to assist managers in this difficult task.

This article provides information about the skills needed to motivate workers of diverse backgrounds. Although its focus is primarily on ethnic and cultural diversity, the principles outlined are useful in managing employees who are different in other ways as well. For example, the importance of accurately interpreting behaviors or finding effective compromises is as central to managing and motivating people who vary in age or gender as it is to managing and motivating people from unfamiliar immigrant cultures.

SEVEN STEPS TO MOTIVATING

Any effective motivation strategy consists of assessing an employee's needs and matching those needs with those of the organization. The challenge lies in the fact that the needs of employees, even within one company and from one culture, are diverse. One worker might value and strive for more money, whereas another might be more responsive to the prospect of increased authority, time off, or something as simple as a better parking spot.

The challenge of motivating effectively is amplified in the multicultural workplace, where something that motivates a worker from one ethnic or immigrant group might be meaningless to a worker from another group. The seven steps listed below and discussed throughout this article are useful in designing

---

[1] This article is based on material presented in the author's books, *Bridging Cultural Barriers for Corporate Success: How to Manage the Multicultural Work Force,* New York: Lexington/Macmillan, 1991, and *Profiting in America's Multicultural Marketplace: How to Do Business Across Cultural Lines,* New York: Lexington/Macmillan, 1991. This material has been adapted with permission of the publisher.

motivation strategies that are sensitive to cultural differences and, therefore, useful in a manager's efforts to maintain a harmonious and productive multicultural workplace. The manager should:

1. Overcome resistance to change.
2. Interpret the behavior correctly.
3. Explain his or her expectations and the expectations of American management.
4. Compromise.
5. Speak the worker's "cultural language."
6. Honor culture-specific needs.
7. Positively reinforce the desired behavior.

Each of these steps can be part of an overall strategy or used individually depending on the specifics of the situation.

In the discussion of these steps that follows, the behaviors used as illustration are those most often mentioned as problematic in the multicultural workplace. This is not to say that these behaviors are intrinsically undesirable and, therefore, targets for change, but merely that in the context of business in the United States they create confusion for managers and colleagues and at least need to be understood better. The behaviors are these:

- Hesitance to take independent initiative on tasks;
- Reluctance to complain or make negative statements;
- Failure to admit lack of understanding;
- Reluctance to seek or accept promotions;
- Reluctance to praise self; and
- Speaking foreign languages in the workplace.

These behaviors should be treated as illustrations only. They do not apply to all members of a given group. Furthermore, the techniques mentioned here can be applied to any behavior and are particularly effective for behaviors that are most deeply rooted in differing values and expectations.

Step 1: Overcome Resistance to Change

Many immigrants are committed to maintaining their cultural identity. This commitment is perfectly understandable; a person's culture is a part of his or her sense of self, an essential component of his or her identity. When a person's culture is compromised, so too is that person. Consequently, when an immigrant employee is asked to behave in a way that runs counter to his or her cultural background, that person naturally becomes anxious and defensive.

Behavioral scientists know that in order for change to take place, the subject—in this case, the culturally diverse worker—must feel psychologically safe and secure enough to make that adjustment. Anxiety about losing one's cultural identity and one's way of life can only interfere with receptivity to new ideas and behaviors. A defensive reaction is even more likely to occur when the employee is already in a state of culture shock, disoriented and threatened by being immersed in a strange culture. To begin the process of overcoming resistance, the manager must offer reassurance that he or she has no intention of changing the employee's culture.

Employees might also be reluctant to adopt new behaviors because they often are asked to do something foreign and unfamiliar. Managers must realize that asking an Asian to praise himself or herself in front of a group, for example, is like asking a native-born American to walk into a party setting and immediately begin bragging to the first stranger who comes along. Similarly, expecting Hispanics to seek promotions over countrymen who are older than they is equivalent to asking a native-born American to sabotage the professional progress of a dear friend just to advance within the company; Hispanics perceive seeking promotions under such circumstances as a source of shame, not pride.

Expecting an Asian or Hispanic employee to take the initiative on a task would be like expecting a native-born American to stride into the boss's office and begin cleaning his or her desk without having been asked to do so. Expecting an Asian worker to complain about something is like expecting an American employee to keep the boss informed of every insignificant negative event that happens on the job—it just does not feel right. These examples are, of course, generalities; but they do help to explain why a worker who is committed to another culture might resist a manager's efforts to encourage behavioral change.

In situations like these, the manager must give workers as much power as possible. By including employees in the decision to change, the manager increases the likelihood that employees will commit to the changes that the manager wants. The manager should not simply tell workers what to do but instead should ask them how far they are prepared to go in modifying their usual way of doing things. By giving employees the power to participate in the decision to change and in the specific details of a change, the manager decreases anxiety and defensiveness and increases the chance of compliance. Even if workers do not wish to contribute to this decision because of discomfort with participative management, the manager still has asked for their comments—a gesture that is, in itself, empowering to the workers.

Step 2: Interpret the Behavior Correctly

The next step to successful cross-cultural motivation is to understand why an employee is behaving in a particular way. This step is important for two reasons:

1. Efforts to understand communicate to the employee that the manager respects him or her enough to learn what might be very culturally specific reasons for particular attitudes and behaviors. A manager who shows such respect and interest enables the employee to feel less defensive and, therefore, to be more willing to cooperate.

2. If the manager does not correctly interpret the behavior, he or she cannot design appropriate and successful motivation strategies for

modifying that behavior. Assessing why workers do what they do can be difficult enough when they and the manager share the same background; it is even more difficult when a worker's values and expectations of proper employee behavior are different from those of the manager.

Figure 1 lists the behaviors most often mentioned as problematic in the multicultural workplace, which were referred to previously, along with some of the possible interpretations of those behaviors. Specific ethnic and immigrant cultures are not mentioned here because the behaviors listed tend to be characteristic of various groups. As the content of this figure reveals, the culture of mainstream corporate America is distinguished in many of its values from much of the rest of the world. Immigrant workers arrive from many different cultures and, much to the manager's surprise, share more values among themselves, despite their diversity, than they do with the native-born American.

Managers should note that it is impossible to generalize about all members of any cultural group. Each person has his or her own character and value system; culture is only one aspect of every employee's personality. Also, it is important to take the time to ask employees why they feel or behave in a certain way. This process not only uncovers valuable information but also communicates to workers that the manager cares enough about their individuality to understand them better.

---

1. **Hesitance to take independent initiative on tasks**

   Possible interpretations: Respect for authority, fear of losing face, desire for anonymity, fear of job loss

2. **Reluctance to complain or make negative statements**

   Possible interpretations: Desire for harmony in relationships, respect for authority, compassion for the other person, fear of a negative reflection on the group, fear of job loss

3. **Failure to admit lack of understanding**

   Possible interpretations: Fear of losing face, fear of embarrassing the speaker, fear of not understanding the message or material if it is repeated

4. **Reluctance to seek or accept promotions**

   Possible interpretations: Desire for anonymity, belief in leaving things to fate, desire not to be elevated above the group, respect for informal group hierarchy, desire to fulfill one's present role, fear of losing face, varying personal needs, wishes of family members

5. **Reluctance to praise self**

   Possible interpretations: Desire for anonymity, desire not to be set apart from the group

6. **Speaking foreign languages in the workplace**

   Possible interpretations: Fatigue, loneliness, forgetfulness, unconscious response to stress and crises, desire for efficiency

---

Figure 1. Interpretations of Employee Behaviors

Pfeiffer & Company

Step 3: Explain Expectations

Employee training is big business in the United States, but rarely are those who are new to the work force—whether they be immigrants or members of other diverse groups—instructed in the values of American culture or the basic desires of American management. Those who are new to the work force are privy neither to the subtle, unspoken "rules of the game" that are essential to any employee's advancement nor to more-obvious expectations such as the assumptions that employees will take the initiative on tasks, will seek promotions, or will keep their managers informed of problems in the workplace.

Explaining what we want from others is not easy. Often it is the most familiar procedures, policies, and expectations that are the most difficult to articulate. For example, explaining how important it is for employees to admit lack of understanding is not a simple task in light of the fact that making such an admission is considered rude and disrespectful in most cultures. One way for a manager to approach this explanation is to point out that the employee who admits that he or she does not understand is seen more positively—is considered to be more enthusiastic, committed, and concerned with doing the job right— than is an employee who does not admit a lack of understanding. Another important point to make is that if workers pretend to understand, they might be thought of as dishonest and are clearly in danger of making errors that will create problems for others.

In many cultures the hesitance to praise oneself stems from a desire to maintain social harmony and balance. In order to explain the necessity of voicing one's qualifications during an interview, the manager must address this basic difference in viewpoint. The manager might say, for example, that in the American workplace, praising oneself is not considered rude but, instead, is gracious in that it helps the manager to make more informed decisions about hiring and promoting. This knowledge, in turn, helps the manager to do a better job and makes the entire company function more efficiently.

These suggestions are not intended to be used word for word; instead, they are intended to generate the manager's own thinking about ways to phrase necessary explanations. The manager's remarks should reflect his or her own personality, the specifics of the situation, the personality of the worker, and the degree of English-language skill that the worker possesses. Here are some guidelines for conducting such a conversation:

1. Before talking with the employee, the manager should think carefully about what is to be said.

2. The conversation should be held in neutral territory rather than in the manager's office. (Neutral territory will be less intimidating to the employee.)

3. The manager should put the message in writing and give the employee a copy. This approach lends importance to the message and gives the employee an opportunity to discuss its contents with colleagues and others from the same country.

It is easy to become frustrated while conducting such a conversation. The manager should remember that this effort may be the first that anyone has made to familiarize the new employee with the expectations of American management.

Step 4: Compromise

Demonstrating a willingness to compromise not only shows respect but also encourages cooperation and change. One way, for example, to deal with the issue of hesitance to complain is to allow complaints to be presented by the group as a whole, thus removing the responsibility from any one worker while honoring the value that is placed on the group over the individual. The manager might also mention that complaints and problems may be presented to management by an informal group leader; this approach also preserves the anonymity of the specific worker. Another compromise is to institute the age-old device of the suggestion box, which workers can use to share their problems without fear of appearing disrespectful. Of course, the suggestion box will not work if employees are required to identify themselves in order to make suggestions about ways to solve problems. Inviting complaints in private and reassuring workers that their anonymity will be honored are also helpful techniques.

A similar compromise can be entered into when the manager wants to encourage the admission that something has not been understood. Giving the worker the opportunity to voice confusion in private can relieve the worker's concern that he or she will appear foolish to others. Requesting that questions be put in writing is another compromise that will minimize embarrassment.

A form of compromise that can apply to many behaviors is to place the worker in a position in which his or her strengths can be used to the best advantage. For example, a hotel restaurant in the state of Washington employed an Asian-born woman who was extremely gracious and hard working but who was also uncomfortable about approaching customers to ask if they needed anything. Instead of continually nagging the young woman to be more assertive, the hotel's management transferred her to the concierge desk, where her formality and graciousness would be appreciated and where she could comfortably wait for guests to come to her.

When behavioral changes are desired, the best way to establish an effective and permanent compromise is for the manager to ask the employees involved for their suggestions. Employees often come up with valuable ideas about how they and the manager can meet halfway to make the workplace more efficient while preserving the integrity of the employee's culture.

Step 5: Speak the Worker's "Cultural Language"

Speaking the worker's "cultural language" means that the manager voices his or her request and the reasons for it in terms that can be understood readily in the context of the worker's cultural values and priorities. Saving face, for example, is a central tenet of Asian, Middle Eastern, and Hispanic cultures and constitutes an important component of vocabulary in the "cultural language" of many immigrant and ethnic workers. As such, it can be used as a way of communicating the manager's position in an effective manner.

For example, the manager may point out to workers that one of the reasons that the failure to take initiative, to complain, or to admit lack of understanding creates problems in the workplace is that each of these practices can cause loss of face for the manager and/or the employer:

- If the initiative is not taken on tasks, the job does not get done—a situation that reflects adversely on the manager's ability to supervise effectively and on the employer's talent at running an efficient operation.

- If the manager is ignorant of problems in the workplace, he or she is incapable of solving them and, therefore, may appear incompetent to superiors and colleagues.

- If the manager is unaware that instructions have not been understood, mistakes will be made; as a result, both the manager and the worker will suffer embarrassment.

Reference to saving face can also be made as part of the manager's efforts to encourage workers to seek promotions and to praise themselves. For example, the manager might explain that if workers do not state their qualifications, the manager will be unable to make correct staffing decisions and will lose face in the eyes of superiors.

Loss of face also affects the issue of speaking a foreign language in the workplace. The manager might explain that when workers speak a foreign language that cannot be understood by others—be they superiors, colleagues, clients, or customers—those other people may feel left out, uncomfortable, and anxious. All of these feelings result in loss of face.

Each of these examples involves a loss of face. As this value is so common to the multicultural workplace, managers might consider using it to motivate behavioral change. When a request is phrased in terms of avoiding the loss of face, not only will that request be quickly understood but also the manager will be demonstrating that he or she cares enough to use a concept that is important to the worker.

Respect for the group as a whole is another component of "cultural language" that can be used as a means of encouraging cooperation. Because of this priority, some workers are hesitant to seek promotions; they believe that to do so calls attention to the individual at the expense of the group and separates the individual from treasured friends and colleagues. A similar rationale applies to self-praise; it is considered inappropriate and disruptive of group harmony. One way to modify these behaviors is to point out that promotions and achievements reflect well on the individual as well as on the group as a whole. The same argument might be made with the worker who does not want to take the initiative on tasks because he or she is concerned about being set apart from the group: If that person does well at the task, his or her accomplishment will make the entire group look good.

Step 6: Honor Culture-Specific Needs

In motivating diverse workers, managers have an unfortunate tendency to project their own desires and needs onto others and to assume that everyone responds to similar rewards. For example, consider the following list of motivators. Which ones are motivators throughout the world, and which are specific to just a few cultures?

Recognition/Respect

Responsibility

Financial gain

Social needs

Professional and personal growth

Advancement

The work itself

Power

Chance to contribute ideas

Chance to see concrete results

Job security

Autonomy

Structure

Chance to compete

Probably the only one of these motivators that is universal is social needs—the desire for human contact, comfort, and companionship. In Thai and Vietnamese cultures, for example, maintaining a positive relationship with others is the most powerful motivator of productive behavior. The remaining items on the list are specific only to certain cultures and, particularly, to Western industrialized societies.

It is important for managers to learn what motivates them so that they can avoid projecting their own needs and wants onto others. Recognition, the chance to contribute ideas, and advancement are important to many American managers because American culture values any forms of reward that singles out the individual for attention. Praise, the prospect of a premium parking spot, a picture in the company newsletter, a prestigious promotion, or the title of "employee of the month" are widely sought by workers who were born and raised in mainstream American society. Indeed, Japanese managers who work with American-born workers marvel at how soon after being hired they seek promotions.

Competition, too, is valued in the West but considered disruptive of harmony and counter to productivity in many other countries as well as in several native American Indian cultures. Even a monetary bonus, so highly valued in the United States, would bring humiliation to the Chinese, Japanese, or Eastern European worker, who would feel that such a reward was in poor taste. We tend to forget that Western culture is almost unique in its emphasis on the material. When deciding how to motivate workers, the manager should look closely at what the individual employee really values and take care not to assume that all workers from all cultures value the same thing.

The family or group is another value that is of paramount importance within most immigrant and ethnic communities. This statement is, of course, a generality; but it serves as a guideline for assessing the needs and desires of workers. For example, it might be appropriate to motivate some Hispanic or Asian workers by offering them time off to return to their native lands for family events and special occasions. The prospect of company-sponsored family gatherings and picnics can also constitute strong motivation for a worker and one that shows that the manager cares enough about the worker and his or her values to seek out ways to satisfy those needs.

A similar value involves the desire to work overtime so that the worker can send money home to family members in another country or can accumulate funds with which to bring family members to the United States. Allowing for the celebration of customary national holidays is another way of providing for family time while showing respect for the traditions of the group.

It is not always possible or necessary for the manager to meet every need encountered in the multicultural work force. Sometimes it is enough for the manager to acknowledge the existence of the need and the worker's right to feel that need. Acknowledging, for example, a worker's need for relaxation, companionship, and identity can diminish his or her desire to speak a foreign language while on the job. For all of us, sometimes just knowing that our needs are understood can encourage cooperation and motivate behavioral change.

Step 7: Positively Reinforce the Desired Behavior

Without positive reinforcement as the final step in this process, the rest of the manager's efforts can come to nothing. Negative reinforcement—criticism—often leaves a worker feeling nervous and self-conscious and produces short-term benefits at best. In contrast, positive reinforcement, especially if provided in the early stages of a new behavior, can be very effective.

Positive reinforcement is usually a simple matter; the manager notices that the worker is behaving as desired and praises him or her for it. But when the manager is trying to motivate across cultural boundaries, this step becomes a bit trickier. For example, not all ethnic and immigrant workers are comfortable with praise. Many dislike being highly praised because they want to avoid having attention drawn to them as individuals, are concerned about maintaining harmony and balance, and are preoccupied with social hierarchy and seniority. Another reason that the manager's praise might not evoke the desired reaction is that compliments sometimes are accompanied by the implication that the manager is surprised that the worker has done well. This situation is similar to the one in which a colleague comes to work dressed particularly nicely and people react by exclaiming, "My goodness, you look good today!"

The manager can minimize the resistance to praise by being discreet, by using a third party or word of mouth, by praising the group as a whole, by putting a complimentary note in the worker's file, and by being careful not to overpraise.

It is a good idea to remember that fewer words are more effective, easier to understand, and less embarrassing.

Another issue related to the need to provide positive reinforcement is that it is difficult to praise someone if he or she has made a serious error. Mistakes will inevitably be made when employees take the initiative on tasks. These errors present a great challenge to the cross-cultural manager, who must correct the error while preserving the pride of the employee and continuing to encourage the taking of independent action. If pride and face are lost through an error, the chances of that employee's being willing to take the initiative again are slim. The solution in this case is to treat the error as a separate issue from the initiative. The manager must point out the mistake but at the same time put greater emphasis on how pleased he or she is that the worker took a chance and acted independently.

Many managers also find it difficult to praise when bad news is brought to them. It is understandably difficult, for example, for a manager to bring himself or herself to praise the worker who arrives bearing news of a missed deadline or a broken piece of equipment. Even though this task is not easy, the manager must try to distance himself or herself from the distress long enough to praise the worker for making the information known and to encourage the worker to continue to do so.

Finally, there is always the danger of taking certain behaviors for granted. For instance, American managers are so accustomed to seeing workers take the initiative on tasks or seek promotions or praise themselves during an assessment interview that it is difficult to remember that these behaviors must be reinforced and encouraged with culturally different workers. The same applies to the speaking of English in the workplace. Managers must stay aware of behaviors such as these; they seem automatic and commonplace but may be very difficult for the immigrant and ethnic employee to execute.

HOW THE HRD PROFESSIONAL CAN HELP

Managing diversity is a challenge that can feel overwhelming. The subtleties of varying communication styles, the complexity of legal restrictions, the necessity of learning about other cultures while avoiding the danger of stereotypical thinking can cause even the most-aware manager to lose confidence and want to avoid the issue.

The good news is that as long as we acknowledge the differences as well as the preferences we hold in common and are willing to ask questions in order to understand the diverse people with whom we work, the answers to even the most-delicate dilemmas will be closer than we think. The HRD practitioner can help managers to deal effectively with diversity in the following ways:

- By giving them copies of this article and encouraging them to read it;

- By helping them to resolve particular problems;

- By offering to assist as a third-party consultant when appropriate;

- By making suggestions about resources to consult (see the bibliography at the end of this article);
- By conducting training on the topic of diversity;[2]
- By conducting special orientation sessions for new employees who are immigrants or members of other diverse groups; and
- By holding informal meetings in which managers can share their experiences as well as tips on managing diversity.

BIBLIOGRAPHY

Fernandez, J.P. (1991). *Managing a diverse work force: Regaining the competitive edge.* Lexington, MA: Lexington.

Fyock, C.D. (1990). *America's work force is coming of age: What every business needs to know to recruit, train, manage, and retain an aging work force.* Lexington, MA: Lexington.

Grote, K. (1991). *Diversity awareness profile.* San Diego, CA: Pfeiffer & Company.

Grote, K. (1991). *Diversity awareness profile* (manager's version). San Diego, CA: Pfeiffer & Co.

Jamieson, D., & O'Mara, J. (1991). *Managing workforce 2000: Gaining the diversity advantage.* San Francisco: Jossey-Bass.

Kogod, K. (1991). *A workshop for managing diversity in the workplace.* San Diego, CA: Pfeiffer & Company.

Loden, M., & Rosener, J.B. (1991). *Workforce America! Managing employee diversity as a vital resource.* Homewood, IL: Business One Irwin.

Sue, D.W., & Sue, D. (1990). *Counseling the culturally different: Theory & practice* (2nd ed.). New York: John Wiley.

Thiederman, S. (1991). *Bridging cultural barriers for corporate success: How to manage the multicultural work force.* New York: Lexington/Macmillan.

Thiederman, S. (1991). *Profiting in America's multicultural marketplace: How to do business across cultural lines.* New York: Lexington/Macmillan.

Sondra Thiederman, Ph.D., has fifteen years' experience as a speaker, trainer, and author on the topic of cultural diversity. Since receiving her doctorate from the University of California, Los Angeles, she has worked with numerous clients in the United States and internationally. She has authored two books about cultural diversity: Bridging Cultural Barriers for Corporate Success *and* Profiting in America's Multicultural Marketplace. *Dr. Thiederman also serves as narrator for Barr Film's training video,* Bridging Cultural Barriers, *which is based on her work and addresses the issue of cultural diversity in the workplace.*

---

[2] See, for example, *A Workshop on Managing Diversity in the Workplace,* available from Pfeiffer & Company.

THE EFFECTIVE USE OF HUMOR IN HUMAN RESOURCE DEVELOPMENT

Ozzie Dean

David Kearns, chairman and chief executive officer of Xerox Corporation, told this joke as he addressed students at the University of Chicago Graduate School of Business (Kushner, 1990):

> There's a story about a Frenchman, a Japanese and an American who face a firing squad. Each gets one last request. The Frenchman asks to hear "The Marseillaise." The Japanese asks to give a lecture on the art of management. The American says, "Shoot me first—I can't stand one more lecture on Japanese management." (p. 39)

After the laughter subsided he added, "You'll be glad to hear I'm not going to talk about Japanese management today. In fact, if we keep on the right track, we may wind up listening to the Japanese give lectures on American management" (Kushner, 1990, p. 39).

Just as the message that David Kearns delivered was an important one, the messages that you deliver during the course of your work as a human resource development (HRD) practitioner—whether in formal speaking engagements, in training sessions, or in informal conversations with trainees or clients—are equally important. If your message is worthwhile but boring, the chances are that it will not be heard, understood, and remembered. Humor enlivens your message and helps listeners to relax and pay attention. Gene Perret (1990), one of America's leading comedy writers, reinforces this point:

> Some people may wonder "why bother using humor when you can make a point as fiercely as possible and get on with it?" Marshall McLuhan answers with: "Those who draw the distinction between education and entertainment don't know the first thing about either." (p. 327)

THE BENEFITS OF USING HUMOR

> As I left home to come down here tonight, my wife gave me some last-minute advice. She said, "I know it's a difficult subject and a tough group. But don't be intimidated. And don't try to be charming, witty, or intellectual. Just be yourself."
>
> Mario Cuomo

By using and encouraging humor and fun, you can have the following positive effects on those with whom you communicate:

1. You show them that you are not afraid to let your guard down.

2. You convey that you are confident about their reactions to you.

3. You demonstrate that you trust them to value your spontaneity as much as, or more than, your stage persona as a speaker, trainer, or consultant.

4. You reduce their anxiety so that they can better deal with the problems they are facing.

5. You help them to gain perspective on their problems and to see those problems in a broader context.

Demonstrating a sense of humor decreases the distance between you and your listeners and increases their trust in you. Listeners tend to develop a quicker rapport with a speaker who encourages laughter than with one who is serious and stern. Also, listeners who laugh experience certain physiological and psychological reactions that not only benefit them but also benefit you as a speaker seeking receptivity: Their facial, torso, and stomach muscles relax; their blood pressure goes down; and a general sense of well-being and euphoria takes over.

Research on the psychology of humor shows that humor has a rejuvenating effect on listeners. Regardless of how accomplished a speaker is, listeners eventually reach a saturation point at which they demand some refreshment or they will absorb no more. A little comedy can provide that refreshment, after which people can listen with renewed interest.

Often HRD practitioners resist the use of humor for one or both of the following reasons:

1. *"I'm not here to win a popularity contest."* Because HRD professionals are more interested in getting the job done—in helping people to learn skills and solve problems, in helping organizations to become more effective, and so on—than in creating an atmosphere of fun and play, they sometimes think that creating such an atmosphere is not an important part of their work. This line of thinking is sometimes expressed in comments like "I'm not here to win a popularity contest. I'm here to work hard for my client." Certainly no one wants to serve a client with anything but the highest standards of competence, diligence, and creativity. However, there is a major difference between taking one's work seriously and taking oneself seriously.

2. *"Having fun is childish."* Another reason that HRD professionals sometimes hesitate to use humor is that they associate play or fun with immaturity. Some seem to think that fun precludes learning, creates an atmosphere of laissez faire, and damages their credibility. In reality, injecting appropriate humor into a seminar or session may enhance one's image, alleviate boredom, and boost retention.

It is important to note that creating humor does not necessarily mean becoming an expert at telling jokes. It means saying things that make people feel at ease and relaxed. Having fun, generating laughter, and sharing that laughter tell people that you are glad to see them, that you are happy to be with them, and that you are enjoying yourself. Often it is humor that sets effective speakers apart and makes listeners remember them and recommend them to others. Those who can both educate and entertain—a rare quality in speakers today—earn high fees. And as an HRD professional, you should not hesitate to increase your fees over those of others if you can both generate learning and provide entertainment.

THE LINK BETWEEN FUN AND EFFECTIVENESS

> If you aren't having some fun, you might wonder just what you are doing in your business life.... If employees, customers, and vendors don't laugh and have a good time at your company, something is wrong.
>
> Paul Hawken

As Hawken implies in the preceding quote, there is a definite link between fun and effectiveness. The following paragraphs describe findings involving teachers, priests, managers, and organizations.

Findings with Teachers and Priests

> When his congregation began nodding off, a preacher said, "Last night I held in my arms the wife of another man." That woke people up, and they looked at him startled. Then he added, "It was my dear mother."

Teachers who used humor or created and/or allowed an atmosphere of fun and play were rated more favorably by their students (Abramis, 1991). Studies with priests (Holland, 1982) yielded similar results: Priests who used humor while delivering sermons were rated by those in attendance as "more likable" and "more effective" than were priests who did not use humor. Furthermore, church attendance was greater for the priests who used humor than it was for the priests who did not.

Findings with Managers and Organizations

> Just think, if Moses were alive today, God could have faxed the ten commandments to him.

One study with a control group and an experimental group of managers found that subordinates in the experimental condition—in which managers created and allowed a "funny" atmosphere at meetings—more frequently rated their managers as "likable" and "effective" than did those in the control groups—whose managers did not create or allow fun and play (Chapman, 1986). In addition, David Abramis (1991) studied office fun and reported that roughly 60 percent of employees have fun at work and 10 percent say that they do so consistently. Furthermore, Abramis (1991), Duncan and Feisal (1989), and Kiechell (1983) reported an increase in creativity, productivity, motivation, and satisfaction among employees when enjoyment in the office was emphasized. A decrease in anxiety and depression was also noted. Abramis predicts that managers will increasingly be allowing fun in the workplace once they become convinced that it might help them to achieve organizational goals.

Organizations are beginning to realize that an environment that encourages fun and humor creates a relaxed atmosphere and enhances effectiveness. Consequently, many are hiring humor consultants to teach their managers to take themselves lightly. John Goodman, head of the Humor Institute in Saratoga Springs, New York, and the only full-time humor consultant in the United States, speaks to companies across the world on the use of humor in management and leadership. He reports that he has to turn down twenty lectures a month. That is how important humor is to some organizations; they know its power in motivating people and in boosting morale and productivity. In addition, some companies have recognized the importance of interrupting boring daily routines with enjoyment and have responded by creating "humor rooms" that are filled with mini-basketball hoops, funny props, and *Candid Camera* videos. Employees are encouraged to visit these rooms occasionally for some comic relief.

HOW TO USE HUMOR EFFECTIVELY

Before you start using humor, first make sure your listeners understand that you are competent in your subject matter. You do this by briefly stating your qualifications for the job that you are there to do.

Caution 1. Never introduce yourself in a humorous manner unless your reputation has preceded you. If the listeners have never heard of you, introduce yourself in a serious manner so that they have a chance to get to know you and to become convinced that you can get the job done. A basic principle of audience psychology is audience resistance to humor: People tend to resist those who try to be funny. They need to hear your voice and to become acquainted with you before you attempt to make them laugh.

Caution 2: Never use humor to conceal a lack of preparation or inadequate knowledge of your subject matter. Humor is only the icing on the cake; it should complement and enhance your message, not replace it.

After you have introduced yourself, you are free to use and encourage humor. Here are ten guidelines that you might find helpful:

1. Make Fun of Yourself—Not Others

When I told people I'm in software, they thought that meant women's lingerie.

In any given audience, you will find "hostages"—people who were forced either directly or indirectly to attend. Using self-effacing humor gives "hostages" as well as others an incentive to pay attention and to become less bored. However, be aware that using humor to make fun of others is inappropriate and will alienate people.

Self-effacing humor shows strength and confidence; it tells your listeners that you are secure enough to laugh at yourself. Charles Gruner, professor of speech communication at the University of Georgia in Athens, has studied humor and persuasion for more than twenty years. He reinforces the importance of self-effacing humor by saying, "A little self-deprecation humor shows that the speaker feels strongly enough to make fun of himself. It creates audience rapport" (Kushner, 1990, p. 79). The important phrase in this comment is "a little." Research shows that self-effacing humor is most effective when used sparingly (Kushner, 1990). Without it, you may appear stuffy; but if you use too much of it, you may cast yourself as a "Woody Allen" character, someone who is always putting himself or herself down. To be effective, you will have to strive for a happy medium.

2. Laugh *with* People—Not *at* Them

Be sensitive to people's feelings and needs. Never share a funny anecdote about a person known to you and the listeners unless you have previously received that person's permission to share it.

3. Select Material That Relates to Your Topic or Your Listeners

Keep in mind that you can tell a good story or joke badly, but you can rarely tell a bad story or joke well. Part of what determines whether your material is "good" or "bad" is its relevance to your topic and your audience. Use material that is suited to your topic or audience: stories about careers for a training session on career development, stories about management for an audience of managers, and so on.

4. Believe in Your Material

To tell a story or joke effectively, you must believe in its concept. You must "buy" the idea. Otherwise, you may subconsciously hold back.

5. Deliver Your Material Well

Musicians often say that many people can play the guitar but few play it well. The same is true of telling stories and jokes. Good delivery takes practice, practice, and more practice so that the material sounds spontaneous and conversational.

6. Learn Techniques for Good Delivery

Here are some tips for achieving good delivery:

- Know your lines.
- Be confident.
- Do not announce that you are going to tell a joke.
- Establish eye contact.
- Pause for the punch line and wait for the laugh.
- Keep it brief.

7. Avoid Ethnic Put-Downs

Jokes that disparage specific cultures are inappropriate. Some professional comedians feel that you can tell an ethnic joke if you are of that ethnicity, but others disagree. This issue warrants careful judgment, especially in light of recent concern about sensitivity to cultural diversity.

8. Avoid Sexist Put-Downs

Although it has never been wise to disparage one sex or the other, it is especially inappropriate now, when the gender gap is widening because of sexual harassment. It is also unwise to belittle particular people in your audience, who will probably resent it. Humor should heal, not hurt.

9. Give Listeners Permission to Laugh

> In these times, a good time to laugh is any time you can.
>
> Ozzie Dean

Listeners typically model their behavior after that of the speaker: If the speaker is serious, they tend to be serious; if the speaker is entertaining, they tend to relax and have a good time. For this reason, it is important to give your listeners permission to laugh. You do this by laughing with them, reminding them of the difference between taking your work seriously and taking yourself lightly.

In the five years that I have been a management consultant and a professional stand-up comedian, I have spoken to a wide variety of audiences: Navy personnel, senior citizens, people who are hearing impaired, religious people, graduate and undergraduate students, and tough comedy-club customers. I have never encountered an audience that did not want to laugh. The reason is simple: There is a child in each and every one of us dying to have permission to laugh. Try to involve your listeners actively in the fun; encourage them to relate funny anecdotes, personal experiences, and so on. Keep in mind that in any audience there are natural jokesters who like to draw attention to themselves and who can contribute to the overall atmosphere of fun. Allow them to do so as long as they do not upstage you or get out of hand.

10. Use "Savers" If a Story or Joke Bombs

A "saver" is a funny comment that is made after a story or joke does not receive the expected laughter. Even the most accomplished comedians tell stories and jokes that bomb once in a while. As one comedian put it, "Dying is easy; comedy is hard." Consequently, all comedians prepare savers to use when their material fails. Either you can compose your own savers to fit a particular situation, or you can use any of the following:

- "Well, I'm going to follow in Saddam Hussein's footsteps and call that joke a victory."
- "That usually works...with my wife (husband)."

- "You know what they say: 'He who laughs...lasts.'"
- "Come on, people, that joke is a killer in Cleveland (substitute any other city)."
- "I should have a sign that says 'How am I dying? Call 555-1212.'"
- "That was one of those scud-missile jokes. You never know when it's going to hit."
- "What's the difference between a consultant and a pigeon? The pigeon can make a deposit on a new car."

REFERENCES AND BIBLIOGRAPHY

Abramis, D. (1991, March 19). There is nothing wrong with a little fun. *The San Diego Union*, p. 25.

Carter, J. (1990). *Stand-up comedy: The book.* New York: Dell.

Chapman, A. (1986). *Humor and laughter: Theory, research, and applications.* New York: St. Martin's Press.

Duncan, W.J., & Feisal, P. (1989). No laughing matter: Patterns of humor in the workplace. *Organizational Dynamics, 17,* 18-30.

Higginbotham, W. (1988). *Mirth in management.* Buffalo, NY: Bearly Limited.

Holland, N.W. (1982). *Laughing: A psychology of humor.* Ithaca, NY: Cornell University Press.

Kiechell, W. III. (1983, December 12). Executives ought to be funnier. *Fortune Magazine,* pp. 206-216.

Kushner, M. (1990). *The light touch: How to use humor for business success.* New York: Simon & Schuster.

Perret, G. (1984a). *How to hold your audience with humor.* Englewood Cliffs, NJ: Prentice-Hall.

Perret, G. (1984b). *How to write and sell your sense of humor.* Englewood Cliffs, NJ: Prentice-Hall.

Perret, G. (1990). *Funny business: Speakers' treasury of business humor for all occasions.* Englewood Cliffs, NJ: Prentice-Hall.

Robin Williams: The king of comedy. (1986, July 7). *Newsweek,* pp. 52-58.

Saks, S. (1984). *The craft of comedy writing.* New York: St. Martin's Press.

Shales, T.. (1989, July). Is comedy making a comeback? America laughs again. *Esquire,* pp. 118-129.

Wilde, L. (1983). *How the great comedy writers create laughter.* Chicago: Nelson-Hall.

Wolmuth, R. (1986, June). Inside comedy. *Time,* pp. 96-106.

Ozzie Dean, Ph.D., *is a management consultant and the president of Diversity Plus, a firm specializing in the management of a multicultural workforce, cross-cultural management, and cross-cultural counseling. In his ten years of experience in human resource development, Dr. Dean has consulted with the U.S. Navy, high-tech corporations, and institutions of higher learning. He is currently teaching psychology, human behavior, and management courses at National University. In addition, he is a professional stand-up comedian and has performed at the Comedy Store, the Comedy Isle, and other comedy clubs in San Diego, Los Angeles, and Hollywood. He has appeared on such television programs as "PM Magazine," "The Kill Them with Comedy Show," and the KGTV news in San Diego. Dr. Dean is currently writing a book on the effective use of humor in management and leadership.*

THE INITIAL INTERVIEW: ASSESSING CLIENT NEEDS

Dan Stone and Robert J. Marshak

INTRODUCTION

In times of confusion and uncertainty, organizations often turn to organization development (OD) consultants for help in addressing troublesome problems. The consultant's first task is to understand the exact nature of the client's concern and then to assist in selecting appropriate strategies. Figure 1 provides a basic set of initial interview questions for a consultant to ask. These questions have been specifically prepared to ensure that all relevant information is considered before a consultant and client commit to a particular course of action.

Although a great deal has been written on the theory and practice of organization development, relatively little mentions the first interview with the client. The importance of this first interview lies in the fact that it forms the basis for the continuing relationship. To help ensure a successful first encounter, the questions in Figure 1 focus specifically on key areas that build the foundation for the helping relationship.

One major task for a consultant is to help the client to reflect and to clarify concerns. Simply leading the client through the sequence of thought in this first interview may be an important intervention. By the end of the initial interview, the client may have found a solution that he or she is fully empowered to enact without further consulting assistance. On the other hand, this first interview may well be the beginning of a productive long-term consulting relationship.

This article begins by introducing the purpose of the first interview and the stance the consultant needs to establish in building a productive working relationship. Next each of the questions is examined in detail to expose any underlying nuances. Several suggestions then are made as to how to use these questions most effectively. Finally a sample work sheet incorporating the questions is provided for consultants to use or adapt.

PURPOSE OF THE INTERVIEW

The first client interview has the following basic purposes:

- To build rapport with client;
- To gather information; and
- To form an agreement for proceeding.

1. What is the problem or the reason that you called me in?
2. What is the impact of this problem?
3. What factors contribute to perpetuating the problem?
4. What have you tried so far to address the problem? What have been the results?
5. Ideally, what would you like to happen?
6. What interventions might bring about this preferred solution?
7. What forces support this intervention?
8. What forces inhibit this intervention?
9. What are you (the client) willing to invest in finding a solution?
10. What do you want from me (the consultant)?
11. Is there anything else that I need to know in order to understand the situation?
12. What are the next steps we need to take?

Figure 1. Initial OD Interview Questions

Typically the initial interview is not intended as a complete diagnosis of the client system. Furthermore, the initial interview may not necessarily result in a contract for conducting an OD intervention. Instead this first interview is designed to help the consultant get a sense of how to approach the overall client system in order to move forward with diagnosis or intervention. Therefore the consultant and the client both need to be clear that the interview is a preliminary stage of the consultant's involvement with the client system.

THE CONSULTING STANCE

Certain basic elements in the consulting stance can help to build rapport, gather information, and form agreements. These elements are outlined in the section that follows.

1. *Be supportive.* In order to establish an optimal relationship, clients must feel safe enough to be vulnerable. Vulnerable areas often are areas of potential incompetence or areas in which the client might be criticized for not addressing the problem successfully. Autonomy is a key to maintaining a person's self-esteem; the very act of calling in a consultant sometimes can threaten that sense of autonomy. Therefore it is important for the consultant to communicate a general message to the client that it is perfectly acceptable to ask for help and that the client will not be judged, blamed, or criticized for the information he or she is about to share.

2. *Be attentive.* Although the twelve questions suggested provide a basic progression of thought, consulting should be fundamentally client centered. Therefore the consultant needs to be aware of the client's progress through the discussion. That may mean following digressions, tolerating apparent irrelevancies, and sharing control of the interview

process. The consulting stance is to view everything the client does as data that may or may not be immediately comprehensible.

3. *Be definitive.* Much of the initial interview consists of the consultant's "taking in" the client's reality, and it is essential that the consultant understand how the client sees and experiences the world. Having done that, the consultant must establish his or her own identity and role in the process. A healthy consulting relationship requires an explicit and concrete understanding of the client's and consultant's mutual expectations.

Although each of these principles is important, their relative emphasis may shift at different phases of this initial interview. For example, it is generally important to avoid being too definitive until the later stages of the discussion; however, showing support may be important throughout the interview, especially with an edgy client.

OVERVIEW OF THE QUESTIONS

Each of the twelve questions is quite simple and—in some senses—obvious. Understanding the rationale for each question will enable the consultant to concentrate on its intent rather than simply to complete a rote sequence of information gathering. Understanding the objective of each question is also important in being able to generate appropriate follow-up questions and probes.

1. *What is the problem or the reason that you called me in?* This is the obvious starting place, inasmuch as clients call consultants to help solve problems or address issues. This question opens the door to understanding the source of the discomfort, pain, or unfulfilled potential with which the client wants assistance.

Sometimes the answer a client initially gives takes the form of a solution, as if the interviewer's question had been "What do you want to do about the problem?" For example, one client was asked what the problem was and replied, "We need a team-building session." A natural follow-up question could be to ask about what had been happening that led to that conclusion. It is important that the consultant have a clear picture of the current situation that the client wants changed and not simply the mechanism the client has established for making that change.

A client may be reluctant to discuss the problem for a variety of reasons. It is helpful to remember that maintaining control is a critical need for many people, especially managers. For some people, to admit to problems that they cannot solve is an admission of being out of control. Therefore getting the client to focus directly and openly on describing the presenting problem may be a delicate task requiring tact and interviewing skill.

2. *What is the impact of this problem?* After exploring the client's perception of the problem, the consultant examines the dimensions of the problem:

- Where is the problem occurring or not occurring?
- To whom is the situation a problem?

- When does the problem occur or not occur?

- When the problem occurs, what is the result?

The nature of problems is that they cause pain; inasmuch as most people prefer to avoid pain, they often choose to avoid looking closely at problems. This question (along with follow-up probes) is intended to support the client in taking a closer examination of the problem—perhaps in new ways.

3. *What factors contribute to perpetuating the problem?* Once the consultant understands the basic dimensions of the problem, it is important to know the client's perception of why the problem is occurring. Despite asking the client to assess the forces contributing to the situation, the consultant must be aware that the client may well bring his or her own sources of distortion to this assessment. The consultant must remind the client that this is a preliminary interview and that in most instances there will be additional data gathering prior to the consultant's drawing any conclusions. In this way, the consultant also opens the client to the possibility of forces other than those that have been previously identified.

This may also be a time for the consultant to offer other possible interpretations, not as conclusions but simply to test ideas and help the client expand the range of possibilities. Note that the phrasing of this question assumes that problems are multi-determined. Although this premise sometimes may be argued, the consulting stance here is one of open inquiry into possible explanations or interpretations without prematurely closing on a single explanation.

4. *What have you tried so far to address the problem? What have been the results?* In general people like to believe that they can solve their own problems. This is especially true of managers, who are paid to resolve management issues. To preserve the self-esteem of the client (a key process goal of the interview), it is essential to acknowledge the client's efforts to address the problem and his or her perceptions about the results. These may be important data for what might not work in the future and for factors that must be considered for a successful intervention.

5. *Ideally, what would you like to happen?* After exploring the current situation, the client may well be ready to focus on the future. This is the time to assess and potentially to tap into the client's energy and enthusiasm for having things change. Although this may well not be the final goal statement, posing the question invites the client to a more empowered position.

In exploring this area, the client should be asked to describe the preferred situation as specifically as possible, using questions such as the following:

- If the situation were how you want it to be, what specifically would people be doing?

- How exactly would people be feeling?

- What would be happening in the environment? (For example, what would customers be saying/doing/thinking?)

- What specifically would the product or service be like?

When the client is finding it difficult to commit to a particular vision for the future, another question might be "What might it be like if the situation were more the way you want it?" This can free up the client to discuss possibilities that he or she is not yet ready to support.

If the client seems reluctant or de-energized by the question, other factors may not be clear to the consultant. It may simply mean that the client is not ready to move forward, in which case the consultant can simply acknowledge that in a nonblaming manner and allow the client to indicate the next move.

6. *What interventions might bring about this preferred solution?* This brainstorming question is intended to elicit a range of possibilities. An underlying premise in much of OD is "equifinality"—in other words, there is more than one way to skin a cat. More precisely, equifinality means that equally valuable results can be achieved through a variety of means. Therefore if the client provides only one option, a good follow-up question might be "What other options might be helpful?"

After generating options for bringing about the preferred situation, it may also be helpful to ask what criteria need to be met by whatever option is selected. For example, criteria might concern costs, timeliness, who is involved, how much data gathering is required, and so on. Once these criteria are known, the various options can be tested against the criteria and a tentative decision can be made.

The consultant should also contribute expertise in terms of options and their likely consequences. If the client is overlooking an important option or is leaning toward an option that the consultant's experience has shown not to work, this is the time to speak. After all, the process consultant is being hired for his or her process expertise.

7. *What forces support this intervention?* and

8. *What forces inhibit this intervention?* After a direction has been determined, it is important to detect any hidden mine fields and to identify additional support that could be enlisted to help ensure success. Examples of forces (either supporting or opposing) include the following:

- The motivation levels of the employees involved;

- The presence (or absence) of key allies within and outside the client system;

- The adequacy of resources, including money and time;

- The level of support for such activities within the organizational culture; and

- The timing of the activities and how they fit with other events or stages within the larger organizational context.

Once these forces have been identified, the client should be asked to reassess how reasonable the selected approach will be. Assuming it is still a "Go," these forces should be incorporated into any plans.

9. *What are you (the client) willing to invest in finding a solution?* By this point in the discussion, the client and the consultant will be much clearer about the nature

of the situation, the potential benefits of addressing it, and the likelihood of success or failure. It is now time to address costs and risks.

For most interventions, the primary costs focus on money and time. Risks may include potential loss of the client's credibility in the organization, the situation worsening, or the emotional pain of going through the intervention.

In asking the client to assess these costs and risks, it may also be necessary for the consultant to help reality-test the situation. For example, the client may wish to know whether a team building approach is likely to succeed. This can be addressed by discussing the consultant's overall experience with the success of team-building approaches.

However it is done, the client needs to be clear about the costs and risks and make choices as to whether or not to proceed.

10. *What do you want from me (the consultant)?* Assuming that the intervention is still a "go," the consultant can move toward exploring his or her role in the effort. Although in some cases the client will be ready to move toward formal contracting, other cases will need additional data gathering or a time lapse before a contract can be developed. In either case, the consultant's role in the intervention should be explored. It is especially important to clarify the following points:

- What specifically will the consultant do and what conditions does the consultant need to meet (time frames, checking out products or processes before use, confidentiality, and so on)? and

- What will the client do and what conditions does the client need to meet (introducing the consultant, handling administrative details, making payments, and so on)?

This discussion needs to produce a mutually satisfactory agreement on roles and conditions for the future relationship, in which the following points are covered:

- The consultant's role is defined in a way that will allow successful performance, and

- The client's role is defined in a way that will ensure the necessary support and commitment.

Before reaching a final agreement, the client and/or consultant may want additional time to gather more data or simply to reconsider this agreement and to renegotiate. This may also be a time to hit the "pause button;" if there is any sense of discomfort or uncertainty about the direction being taken, either party might request or suggest a delay. However, if it seems that both parties are comfortable and committed to moving forward, the time may be ripe for concluding an agreement.

11. *Is there anything else that I need to know in order to understand the situation?* This is a catch-all question. Experience also shows that human communication is not always a linear process; questions that are addressed early in a discussion might be answered in a different light or with different information later in the interview.

This is a last check so that the client may reflect on the total discussion and add whatever additional thoughts he or she might have.

12. *What are the next steps we need to take?* Before ending, there need to be agreements about how and when further communication or contact will occur. If the results of the meeting need to be documented or contracts prepared, responsibility needs to be assigned.

In addition, this might be a time to recognize that a relationship has begun. Two or more individuals have come to know things about one another that may be quite intimate, perhaps exposing vulnerabilities that normally are not shown. There may be value in acknowledging the level of discussion that has taken place and reassuring the client that their problems and concerns will be handled with care. If appropriate, it may also help to offer whatever level of reassurance can be genuinely provided on hopes for improvement or on the likely success of what the client is attempting to achieve.

USING THE QUESTIONS

These twelve questions are intended as a general framework for discussion and are not meant to be restrictive or a prescriptive formula for success. Clearly there are variations on questions and avenues that either extend the questions posed or go off in other directions. The first rule is to follow the client. However, having so followed the client, the questions may help the consultant to reorient by providing a checklist of areas to have covered prior to finalizing an agreement for further work with the client.

The questions primarily focus on the client's perspective on the problem and what is needed. This is not to preclude the consultant from providing his or her own expertise and perspective in either suggesting interpretations or providing options for proceeding.

Further, the questions are primarily intended to orient the consultant to areas of inquiry and do not necessarily represent the optimal phrasing or level of detail. For some areas, it may be necessary to employ numerous probes; in others, the simplicity of these questions may suffice. These questions should not preclude the consultant from following additional lines of inquiry based on the information the client is providing, nor from phrasing questions in a manner that is natural to the consultant and the situation.

VERBAL INTERVIEWING TECHNIQUES

In exploring the client's answers to the questions, the consultant may use a variety of interviewing techniqus to draw out, probe, or extend the client's responses. Three primary sets of techniques have been described by Jones (1973). These techniques, outlined in Figure 2, help to ensure that the client and the consultant have a highly productive discussion around the questions and the answers.

Probing Responses	Understanding Responses	Supporting Responses
• General leads: questions that are nonspecific • Binary questions: yes/no questions • Follow-up leads: specific questions based on prior responses • Cue-exploration leads: questions phrased in responses to cues given by the client • Continuation leads: questions designed to keep the client talking about a particular topic • Amplification leads: requests for further explanation • Testing: questions that test out theories that the consultant is forming	• Restatement: repetition of the client's words • Paraphrase: restatement of the client's response in the consultant's words • Reflection: mirroring back to the client of the feelings that the consultant believes the client is experiencing • Summarization: recapitulation of the data gathered thus far	• Sharing: descriptions of situations that the consultant has experienced that are similar to those being described by the client • Consoling: sharing feelings of concern for the client • Expressing caring: demonstrating that the client and the consultant are building a relationship

Figure 2. Verbal Interviewing Techniques

FINAL THOUGHTS

Although the questions are presented in a set sequence, the interview may not flow in such a linear fashion. It may be necessary to jump around or cycle back through questions that were addressed earlier.

Finally, these questions are intended for use during an initial diagnostic interview; however, there may be situations in which the consultant might provide the questions to the client in advance of the interview. This might be particularly helpful under any of the following conditions:

- The presenting problem is particularly complex or requires extensive thought as to its roots;

- Time for the initial interview is limited;

- The organization's norms are more consistent with the submission of written questions in advance of meetings; and/or

- This particular client prefers to reflect in advance on the questions.

This set of twelve questions is a general framework for dialogue. Used skillfully, the questions allow the consultant to draw on all of his or her powers of observation and skills so as to establish rapport and ensure a productive and valuable client-consultant relationship. Figure 3 shows an example of how these questions could be incorporated into an Initial Diagnostic Interview Work Sheet.

Note that the client's responses and the rationale behind the questions should drive the dialogue, not the specific words or order of inquiries on any protocol.

CLIENT: _____ DATE:_____

1. What is the problem or the reason that you called me in?

2. What is the impact of this problem? (For whom is it a problem? Where is the problem occurring or not occurring? How big is the problem? What would be the consequences of not addressing problem?)

3. What factors contribute to perpetuating the problem? (What are people doing or not doing that is creating or sustaining the problem? How might such things as organizational reward systems, structures, rules, policies, relationships, and so on contribute?)

4. What have you tried so far to address the problem? What have been the results? (What has worked? What has not worked? Why?)

5. Ideally, what would you like to happen? (What would it be like if the situation were the way you want it to be?)

6. What interventions might bring about this preferred solution? (Which do you see as most likely to succeed? Why?)

7. What forces support this intervention? (Key people, resources, time, outside events, and so on.)

8. What forces inhibit this intervention? (Key people, resources, time, outside events, and so on.)

9. What are you (the client) willing to invest in finding a solution? (Your time? The time of others? Money? Risk? Involvement? Commitment? Resources?)

10. What do you want from me (the consultant)? (Support? Active involvement? Resources? Type(s) of consulting services? Nature of the relationship?)

11. Is there anything else that I need to know in order to understand the situation?

12. What are the next steps we need to take? (Who? What? When? How? Where?)

Figure 3. Initial Diagnostic Interview Work Sheet

REFERENCE

Jones, J.E. (1973). The sensing interview. In J.E. Jones & J.W. Pfeiffer (Eds.), *The 1973 annual handbook for group facilitators* (pp. 213-224). San Diego, CA: Pfeiffer & Company.

Dan Stone is chief of organization development for the U.S. Department of Agriculture — Animal and Plant Health Inspection Service. He and his staff provide consulting services to departmental managers in areas such as organizational diagnosis, change planning, team building, and strategic planning. He supervised the implementation of one of the first self-directed work teams in the federal government. Mr. Stone also maintains a private OD consulting practice specializing in strategic planning for human service agencies. He is a professional member of the National Training Laboratories and an occasional presenter at the Organization Development Network.

Robert J. Marshak, Ph.D., is president of Marshak Associates. He has been an organizational consultant for over twenty years, focusing primarily in the areas of strategic change, managing conflict and differences, and the development of executives and change agents. Dr. Marshak is on the adjunct faculty of The American University and is a member of the NTL Institute. He has written numerous publications and is the co-creator of The Covert Processes Model *for understanding the hidden dimensions of group and organizational dynamics.*

GROWING BY LEAPS AND BOUNDS: MANAGEMENT DEVELOPMENT THROUGH KEY GROWTH EXPERIENCES

Jason Ollander-Krane and Neil Johnson

The dilemma of developing and retaining quality managers is one that human resource development (HRD) consultants confront frequently. Consider the following scenarios:

- A consultant flies to San Francisco to meet with the top executive of a leading advertising agency. As they settle down to enjoy lunch, the executive spreads out a large piece of paper marked in squares like a chess board. In each square is the name of a manager in his agency. "Now," he asks the consultant, "tell me what happens if I leave my job. In which order should I promote these people?" They talk for a while, and it turns out that there is no manager whom the executive would rank above the others; he feels that no one is ready for major responsibility. The executive concludes, "I need to change that and I need to change it fast. What do I do?"

- The president of an organization asks a consultant this interesting and revealing question: "Where do I get the talent I need to manage this company? We lose all of our best people. We need to grow our management talent by leaps and bounds each year, and yet we have fewer resources than we did in past years. How will we get smart, hard-working, results-oriented managers to take us toward the year 2000?"

- In a small service company, a junior executive works for a person widely reputed to be a tough manager of people. The junior executive is highly prized by her company and carefully watched to be groomed for greater things. After three years, she is promoted to a more senior job. That year she is responsible for an incremental 33 million dollars in profit. At the end of the year, she resigns to start her own company.

Scenarios like these are not uncommon in companies today. Organizations want to grow talented managers quickly and keep them longer, yet they are thwarted at each turn. The employees whom they do manage to develop often leave before their talents can be utilized fully or after having made significant, one-time contributions, exiting their companies without providing a sufficient return on the considerable investments that have been made in these people. Organizations need ways to help employees to make huge leaps in experience—experience that results in enhanced creativity and increased profits.

From 1980 to 1990, in a casual but meaningful study, the authors surveyed almost three hundred managers. These managers were asked about their biggest growth experiences, and it was discovered that these experiences have a number of things in common. Chief among them is that they defy the conventional HRD logic. Not only do they defy this logic, but everything about the factors that produced growth for these employees opposes traditional thinking about how people in companies grow. Yet the people surveyed did grow—and quickly. The authors have developed a term for these development activities: "key growth experiences" (KGEs). The process of participating in a key growth experience is known as "leaping" because the experience involves a significant leap in responsibility. This article offers a detailed look at KGEs and leaping, including how these experiences can be captured and used in organizations and how to avoid the common occurrence of a participant's leaving one company for another after a key growth experience.

WHAT ARE KEY GROWTH EXPERIENCES?

One way to describe the concept of KGEs is to say that they provide development through on-the-job *experience* rather than on-the-job *training*. The typical method of on-the-job development is to place an employee in a job, provide job-content and skill training, and then stand back and watch the employee grow. This method works; but it works slowly and gradually as people learn, try, make errors, relearn, and try again. Key growth experiences spring from a different idea. They begin with the concept that when people need to get a job done they do it, do it well, and instinctively try to make the best choices. In fact, most learning in life takes place through such a process. Similarly, KGEs provide life learning in the workplace. The fascinating outcome is that participants learn faster and more completely than they do with the traditional method; they put their learning to work more readily; and they learn much more than conventional training could ever teach them.

Implementing key growth experiences is easy; the idea is to match employees with job experiences that have special attributes, such as those described here, and let them do their best. The most amazing and special aspect of these experiences is that they do not involve the creation of an educational model that one needs to learn and then apply rigorously in a company. All that is needed is an understanding of the process, an ability to identify KGEs, and a willingness to put them to work. The theories about these experiences are based on empirical evidence that KGEs already exist in companies—in every company.

THE CHARACTERISTICS OF KEY GROWTH EXPERIENCES

Key growth experiences share these characteristics:

- They begin with big leaps in responsibility.
- They involve leaps of faith (as well as responsibility).
- They are unique, once-in-a-lifetime responsibilities.

- They involve people in a way that builds lasting social and professional bonds.
- They take place in flat, nonhierarchical organizations.
- They are an efficient, low-cost way of providing development.

Leaps in Responsibility

Trainers are always hoping that the people they train will learn not only how to do but how to think, to change not how people act but how people are. Leaps in growth and responsibility seem to teach just these things. Participants in key growth experiences report that the situations they find themselves in are like real-life survival simulations. They have limited resources, a huge amount to do in a short amount of time, lots of pressure for results, and high expectations from their bosses. They need to make things work. In situations such as these, logic and learning have little to do with success; instead, flexibility and an ability to think creatively promote success. It is not surprising, then, that participants find themselves jumping into the rapids and swimming like crazy. In doing so they discover that they can swim, often better and with more stamina than they ever suspected.

The idea of putting young managers in over their heads certainly flies in the face of traditional development logic and may sound crazy to some. Most managers advocate slow, carefully planned growth for their people. Yet it is known that most growth takes place when people are required to stretch, to wonder if they will succeed, and to rely on instinct more than intellect. In the study conducted by the authors, hundreds of managers validated this intrinsic, instinctive way of learning as they recalled when they had grown most. They all said that they learned best when they made giant leaps in their levels of responsibility. From these testimonies it can be concluded that the typical HRD paths are old-fashioned, slow, and expensive. Although leaping may seem to be risky and to involve outcomes that are too unpredictable, in fact, neither is true. The overwhelming majority of participants report that KGEs work precisely because participants are "in over their heads," resulting in the feeling that they are "up the creek without a paddle," that they simply must "get the job done in the best way they know how." Participants say that the risky, unpredictable aspect makes the experiences work better. Fortunately for companies, the outcomes are far from unpredictable.

Leaps of Faith

Many participants identify a crucial element in the success of their key growth experiences. Essential to their growth, they say, is the fact that they are forced (often along with the managers who select them for the assignments) to rely on a belief that they can survive and complete their assignments successfully. Many report that at the beginning of their experiences they themselves did not believe they would succeed. Instead, they had faith because the managers who made the assignments (or with whom they worked) thought they could succeed. The faith that a participant has in the manager who makes the assignment is critical in facilitating a leap. Although the importance of such faith makes sense given all that is known about the power of expectation and self-fulfilling prophecy, very few job assignments are made with this in mind.

Once in a Lifetime

Participants often say that they would repeat the experiences tomorrow but hope they never have to. This mixture of feelings seems to be another aspect of KGEs that makes them work. Often the assignment is a one-time-only proposition (a start-up, an overseas branch opening, a promotion that skips several organizational levels, and so on). The experience is generally unexpected and unrequested. Participants often say, "I never would have asked for it, but it needed to be done" or "I'll never do that again; I learned something from the last time!" In fact, they learn so much from their experiences that they feel they cannot go back to their previous ways of working—their lives have changed too dramatically.

The Social Aspect

Many participants report changes in their social circles. Although participants report having barely enough time to eat and sleep during a KGE, social attachments seem central to the experience. Research shows that during KGEs participants spend more time in closer contact with co-workers than before and that they share more openly about their private lives. What is more interesting, however, is that participants report more openness *professionally* as well. In projects such as these, managers share ideas more openly and are more open to feedback and criticism. Also, they are more emotional and have more chances to witness the emotions of their co-workers. In other words, the people involved in these projects have a chance to be more fully human and open than they might be in a typical working environment; the open environment of KGEs produces better learning for everyone.

Nonhierarchical, Flat Organizations

Traditional employee-growth strategies would not advocate that a senior vice president work hand in hand with a recently hired junior manager on a major assignment, the results of which were central to the survival of the company. Yet these are the arrangements that foster talent and make leaps in growth happen. Not only do people of various levels work together during KGEs, but they work side by side with equal responsibility for producing results. One participant reported that he grew the most when "senior people asked for my advice and took it, and what I advocated worked!" Some reported that they grew because "we worked together every day and the issue of seniority never came up." Organizations that create flat, flexible, web-like work groups that emphasize open, lateral, cross-disciplinary communication work best in creating big leaps of growth. Often these are temporary groups that last no longer than the KGE but account for significant development during it.

Efficient, Low-Cost Development

Many companies have accepted as fact the concept that gradual development of employees works best. This is especially true today when many companies have limited resources that they are willing to devote to education and development. Whether due to flat structure, lean staff, or a need to respond flexibly to changes in the economy, many companies are placing increasing emphasis on employees' taking charge of their own career development. This short-term solution may lead to long-term problems. Key growth experiences provide a valuable alternative to gradual growth and do not require significant increases in spending or re-allocation of resources. In fact, KGEs thrive in a low-budget environment and often at no additional cost to the company. Key growth experiences can develop many employees at once or only a few hand-picked employees at a time. These experiences become most cost effective when used widely in companies because they provide the advantages of individualized development with the efficiency of training several people simultaneously.

EXAMPLES OF KEY GROWTH EXPERIENCES

The characteristics of KGEs begin to take shape when viewed in light of actual examples. Here are some examples of KGEs that have been captured in companies:

- At a major West Coast Bank, managers routinely rotate through the signature verification unit, noted for its fast pace and high volume of transaction. "If managers can survive in that area, they can survive anywhere," said a senior manager in the division. "It's sink or swim. We made a six-month rotation into this job part of every manager's growth in our manager-development program." The next step is into one of two equally challenging areas: Safe-Deposit Box Administration or the grave-yard shift, Returned Items. These departments were chosen because they have the slowest pace in the division. The bank has identified both kinds of experiences as key for the growth of future managers.

- A temporary-help supplier has identified particular branches as growth branches because of their management and client base. Fast-track managers are moved into these branches for short assignments and then into other key branches that will provide them with similar experience. While at the growth branches, they are involved in a combination of fast-track seminar training and structured KGEs. "These managers could not survive without the growth branch," said the area vice president. "They would fail without the kind of quick immersion the growth branch experience gives them." As part of a pilot program, Chicago was selected as a "KGE area" where all managers are being groomed using key growth experiences.

- At a major advertising agency, a ten-week workshop is well known as a KGE. Groups of participants come from all over the world for immersion in the study of sophisticated elements of creating advertising. One highly social group finished the session with a 72-hour, new-business-development project that involved working through the night to finish a presentation on the project that would be given to top managers. Although a majority of graduates from this particular group left the company within two years of completing the workshop, many of them are still in touch socially and professionally. Many believe that this KGE was a turning point in their careers.

HOW TO CAPTURE KEY GROWTH EXPERIENCES

Capturing key growth experiences is really quite simple. The first, and possibly most daunting, step is to be open to an idea that is so different from what intuition says will work. Once past this obstacle, the following steps can be used to implement KGEs:

1. Collect information already available in the company about which experiences have provided the greatest leaps in growth for people in the past. Use this information to create a blueprint for identifying these experiences.

2. Identify ways in which managers contribute to employee growth and then target mentors (managers who are excellent developers).

3. Identify assignments that fit into the blueprint already made.

4. Match assignments to the employees to be developed. Incorporate the assignments into managers' development plans.

5. Create career tracks that keep participants moving quickly in the company after their leaps.

Step 1: Collecting Information

Conducting a meeting that includes eight to ten of the best-performing managers in a company is the first step in collecting information. The chosen managers should be from as high in the organizational hierarchy as possible in order to gather data about what promotes the best growth and development. Their experiences can help to determine KGEs for the entire company, division, or group.

This meeting has two goals: (1) to gather data and (2) to create acceptance of the idea of KGEs in the company. Capturing the ways in which the strongest managers grew strengthens the case for repeating the process throughout the company. Most senior employees grew through leaps in responsibility, but this fact usually goes unnoticed. Once high-level managers see that their best growth occurred this way, they can help sell the idea in the organization.

Step 2: Identifying Experiences and Choosing Mentors

In the initial meeting, the following steps can be used to identify KGEs and to introduce the concept of mentoring. The meeting members should be informed that they will not be compelled to share responses and that they may think of work- or nonwork-related experiences.

1. Ask each manager to think about three experiences that produced tremendous growth in his or her life and to write brief descriptions of these experiences.

2. Have each manager make a list of attributes common to all three experiences that made them ideal for growth.

3. Ask for volunteers to share items from their attribute lists with the group. Write the responses on a newsprint flip chart.

4. Next ask each manager to determine how many items on his or her own list were mentioned by others.

5. Then ask these questions and record volunteers' responses on a flip chart:

   • What job-related experiences seemed to produce big leaps in growth?

   • Given the attributes outlined, what experiences, important projects, or job assignments might exist now in the company that could provide this growth?

6. Share the guidelines for key growth experiences that have been agreed on and compare and contrast them to the attributes that the group offered.

7. Ask what projects are being planned in the next year that could be structured according to the determined guidelines. Record the data for use later.

8. Next ask each manager to think about three people who were instrumental in his or her growth and to record the names of these people.

9. Have each manager record what attributes these people exhibited that inspired his or her growth.

10. Ask for volunteers to share the attributes they listed and then record these attributes on a separate sheet of newsprint.

11. Then ask these questions and record the data to create a blueprint or model for identifying KGEs:

   • How many of the recorded items were on everyone's list?

   • Which attributes about managers seem to be universally associated with people who encourage growth?

   • Given these attributes, who might be good choices for mentors to help people make big leaps in growth?

Interestingly, some of the attributes mentioned may be negative. Tough mentors are often better than gentle mentors for promoting growth and learning. In fact, the authors' research seems to point heavily to experiences with tough, exacting mentors as key to managers' growth if those mentors also have faith that subordinates will do a good job.

The group should be provided with the following list of attributes exhibited by effective mentors involved in key growth experiences:

- They have little interest in asserting their power.
- They openly share their expertise.
- They ask for feedback and input from junior team members.
- They make their personal faith in the success of the projects a major motivator.
- They employ a hands-off approach until their help is needed.
- They socialize freely with other team members.
- They do not pull rank, but rather encourage team members to work without interest in organizational power or level.
- They consistently model shared, creative problem solving.

It is important to ensure the involvement of high-level managers before beginning a KGE program because these managers are the ones who will serve as mentors. Managers should be carefully selected based on the level of support and involvement that they can provide. It is important to select mentors who can nurture and develop both the program and the participants.

Step 3: Identifying Appropriate Assignments

As mentioned previously, the process of capturing KGEs is not about creating experiences but about identifying experiences that fit the KGE model and already exist in a company. Once enough information has been obtained about the experiences that have resulted in fast growth for organizational members, the HRD consultant can identify which of these experiences are recurring projects or assignments that can be captured and used regularly for employee development. The managers in a company can be trained to recognize potential KGEs by being familiar with what they are and how they work.

Recurring assignments are designated as KGEs by letting everyone involved in promotion decisions know that these assignments are for key growth use only. Key growth experiences may be tasks or positions. Examples of the kinds of *tasks* that might currently exist or be available soon include the following:

- Start-up assignments;
- Branch openings;
- Annual inventory management;
- Assignment in a foreign office;
- Implementation of new federal legislation;
- Installation of a new computer system;
- College recruiting;

- Organization development; and
- Strategic planning.

Types of *positions* providing key growth experiences may include these:

- Training facilitator;
- Large-volume outlet manager;
- Regional or area manager;
- Profit analyst working with senior managers;
- Public-relations director;
- Product manager for a product launch;
- Franchise-sales manager; or
- Task-force chairperson.

Step 4: Identifying Participants and Matching Assignments

After appropriate key growth experiences have been selected, participants are chosen to be on a KGE career track. Often participants are high-potential managers who need (or would welcome the opportunity) to grow quickly in order for the company to reap maximum return on its investment in human resources. Once these participants are identified, they are matched with KGEs as they normally would be matched with their next assignments. Particular attention should be paid to the outcome of each KGE and how it will catalyze growth for the participant.

The trick to making these assignments work, whether they are created or captured assignments, is to make them challenging. Giving lip service to KGEs without supplying a truly once-in-a-lifetime experience will quickly reduce their effectiveness. Excitement, rarity, and a focus on bottom-line results are catalysts for KGEs and cannot be synthesized or grafted onto job assignments already held by participants.

However, the knowledge gained from implementing KGEs can be used to make sure that every growth experience that a person has in a company contains some of the elements identified with KGEs. Key growth experiences should be kept for the best, fast-track performers; but other experiences can be carefully constructed to contain some of the growth-giving elements of KGEs. Opportunities to become involved in a leap experience may arise for each employee as he or she advances to an accelerated career track. Managers who are encouraged to make every growth experience incorporate elements of KGEs will be fostering the fastest and longest-lasting growth.

Step 5: Creating a KGE Career Track—Keeping People After They Leap

It is 1:30 a.m. and seven managers are sitting in a hotel room in suburban New Jersey. Their location is secret, and their job descriptions are privileged information. They constitute a varied group; each has been chosen for particular skills and experience, ranging from a newly hired junior executive to a senior vice president who heads the project. The president of the company, who is visiting the group to discuss its progress, asks each manager, regardless of rank, what he or she thinks will happen as a result of the work. The managers have been there every night for nine weeks, meeting into the early morning. By day, they work in cramped offices at a manufacturing site nearby. Their mission: to solve serious employee-relations, morale, and productivity issues.

Two years later the secret mission has been lauded as an astounding success; it has exceeded all expectations. The senior vice president who worked on the project and the company president meet for lunch to discuss a strange phenomenon. Of the seven managers, each hand picked for the assignment, none remain in the company. They all occupy significantly more responsible jobs at other companies. They socialize together regularly and share success stories. In fact, as a group they have gained a reputation as some of the best results-oriented managers in town. The companies they work for would agree. Yet even after making a major contribution to the success of their company, they left without looking back. What the president does not yet know is that in another year, the senior vice president with whom he is speaking will leave to start her own consulting firm.

This example illustrates what often occurs after employees have been involved in major career leaps. Thus, when employees are participating in KGEs, it is very important for the company to protect itself from losing its newly developed talent. Following are some guidelines for retaining KGE participants:

1. *Make all growth in the company a top priority.* Let employees know that their assignments are carefully designed to create the most and best growth for them.

2. *Involve senior management with participants in the KGE program.* Encourage high-level managers to mentor participants during, after, and between their leaps. Widely communicate senior management's involvement so participants understand that they are receiving special development.

3. *Three to six weeks before the end of leap assignments, map out long-term growth strategies for the participants.* It is the responsibility of the mentors to guide the participants at this time. The strategies need not outline specific future assignments but should include general goals; areas for further work or exposure; and measurable, bottom-line results. This discussion can also outline future salary growth or the potential for growth based on results.

4. *Keep KGE participants focused on the bottom line.* Once participants have seen the view from the mountaintop, it is hard for them to get used to being back in the valley. After their leap assignments, participants should encounter a continued expectation of results so that they will be encouraged to remain productive. Participants need to know that they are expected to retain their closeness to and impact on the day-to-day running of business.

5. *Make sure participants' next assignments involve as much independence as their KGE assignments.* Participants often complain that after they have learned to work on their own in the rarefied company of senior managers, they are then returned to "boring, middle-level jobs in the 'real world.'" Ideally, their next assignments

should allow them the independence that they just experienced. One way to do this is to assign the participants to the same mentors with whom they worked during KGEs for a year or two after the leaps. Retention of KGE participants can be designated as a performance goal for each of the mentoring managers.

6. *Create opportunities for participants to meet or work together after a KGE.* Participants report that after KGEs they feel symptoms of depression associated with losing their KGE teams. The social, networking, team aspect of KGEs is vital to the experiences and needs to be nurtured and preserved after the conclusion of the experiences.

7. *Plan the transition to regular (or new) assignments.* As mentioned in the previous paragraph, participants in KGEs report strong emotions as they deal with the break-up of their KGE teams; they miss the close working relationships, the free sharing of ideas, the intensity of focus on a goal, and the aspect of being in over their heads. One way to aid transitions is to provide work similar to that of the KGEs in participants' new assignments or to build special projects into their jobs. Another way is to assign tasks that will encourage them to mentor others or to help others make career leaps. It is important to remember that many KGE participants report feeling underused after their leaps. It is up to the company to nurture the new-found skills of participants; otherwise, the company risks losing these employees.

8. *Compensate participants based on their worth after KGEs.* The growth that KGE participants experience defies job grades and salary structures. During the times when they are being encouraged to grow, they become exceptions to many rules. To encourage them to stay, they need to be paid as exceptions as well.

9. *Begin a participant's role as mentor for others as soon as possible.* As developers of others, KGE participants cannot be underestimated. This is especially true immediately after they have completed leap assignments and have learned new skills, many by watching the effective senior managers with whom they have worked. It is vital to capture their enthusiasm and ability and use these qualities to the company's advantage.

RESULTS OF KEY GROWTH EXPERIENCES

As mentioned previously, the results of KGEs are far from unpredictable. The authors' research shows that KGEs create some common results. Participants are known to attain the following:

- Geometric leaps in growth;
- Growth that is not readily associated with traditional management development;
- Excellent leadership skills;
- Outstanding business results;
- Catalyzed career development; and
- Trouble remaining in conventional career tracks.

Geometric Leaps in Growth

One amazing outcome of KGEs is the kind of growth they produce. Unlike the usual measured growth that is seen in organizations, the growth attained as a result of KGEs is described by participants as giant steps in their ability to perform their jobs. This growth is reported to occur not only in job-specific areas but in totally unrelated areas.

In one scenario a junior manager may be asked to handle her boss's in-basket while the boss is away on disability leave. Over a period of three weeks, the junior manager is required to handle a number of in-basket items in areas that she has never dealt with before. In addition, she seeks advice from senior managers in other departments that she has not worked with before. Eventually she is asked to attend the boss's staff meeting to discuss a number of her decisions. By the time the boss returns, the junior manager has taken a big leap in the kinds of activities that she can reasonably be expected to handle. She suddenly feels comfortable in planning the budget, counseling employees, and dealing with managers above her in the organization. In fact, in some ways her knowledge is more up-to-date than that of her boss. She can now see projects from a different vantage point; able to see both the forest and the trees, she is more confident and able.

A Different Kind of Growth

Day-to-day work provides steady growth in many companies that use performance reviews and lists of objectives to focus employees. Workshop experiences produce concentrated growth in a short period of time, but it takes some effort for most training experiences to be transferred to the job. Key growth experiences seem to provide broad-based growth in many directions at once. This growth is extremely fast, is very powerful for the participant, and seems to be immediately applicable on the job.

For example, a young manager in his second assignment with a well-known service company spent nine months as employment manager during the toughest new-facility opening that his company had experienced. While doing so, he worked with the company's most talented employee-relations manager. When the young manager returned to a mid-level site-management position, he excelled at his usual job and, in addition, produced outstanding results in employee relations. That year he established and maintained the highest employee retention in the company.

Extraordinary Leadership Skills

American companies will need two resources in the future: better leadership and global strategies that work. Key growth experiences create better leaders by nurturing them in an environment that emphasizes both individual and group leadership. When participants emerge from KGEs, they have worked in stressful environments that forced them to work effectively with others with different points of view, ways of working, and levels of experience. These skills are transferred quickly and efficiently to create more flexible, more open leaders who enjoy and welcome diversity.

During leaps, participants not only see leadership modeled by other managers, but they also have a chance to lead. Because they are working in flat organizations, they often get a chance to lead or influence people who are organizationally more senior and who would, in other situations, be outside their sphere of influence. This situation produces a number of valuable outcomes. Participants become both more disposed toward and more skilled in teamwork. They become open to the possibility that others may provide insights and solutions, and they become better at asking for and accepting input gracefully. Working in this way changes the likelihood that they will act as rugged individualists and increases their willingness to build and use a network composed of co-workers at many levels with various areas of expertise. Many participants become avid gatherers of information from varied sources, perfecting their data-gathering and decision-making skills. All in all, the leadership skills that so many companies are seeking to synthesize—including gathering information, making decisions, managing resources, building consensus, and staying in touch with employees—are acquired naturally in key growth experiences.

Outstanding Business Results

Most KGE participants report that their results during KGEs are the best they have ever produced. In fact, they report that they are more (or differently) focused on results. In each case the result or goal of an assignment seems to overtake limiting factors that a participant might otherwise apply to work or have experienced in the past. Participants work longer hours, concentrate intensively for longer periods of time, take fewer breaks, and want less sleep. While many report that intense social and professional relationships come out of these experiences, they spend less time socializing away from work during the assignment. As a result, KGE participants produce outstanding, measurable results directly tied to the goals of their assignments.

Catalyzed Career Development

The increased focus on results seems to create a heightened attention to participants' own career development. At the conclusion of their leap assignments, they seem to have a new instinct for how to wring development from any experience; and they seek to do that whenever they can. They are more likely to welcome risk, to make decisions based on intuition, to take on new experiences willingly (especially those that require fresh insight), to break through to new technology, and to expect and receive the most from others. They also drive harder toward a goal than they previously did. When their energy is directed toward tasks, it translates into results. When it is directed toward the development of others, it translates into an ability to coach for improved effectiveness and creativity. When it is directed toward their own career development, it translates into impatience, high expectations, and an unwillingness to compromise their own growth.

Trouble After a Leap

Regardless of the success experienced in KGEs, many participants leave their companies not long after they finish their assignments. It is hypothesized that the company is responsible for this, not the participant. Sometimes companies make promises predicated on producing results and forget about or break those promises after the desired results are produced. At other times participants find that once they have completed their assignments the company does not subsequently provide equally challenging assignments for them. Some participants report that their companies keep them on a typical growth and promotion track after the leap assignment and that they feel they can find better opportunities by taking their newly wrought skills elsewhere. Part of the problem is the failure of the organization to update the profile of KGE participants to include new expertise. Companies may think of them the way they were before their leaps, thus failing to capitalize on their talent and forcing them to go elsewhere.

SOFT TECHNOLOGY TO DEAL WITH HARD ISSUES

As HRD professionals, many of us are looking for the latest technologies, theories, or statistics that will be useful to us in helping companies to solve the day-to-day business problems they face. Lately, companies have made it a priority to seek, hire, and keep better people and to put new talent to work faster. If companies can make leaps of their own, toward the possibility that a simple solution may solve a complicated problem, they can begin systematically hiring and growing the best people by matching them to one-of-a-kind key growth experiences. By capturing the experiences and applying them more intentionally, companies can develop talent in a more effective, planned way. By treating these employees as valued resources as they leap from experience to experience, companies can be assured of keeping these well-prepared people longer. If companies are able to recognize the unique challenges that these employees face when they grow, participants will be helped to make transitions that will strengthen their network, keep them in touch with more of their peers, and create cross-disciplinary skills. By retaining these super-charged employees instead of losing them to competitors, companies can realize the benefits of having more fully rounded, able managers. In many ways KGEs are a simple, low-cost answer to questions that many believe require complicated, expensive solutions.

Jason Ollander-Krane is a managing partner of Ollander-Krane/Johnson, a consulting company specializing in practical, innovative ways to grow and plan business growth, develop people, deliver the best products, and improve sales and service. He has held training and development positions with Wells Fargo Bank, Young and Rubicam, Macy's, and Adia Personnel Services.

Neil Johnson is also a managing partner of Ollander-Krane/Johnson. He designs and delivers custom programs in management development, selling and service, visioning, and planning for groups and individuals. Organizations also draw on his expertise in facilitating, team building, and other interventions.

Jason Ollander-Krane and Neil Johnson have been working together for twelve years. Their current clients include Hewlett Packard, Saatchi & Saatchi DFS, Procter and Gamble, The City of San Francisco, Bermuda Department of Tourism, and Remedy Temporaries.

SEXUAL DIFFERENCES IN THE WORKPLACE: THE NEED FOR TRAINING

Arlette C. Ballew and Pamela Adams-Regan

THE WORK FORCE IS CHANGING

Since the Second World War, women have entered the work force in increasing numbers. Sex-role expectations have changed as a result of economic necessity. Women have become a factor in the success of business and industry in most Western nations and in many other parts of the world as well.

In the U.S., Canada, and the U.K., the increased number of women in the work force has prompted legislation regarding sexual discrimination and harassment. But legislation alone cannot help men and women to learn to work together.

Making the transition from a home environment to a business environment has been difficult for some women; they also need help in "catching up" in terms of job skills, professional connections, and job opportunities. Making the transition from a male-dominated work environment to a male-female work environment has been difficult for some men; they need help in learning to deal with women in a manner that is appropriate to the business environment.

The success of many women in today's businesses and industries reinforces the fact that women are an integral part of today's work force; it also may increase the resentment and resistance on the part of some males to the encroachment of women into the workplace. Without a doubt, women will continue to be a major presence in modern business life. Trainers and consultants will have to address the unique challenges of integrating women into the workplace if the full productivity of men and women working together is to be realized.

MALE-FEMALE DIFFERENCES CREATE ISSUES IN THE WORKPLACE

In training and developing women to take positions in the work force and in management, it is not enough to focus on traditional areas of employee development: career management, résumé writing, presentation skills, interviewing techniques, technical skills, project management, and meeting management. These areas of training are just as relevant to men as they are to women, although men tend to receive more information about them in school and from the mentoring process. Training programs also must begin to address the interpersonal differences and the relationship issues that create problems between and for men and women in the workplace.

In *Developing Women Through Training,* Willis and Daisly (1991) claim that training activities in the U.K. are "planned by men, set up as a male-oriented venue in every way." They say that if women attend, they are there as an afterthought. According to them, trainers in the U.K. do not focus particularly on male/female generic training; they focus on male training. If women want to be trained, they have to learn the "male way." In other words, women are expected to learn to work like "men" rather than to work like workers. To some degree, this probably is true wherever women work.

However, with the increasing awareness of the existing inequality in the workplace for women, and with the increasing governmental action on both sides of the Atlantic to promote equality, it is of critical importance to address the male-female issues that can arise when men and women work together on the job. These issues can be addressed in a number of ways: as communication issues, as value issues, and so on. For example, past training groups have generated the following perceptions of basic differences between men and women:

- Men tend to be highly oriented toward the task.

- Women tend to be highly oriented toward the maintenance of the relationships with the people and environment that impact the task.

- Men tend to be comfortable with or, at least, expect competition (most of them have been raised with team sports in some form or another).

- Women tend to be less comfortable with even friendly competition and take the competitive aspect of work much more seriously.

- Men tend to tease one another a lot as part of ongoing relationships.

- Women tend to take kidding more seriously, especially when it may reflect on their sense of competency in a job.

- Men play one-upmanship games with one another. When men try to play this game with women, it can translate as discrimination.

- Men are rewarded for showing emotion only about sports and other "male-acceptable" pursuits; they are confused when emotion is shown at work in regard to tasks and teamwork.

- Women sometimes can deal better with personnel issues because they listen well and take care in maintaining relationships.

- Women often are trained in the model of successful men, rather than successful women. They may, therefore, be unsympathetic toward other women's problems in the workplace because they have been rewarded for male-like behavior. They may even suppress female-oriented behavior and penalize other women for exhibiting it.

- Women in the workplace may feel isolated from the mainstream of business because men exclude them regularly from mentoring and "bonding" activities.

- Women do not grow up being rewarded for successful confrontation (saying how one feels about something or facing a situation or person

Pfeiffer & Company

head on). Instead, women tend to be rewarded for serving as the peacemakers; therefore, they may have to learn the confrontation skills that are necessary in order to keep tasks on track.

- Men can learn to share their skills, their task-management strategies, and their teamwork expertise with women in order to create a better work environment.

- Women can learn to share their relationship and listening skills, their multi-task management skills, and their detail orientation with men in order to create a better work environment.

- Women can learn to express their emotions in ways that focus on task-related issues.

- Men can learn to focus more on implementation, rather than just on "the big picture."

Many of the perceived differences between men and women are, in fact, backed up by research. Gilligan (1982), a psychologist and professor at Harvard University, studied developmental differences between men and women. She concluded that men and women speak differently; hence, the title of her book, *In a Different Voice.* Gilligan also maintains that the theory of separation or "individuation" from the mother as a developmental process has been formulated by men (Erikson, 1963; Levinson, 1978), whose theories assume that development then proceeds toward autonomy. Gilligan argues that this focus emanates from a male point of view but that, in reality, males and females experience maternal contact differently. Mothers perceive sons as being different from themselves. Consequently, separation and the formation of "ego boundaries" are more emphasized with males, and they become more associated with the internal world. Mothers experience female children as being like themselves, so they tend to parent them differently. Female separation and individuation occur at a slower rate; thus, female children perceive themselves as less differentiated from others, as more connected to the external world. Gilligan concluded that these primary parenting differences lead to a strengthened capacity for empathy among women, along with a stronger basis for experiencing the needs of others.

In other words, young males and females experience relationships and issues of dependency differently: Masculinity is defined through separation; femininity is defined through attachment. Women define themselves in terms of relationships, are threatened by separation, and have difficulty with individualization. Men define themselves in the context of individualization, are threatened by attachment, and have difficulty with relationships. Gilligan does not say that one or the other is preferable; she merely presents the data in the hope of increasing understanding.

Lever (1976) has documented that attachment to and separation from others often are expressed in the games of children. Males more often play outdoors, in large groups with a wide age range. Females more often play indoors, in smaller groups with a narrow age range. Males more often play games that emphasize competition and they quarrel more often. Females more often play games that emphasize relationships, and when quarrels or disputes arise, they often end the games. Furthermore, males play with enemies and compete with friends, in accordance with the rules. Females play mostly with friends in smaller, more intimate groups that are more willing to make exceptions to the rules.

The best-selling book *You Just Don't Understand: Women and Men in Conversation* (Tannen, 1990) also cites the basic differences between the orientations of and assumptions made by men and women. These assumptions cause them to view things differently and, in fact, to communicate in what amount to "different languages." Among other things, men are concerned with data, and women are concerned with interrelationships (between things as well as people).

Interpersonal training has revealed that there may be significant differences between men and women with regard to how they perceive their own work styles, as well as what they perceive as acceptable work styles in others.

Malcolm Hornby (1992), Director of Delta Management in the U.K., says that in his interpersonal skills training programs, he finds that, "Men expect themselves to be seen as drivers, or task-oriented individuals who are tough-minded decision makers with strong leadership styles. But men see women as more amiable, less assertive, and more emotionally responsive. This can cause men to regard women as more indecisive and participative in their leadership approaches."

Hornby goes on to note that a woman sometimes can be perceived unfavorably by both sexes if she demonstrates more task-oriented, driving behavior. "She may be seen as unresponsive, single-minded, aggressive, stubborn, hard-nosed, unfeminine, insensitive, selfish, and threatening," he says. "Many of these attributes would be seen as strengths in her male counterparts. But from a woman, it can sometimes break the man's paradigm of expected female behavior."

On the other hand, men who exhibit analytical or emotionally responsive behaviors may be viewed as indecisive, amiable, chatty, soft, and unbusinesslike. The essential element in interpersonal skill development is to recognize that all work styles are needed to make a productive workplace. "When one worker's behavior does not conform to another worker's expectations, it is the worker with the expectations who needs to demonstrate greater versatility in his or her own work style," explains Hornby. In other words, learning to understand and to value other people's approaches to work can be invaluable in enhancing overall productivity.

Clearly, if men and women are to work together effectively, they need to understand some of the basic psychological differences between them and they need to learn to respect and to deal with those differences in a way that provides a win-win opportunity for both. If they do not do this, individuals will suffer, the work will suffer, the organization will suffer, and the overall productivity and health of the economy will suffer.

SEXUAL DISCRIMINATION AND HARASSMENT IN THE WORKPLACE: AN URGENT ISSUE

Sexual harassment in the workplace has received increased attention lately in the U.S., Canada, and the U.K. There are several types of sexual harassment. The most common, of course, is sexual discrimination. In short, this is any action that does not extend to a woman the same job conditions, courtesy, benefits, salary, training and development, and advancement opportunities as are extended to a man.

Some sexual discrimination (for example, paying a woman less than a man for the same job) is built into an organization's system. Some of the more subtle forms—which include exclusion from job-based benefits such as equal access to professional affiliation—are receiving increased attention. Although all forms of sexual discrimination and harassment are based on the fact that the harassee is of a particular sex, not all are "sexual" (Pfeiffer & Company, 1992).

Much sexual harassment is based on an unwillingness of those in positions of power or control (for example, males) to share that power or control with others whom they perceive as different from themselves (for instance, females). This type of harassment is more about "keeping women in their place" than it is about sex. Women who are most vulnerable to being sexually harassed on the job are the pioneers—the first of their sex to break into an area of employment. When women make up less than 25 percent of the work force, the number of complaints amounts to about two per 1,000 women. The complaint rate drops by half when women make up more than 50 percent of a corporate population. Thus, females who enter previously male-dominated positions often find themselves to be the objects of harassment. Female police officers, fire fighters, gas and electric workers, maintenance and repair persons, and so on, report a wide array of discrimination and harassment techniques. Many of these are intended to actually cause the harassee to be fired or to resign from the job. It has been found that men who are pioneers in occupations typically held by women also are more vulnerable to harassment. It is likely that the first male nurses or telephone operators, for example, may have experienced harassment.

Other forms of sexual harassment are related to sexuality. They are intended to initiate some type of interchange between the harasser and the harassee. Some are motivated by feelings of power, anger, or cruelty, and some are motivated by sexual desires.

There also is evidence that men tend to exclude women from mentoring and other developmental opportunities in the workplace.

In the U.S.

Training magazine (Lee, 1992) reports the following:

- The National Association of Female Executives surveyed its members in 1991 and found that 53 percent of the 1,300 women had been sexually harassed or knew someone who had been.

- A survey conducted by *Working Woman* magazine in 1988 found that 90 percent of *Fortune 500* companies had received sexual harassment complaints; one third had lawsuits filed against them; and 64 percent of their personnel officers said most complaints were valid.

- The American Management Association surveyed 524 of its member companies in November, 1991, and found that 52 percent have dealt with allegations of sexual harassment in the past five years.

Additionally, the U.S. Navy recently suffered a major embarrassment when it was revealed that Navy aircraft carrier aviators who were attending a 1991 "Tailhook" convention had sexually harassed and assaulted female Navy personnel at the convention. Two women who were present at the 1991 Tailhook convention took photos of male attendees exposing themselves and demonstrating other lewd behavior. At least thirty-six women claimed to have been molested by men lining the third-floor hallways. The resulting scandal led to the resignation of Navy Secretary H. Lawrence Garrett II in June, 1992, and to an intensive investigation of sexual harassment within the armed forces.

In the U.K.

In his book, *Mind Your Manners: Managing Culture Clash in the Single European Market*, Mole (1990) states that 45 percent of the U.K. work force is made up of women. This is the largest percentage of female workers in any of the European Community countries, despite the fact that female workers in the U.K. have the lowest maternity benefits and negligible childcare facilities.

The *Financial Times* reported in March, 1992, that "Three quarters of female company directors believe women are discriminated against in the workplace, according to the first survey by the Institute of Directors of the views of its members" (Summers, 1992). A third of these directors said that they had had a direct experience of sexual discrimination, particularly in the early stages of their careers. Male attitudes at work and employers' failure to take into account the childcare and domestic responsibilities of their employees were blamed as the chief causes of the discrimination.

The *Independent* reported in March, 1992, that despite some legislation designed to advance equality and years of campaigning, women in the U.K. still remain almost invisible in the top of public and commercial businesses and institutions (Mills, 1992). There are no female House of Lords judges, no female Cabinet ministers; and before the recent appointment of Barbara Mills as Director of Public Prosecutions, there were no female permanent secretaries in the civil service. In addition, only one in every two hundred company directors are women, even though more than 40 percent of private-sector workers are female. *Labour Research* magazine published a report early in 1992 that showed that although women represent 49 percent of all nonindustrial civil servants in the U.K., fewer than 7 percent are at the levels of under-secretary or above (Mills, 1992).

THE COSTS OF SEXUAL DISCRIMINATION AND HARASSMENT

The costs of sexual discrimination and harassment are many (Gracy-Robertson, Grant, Richmond, & Woodard, 1992). First, the effects on the victims include psychological damage, loss of productivity, loss of wages and other benefits, loss of employment and future benefits, and so on. If a claim or lawsuit is filed, there may be compensatory or punitive damages. Second, the effects on others in the work force include psychological damage (such as anger, resentment, fear), loss of productivity, loss of esteem for the harasser and/or supervisors involved, and possible formation of factions in the work environment as people "take sides." All of this can severely impact the contribution that workers can make to the organization.

Investigating or dealing with a complaint also has costs: people may need to be reassigned or removed from positions; inquiries or in-depth investigations may need to be conducted; in-house personnel may be required to spend time on this or outside personnel may have to be hired to conduct briefings, interviews, and so on; there are administrative costs; and there are counseling costs (which may be both internal and external). Other costs include absenteeism; rescheduling; training of new employees; impact on other workers, supervisors, and personnel relationships; and loss of morale.

In the article, "Sexual Harassment: After the Headlines," in *Training* magazine, Lee (1992, p. 25) states, "Most corporate sexual-harassment training programs aim to protect the company from litigation by familiarizing employees with the company's policy and internal complaint procedures. Often, that knowledge brings a jump in the number of reported incidents—considered a positive sign." And, later, "Lawsuit costs are high...to everyone involved....Everything you can do to prevent sexual harassment before a lawsuit occurs is worth every penny" (Lee, 1992, p. 25).

LEGISLATION ADDRESSES THE ISSUES (BUT NOT THE CAUSES)

The U.S., Canada, and the U.K. all have legislation that prohibits discrimination based on factors such as gender, race or national origin, age, disability, and so on. All three provide remedies for sexual discrimination and sexual harassment. Furthermore, all three hold the employing organization responsible for the actions of its employees and for establishing a working environment that is free from unlawful discrimination and harassment.

U.S. Initiatives

The U.S. government passed the Civil Rights Act of 1991 in order to extend the provisions of Title VII of the existing Civil Rights Act to "protect against and deter unlawful discrimination and harassment in the workplace," including sexual discrimination and harassment.

The U.S. law defines sexual harassment as follows:

> Unwelcome sexual advances, requests for sexual favors, and other verbal or physical conduct of a sexual nature constitute sexual harassment when:

1. Submission to such conduct is made either explicitly or implicitly a term or condition of an individual's employment; or

2. Submission to or rejection of such conduct by an individual is used as the basis for employment decisions affecting such individual; or

3. Such conduct has the purpose or effect of unreasonably interfering with an individual's work performance or creating an intimidating, hostile, or offensive working environment.

These definitions cover both men and women and apply to all types of job-related interactions. A third party also may file a complaint if such behavior offends him or her, even if neither of the two persons involved has complained. For example, if two persons are telling sexual jokes in the work setting and a third person who overhears them is offended, that person may complain.

In recognition of the lack of developmental opportunities for women (and other minorities) in the workplace, the U.S. Congress included the "Glass Ceiling Act" in the Civil Rights Act of November, 1991, stating that "despite a dramatically growing presence in the workplace, women and minorities remain underrepresented in management and decision-making positions" and citing "artificial barriers exist to advancement....lack of access to credential-building developmental opportunities and the desirability of eliminating artificial barriers to their advancement" (Pfeiffer & Company, 1992, p. 53). This act establishes a commission to study the artificial barriers to the development and advancement of women and minorities, the manner in which business fills management and decision-making positions, the developmental experiences that foster advancement to such positions, and the compensation and reward structures currently used in U.S. business.

Two Types of Harassment

Two types of sexual harassment have been defined in the U.S. (Carbonell, Higginbotham, & Sample, 1990). *Quid pro quo* harassment occurs when a sexual act is the prerequisite condition to employment, promotion, or any other job benefit or when refusal to engage in a sexual act results in being fired, denied promotion, or having a job benefit withheld.

Hostile environment harassment occurs when the work atmosphere is made intimidating, hostile, or offensive (for instance, by such things as unequal treatment of the sexes, nude pinups, off-color jokes and remarks, sexually based staring or gestures, repeatedly asking a co-worker for dates after initial refusal, and so on) and when such conduct has the purpose or effect of unreasonably interfering with an individual's work performance or creating an intimidating, hostile, or offensive working environment.

Harassment can include insulting, degrading, hurtful, or rude comments; offensive talk, language, pictures, or physical actions; bad reviews; and attempts to force the person out of the job.

In the case of *Hall v. Gus Construction Company* (1988), three female employees were subjected to repeated acts of harassment by male co-workers. Although the harassment included requests for sexual favors, the majority of it consisted of obscene or hostile acts whose apparent intent was to force the women out of their jobs.

Sexual harassment must be based on the harassee's sex, but the type of conduct can vary; it need not be amorous or involve a request for sexual favors. The conduct can be physical (such as touching), verbal (such as lewd or suggestive comments), or visual (such as the display of pornographic pictures). It may occur in the office or outside the workplace during business-related events. The harassment need not be directed at the victim; something that is overheard or seen can affect the motivation and work environment of those whom it upsets or offends. Harassment directed at men by women or at homosexuals also may constitute unlawful sexual discrimination.

A single event may constitute harassment (Baxter & Hermle, 1989), as in *Boyd v. James S. Hayes Living Health Care Agency, Inc.* (1987), in which the incident occurred during an out-of-town business trip; and in *Joyner v. AAA Cooper Transportation* (1983), which also involved only one incident.

The most significant factors in judging whether an act constitutes sexual harassment are the nature of the conduct, the degree to which the conduct relates to the victim's terms and conditions of employment, whether the conduct is an isolated incident, and how seriously the conduct was intended or perceived.

Canadian Initiatives

The Canadian Human Rights Act, Section 2, states that "Every individual should have an equal opportunity with other individuals to make for himself or herself the life that he or she is able and wishes to have, consistent with his or her duties and obligations as a member of society." It prohibits discrimination on the basis of sex and nine other characteristics. It covers discriminatory acts in employment, employment applications and advertisements, pay, employee organizations, provision of goods and services, reasonable accommodation, discriminatory notices, harassment, and so on. The Canadian Human Rights Commission investigates complaints; monitors annual reports filed by Federally regulated employers; monitors programs, policies, and legislation affecting designated groups; and develops and conducts information programs to promote public understanding of the provisions of the Act.

Harassment is defined as any unwelcome physical, visual, or verbal conduct (Canadian Human Rights Commission, 1991). It may include verbal or practical jokes, insults, threats, personal comments, or innuendo. It may take the form of posters, pictures, or graffiti. It may involve touching, stroking, pushing, pinching, or any unwelcome physical conduct, including physical assault. Unwelcome sexual acts, comments, or propositions are harassment. Offensive acts such as leering or similar gestures also can constitute harassment. A person does not have to be touched or threatened to have been harassed. According to the Canadian Human Rights Commission, any behavior that insults or intimidates is harassment if a reasonable person should have known that the behavior was unwelcome.

In the case of *Bonnie R. v. the Department of National Defence*, the department was held responsible for the acts of a foreman. The Supreme Court of Canada stated that an employer has a responsibility to provide a work environment free of harassment and added: "...only an employer can remedy undesirable effects [of discrimination]; only an employer can provide the most important remedy—a healthy work environment" (Canadian Human Rights Commission, 1991, pp. 4-5).

U.K. Initiatives

In 1990, Prime Minister John Major launched a business-led campaign called "Opportunity 2000" to increase the quality and quantity of women's participation in the work force. This program provides a manual of "how-to's" to assist organizations in planning how to utilize women more effectively in organizations. A key factor is the development of training that helps them not only to prepare for business and the workplace but also to optimize the unique skills that women can bring to a male-oriented work environment.

In the U.K., *Today* reported in March, 1992, that "Sex pests are in for a shock under new Government guidelines. They will be hunted down by a new generation of 'sex spies' and then taken to court" ("Spies in Office," 1992, p. 2). The government is to order firms to set up teams to crack down on sexual harassment at work. More than 40,000 firms will be issued guidelines by Employment Minister Robert Jackson. *Today* goes on to say that firms will be urged to "pull down girlie pin-ups, stop wolf-whistling, and end dirty talk that can lead to humiliation for women" ("Spies in Office," 1992, p. 2). Jackson has said that he is "determined to show that women do not have to put up with sexual harassment" ("Spies in Office," 1992, p. 2).

Under the Employment Protection (Consolidation) Act of 1978, it may be possible for a U.K. employee to claim constructive dismissal where sexual harassment results in the person's working conditions becoming so intolerable as to cause the individual to leave. The person also may make a claim under the Sex Discrimination Act whereby, in addition to employees' liability for their own actions, employers also can be held liable for the discriminatory actions of their employees. Furthermore, sexual harassment may amount to indecent assault (a hostile act accompanied by circumstances of indecency). In this instance, hostile means that the person receiving the act is an unwilling victim, and the act is a criminal offense.

The European Community

The European Community Code of Conduct, which was formally adopted on November 27, 1991, seeks to encourage the development and implementation of policies and practices that establish working environments free from sexual harassment and create a climate at work in which women and men "respect one another's integrity."

WHAT TRAINING NEEDS TO DO

Obviously, the extent of these laws will raise many questions. How is one to know where to draw the line? One answer is to ask whether the harasser's wife/husband or daughter/son would want to be treated in such a way. Another way is to help harassers to realize the true motivation for some of their "kidding" behaviors. This may be difficult for some people. They must learn to differentiate between complimenting, patronizing, and soliciting. They must be given specific examples of what is and what is not considered sexual harassment, so that they have some concrete standards by which to judge their own behavior.

Women, too, have a responsibility for dealing with sexual harassment, and they will need training in learning how to do this. Trainers should help participants practice making and receiving complaints. Furthermore, women have to learn how to confront undesired behavior openly the first time it occurs. This may be as simple as saying assertively, "When you (describe actual behavior), it makes me uncomfortable/offends me, and I would like you not to do it again." Role playing can help people to learn how to respond to harassing behaviors (for example, how to discourage the harasser) and what behaviors of theirs might actually be encouraging the harasser.

Women must learn which behaviors of theirs are sending confusing messages to their male co-workers. For example, passive reception of sexual harassment may be a stalling tactic on the part of the harassee but may be interpreted as acceptance on the part of the harasser. This understanding on both sides will require some honest communication about past assumptions and present confusions. The input of other participants also can help to clarify situations and perceptions.

Rationally talking about responses to the issues of sexual discrimination and sexual harassment in the safety of the training session (such discussions should be confidential to the training setting) often leads to greatly increased awareness and sensitivity about what is generally considered to be an embarrassing topic. During sessions, participants may learn that they share some of the same reactions and fears.

Care must be taken not to make anyone hypersensitive to dealing with male-female issues, as this could lead to "backlash" behaviors. People should not be led to become paranoid about working with or being friendly with someone of the opposite sex.

It is becoming more and more obvious that women are an integral part of the work force. It is equally obvious that many people, both male and female, can benefit from training that is designed to facilitate the acceptance and development of women on the job.

MANAGERS AND SUPERVISORS ALSO NEED TRAINING

Business owners, managers, and supervisors also have much to learn. Businesses must establish policies regarding sexual discrimination and sexual harassment and convey those policies to all employees and supervisors. Both supervisors and organizations can be sued if sexual harassment occurs on the job, even if they were not aware of it, because it is their responsibility to see that it does not occur.

Managers and supervisors must understand, communicate, model, and enforce the organization's policies. They also must be trained in the procedures to be followed in receiving complaints, investigating them, and enforcing policies.

Moreover, they must establish an atmosphere in the workplace in which people are not afraid to ask for guidance or to report harassment. They also must ensure that there are no reprisals, either for the alleged harasser or the harassee, while the complaint is being investigated and that there are no reprisals for the harassee or for any witnesses afterward.

In addition to establishing policies and procedures, organizations must require that supervisors treat all employees (including complainants) with respect and dignity. It has been suggested that some organizations may want to train some supervisors or workers as change-agent seeds—people (men and women) who take on the responsibility for calling subtle or not-so-subtle instances of discrimination or harassment to the offender's attention. Of course, this should be maintained as a learning experience and not be allowed to become a "Gestapo-like" operation.

UNDERSTANDING OF ISSUES LEADS TO GREATER PRODUCTIVITY

Much interpersonal training is based on the assumption that effective communication and clarification of differences contribute to increased understanding, which leads to greater harmony and increased ability to focus on the task. In any training session designed to explore and clarify male/female issues, an emphasis should be placed on listening and feeling free to express feelings about those issues. This may be easier for women to do than it is for men, so helping the male participants to express their beliefs, attitudes, and feelings is one of the trainer's major goals. Similarly, the trainer must ensure that the women have the opportunity to express their views and are not overruled or cut off by the males, who may not be used to such sharing.

Some of the training objectives in such a situation are as follows:

- Increase listening skills;
- Become aware of one's own values and assumptions;
- Learn about the values and assumptions of others;
- Practice constructive confrontation techniques;
- Learn to use third-party intervention;
- Learn to use direct statements and "I" statements;
- Distinguish between thinking and "feeling" statements;
- Explore and understand different social styles; and
- Understand others' task focus.

WHY EXPERIENTIAL LEARNING IS WELL-SUITED FOR SEXUAL-HARASSMENT-AWARENESS TRAINING

The experiential learning process, in which participants—both male and female—can "experience" a business activity in a comfortable, facilitated environment, is a productive means of exploring underlying issues and of learning communication and listening skills, problem-solving skills, and so on. In the safety of the educational environment, people can sort through their feelings, their assumptions, and their values as they hear about and relate to the values of others.

Training activities that are experiential in nature are well-suited to sexual-harassment-awareness training. In such designs, the participants learn from their own experiences, including their emotional responses, reflections, insights, and discussions with others. This differs substantially from didactic learning, in which predetermined "facts" are imparted to the learners. In experiential learning, although the situation is structured, much of the actual learning content is elicited from the participants themselves. Such an outcome takes skill on the part of the trainer; it is the part of training that often is called "facilitation."

The popular Adult Learning Stages cycle described by Kolb (Kolb, Rubin, & McIntyre, 1971)—and subsequently developed and packaged by Honey and Mumford—has been used extensively throughout the U.K. in many training programs. In the U.S., Pfeiffer & Company has developed the "Experiential Learning Cycle" (Jones & Pfeiffer, 1975; Pfeiffer & Company, 1990), which elaborates on Kolb's model. In brief, the ELC is as follows:

Experiencing. In the "activity" phase, participants *do* something that generates a common data base to be discussed, or "processed," in the later stages. The activity may be making something, solving problems, sharing information, giving and receiving feedback, ranking, competing or collaborating, role playing, and so on. This is not the most significant part of the overall activity; if the process is shortchanged after this stage, it is simply a "game," and learning is left to chance.

Publishing. During this step, individuals share their experiences—what happened to them and what their reactions (behavioral, emotional, and cognitive) and observations were during the previous stage. In this way, all members of the group know "what happened." It is important to stick to reactions and observations at this point and not to skip ahead to generalizing.

Processing. This step is a systematic examination of what happened, achieved by discussing patterns and dynamics. It can be done by means of process observers giving reports, thematic discussions, questionnaires, or other activities that help to identify recurring topics, trends, key dimensions, and the effects of particular behaviors within the artificial situation set up by the experiencing phase.

Generalizing. At this point, the focus is taken off the initial activity and put on what happens in the real world. The emphasis is on "what tends to happen," not on "what happened in this group." The participants now are ready to take what they have learned and generalize it to broader situations. These generalizations may include styles of interaction and their effects, situations that evoke common behaviors, and basic "truths." This is the part of the activity that answers the question "So what?" It is a good idea to have the participants create lists or other visual products to show what has been learned. If the trainer/facilitator wants to introduce conceptual data at this point, it must be linked directly to the points that have been generalized by the participants.

Applying. The question in this stage is "Now what?" This is the time to plan effective use of what was learned. The trainer/facilitator can help the participants to apply their generalizations to actual situations in which they are involved. This increases the chance that the learning actually will be utilized. Participants can engage in subgroup discussions, goal setting, contracting, consulting, and practicing in order to reinforce planned applications. This is the end of the activity, but it is not the end of learning. Going out and "doing" something differently afterward is the experiencing step of a new learning cycle.

Activities that ask a question about sexual values can be very useful in getting the training participants to examine their own values and assumptions and to listen to others as they communicate theirs. It is best if the situation on which the activity is based is artificial, so that it does not threaten specific participants or relate too closely to their particular work environment. In this way, the discussions can be focused on values, concepts, and feelings, rather than on past incidents or old resentments. Other activities that can be useful include listening and communicating exercises, surveys and questionnaires that generate discussion, structured role playing, and activities that demonstrate different approaches to communicating, relating, problem solving, and so on.

Although free-form role playing can be inflammatory, structured role playing can be quite revealing to the participants, especially if each role player plays both roles in order to experience both sides of the issue.

The trainer must be prepared to handle the questions that will arise. In many cases, this does not mean answering the questions directly, but saying, "What do you think?" or encouraging the group members to volunteer their own answers. This is especially helpful if the question does not have just one answer but is one of the realities of everyday life that must be assessed in terms of the situation.

CONCLUSION

Integrating the skills of both men and women in the workplace is a challenging task for any employee-development professional. Trainers in the next decade will have the great responsibility of helping people learn to understand, communicate with, solve problems with, and work with one another.

Developing training that can meet the needs of both men and women will help significantly to maximize the productivity of the combined work force. Particularly if issues such as male-female differences and sexual discrimination and harassment can be explored and diffused with awareness training, the greater will be the chance that men and women will learn to treat each other with more understanding and respect.

This will accomplish much more than avoiding undesired or unproductive behaviors. It will allow both men and women to work together in a professional manner that enhances both their own careers and the overall productivity of the organization. Sooner than later, our society will require that everyone grow and change. Trainers in the next decade will have the great responsibility of helping people learn to understand, communicate with, problem solve with, and work with one another. Now is the time to begin.

REFERENCES

Baxter, R.H., Jr., & Hermle, L.C. (1989). *Sexual harassment in the workplace: A guide to the law.* New York: Executive Enterprises Publications.

Canadian Human Rights Commission. (1991). *Harassment casebook: Summaries of selected harassment cases.* Ottawa, Ontario, Canada: author.

Carbonell, J.L., Higginbotham, J., & Sample, J. (1990). Sexual harassment of women in the workplace: Managerial strategies for understanding, preventing, and limiting liability. In J.W. Pfeiffer (Ed.), *The 1990 annual: Developing human resources* (pp. 225-238). San Diego, CA: Pfeiffer & Company.

Erikson, E.H. (1963). *Childhood and society* (2nd ed.). New York: W.W. Norton.

Gilligan, C. (1982). *In a different voice: Psychological theory and women's development.* Cambridge: Harvard University Press.

Gracy-Robertson, G., Grant, J., Richmond, E., Jr., & Woodard, M.D. (1992). *The problem of sexual harassment: A supervisor's guide* (booklet and audiotape package). San Diego, CA: Pfeiffer & Company.

Hornby, M. (1992, May). Personal interview.

Jones, J.E., & Pfeiffer, J.W. (1975). *The 1975 annual handbook for group facilitators.* San Diego, CA: Pfeiffer & Company.

Kolb, D., Rubin, I.M., & McIntyre, J.M. (1971). *Organizational psychology: A book of readings.* Englewood Cliffs, NJ: Prentice-Hall.

Lee, C. (1992, March). Sexual harassment: After the headlines. *Training,* pp. 23-31.

Lever, J. (1976). Sex differences in the games children play. *Social Problems,* pp. 23, 478-487.

Levinson, D.J. (1978). *The seasons of a man's life.* New York: Alfred A. Knopf.

Mills, H. (1992, March 2). Senior jobs still eluding women. (U.K.) *The Independen,* p. 7.

Mole, J. (1990). *Mind your manners: Managing culture clash in the single European market.* London: Industrial Society.

Pfeiffer & Company. (1990). *The experiential learning cycle.* San Diego, CA: Author.

Pfeiffer & Company. (1992). *Addressing sexual harassment in the workplace* (trainer's package). San Diego, CA: Author.

Spies in office hunt sex pests. (1992, March 2). (U.K.) *Today,* p. 2.

Summers, D. (1992, March 19). Female directors report widespread inequality. (U.K.) *Financial Times,* p. 9.

Tannen, D. (1990). *You just don't understand: Women and men in conversation.* New York: Ballantine.

Willis, L., & Daisly, J. (1991). *Developing women through training.* London: McGraw-Hill.

Arlette C. Ballew *is a developmental senior editor at Pfeiffer & Company in San Diego, California.* She is co-author of University Associates Training Technologies *and associate editor of* Theories and Models in Applied Behavioral Science. *Ms. Ballew specializes in developing, writing, and editing HRD materials for professional consultants and trainers.*

Pamela Adams-Regan *is a business consultant, author, and professional speaker, specializing in the areas of sexual harassment, effective presentations, management, team building, and direct marketing. She also provides attorney training in the areas of sexual harassment and presentations. Ms. Adams-Regan is co-author of* WordPerfect 5.0 Macros *(McGraw Hill),* WordPerfect 5.1 Macros *(McGraw Hill), and* WordPerfect Macros, the Windows Version *(McGraw Hill). In addition, she has published articles and pieces in* Training & Development Journal *(United Kingdom),* San Francisco Chronicle, Meetings Magazine, *and* Inc. Magazine. *She also coaches technical and management professionals on effective team presentations.*

STRESS-MANAGEMENT TRAINING FOR THE NINETIES

Beverly Byrum-Robinson

Stress is everywhere: in the workplace, in the home, in the streets. At no time in history has stress been so much discussed nor considered such a problem. In a survey of six hundred workers, 46 percent reported their jobs to be highly stressful; in fact, 34 percent reported so much stress they were contemplating quitting (Farnham, 1991). Whether or not the people who feel stressed really are stressed is almost a moot point. The fact is that as more and more people talk and behave as if they are stressed, stress has become the career buzzword of the Nineties. Moreover, American society appears to promote stress as the socially desirable road to and outcome of achievement. As Farnham (1991, p. 71) notes, "Inner peace is seen as the prerogative of dweebs. It's hip to be stressed."

Managing stress appears to be a real need rather than a fad. In a survey of people currently employed, 80 percent desired more information on stress (Sailer, Schlacter, & Edwards, 1982). Stress affects everyone from factory workers to executives. Because of the high incidence of perceived stress both on the job and in external arenas that may affect job performance, human resource development (HRD) professionals must take an interest in this national phenomenon. This article defines stress, explains the importance of stress to HRD professionals, reviews what is being done and recommended in terms of combating stress, outlines a feasible cognitive-centered stress-management training program, and discusses the advantages and disadvantages of such a program.

A DEFINITION OF STRESS

In defining stress, there are three terms to consider: stress, distress, and eustress. Selye (1974, p. 14), considered to be the father of stress research, defines stress as "the nonspecific response of the body to any demand made upon it." *Nonspecific* refers to the adaptation or effort required in order to resume normal bodily functioning. A specific demand on the body, such as running, requires nonspecific adaptation to return the body to a less active state. Another scientific definition of stress, which includes the consequences of stress, states that stress is "a fairly predictable arousal [referring to Selye's nonspecific demand for adjustment] of psychophysiological (mind-body) systems that, if prolonged, can fatigue or damage the system to the point of malfunction or disease" (Girdano, Everly, & Dusek, 1990, pp. 1-2). Complete damage of the biological system is known as physical exhaustion or death. Complete damage of the motivational system is known as emotional exhaustion and withdrawal, or burnout (Matteson & Ivancevich, 1987a; Watts, 1990).

Stress, or the stress response, is triggered by a stressor, which is any stimulus, internal or external, with the potential to set off a physiological fight-flight response (Greenberg, 1990). *Stress reactivity* is the individual's tendency in the moment to be vulnerable to stress by perceiving an event as a stressor. Therefore, stress can be viewed as the combination of a stressor and stress reactivity or the interaction of a person's ability to deal with alarming external and internal events. For example, Terry's boss has issued the team a tight time frame for a big project (stressor). Terry has a tendency not to delegate and to feel fully responsible for results (stress reactivity). The combination of the deadline and Terry's anxiety about results might result in tension headaches every day (stress response).

Stressors that are negative or cause damage are called *distressors*. However, not all stressors are negative or cause damage. Stressors that are positive and challenging enough to promote action are called *eustressors*. However, any change—whether positive or negative—still requires a response from the body or an adaptation to an event. For example, Terry's receiving a promotion for being able to meet deadlines is a positive consequence, produces new challenges, and still is an event to which Terry will need to adapt.

Stress management refers to any program that reduces stress by understanding the stress response, recognizing stressors, and using coping techniques to minimize stressors, stress reactivity, and/or the negative consequences resulting from stress. *Coping techniques* are thought and/or behavior patterns that neutralize stressors or establish resistance to negative stress outcomes. *Coping* is the effort to manage stressful demands, which can take two equally valid forms. The first form is *problem-focused coping*, activities designed to alter a stressful situation. The second form is *emotion-focused coping*, activities designed to regulate distress by a change in perception or attention, very often when the situation cannot be changed. For example, Terry could refuse the promotion (problem-focused coping to reduce the stressor). Alternatively, Terry could decide to get done what needs to be done (emotion-focused coping to relieve stress reactivity). Or Terry could practice relaxation to lower the potential for headaches (problem-focused coping to reduce stress consequences).

These definitions demonstrate that stress is unavoidable; people will always have demands placed on them. In addition, people seem to need a certain level of demand in order to avoid boredom and stagnation. The point at which the HRD professional needs to become involved is when stress begins to reach the debilitating level.

STRESS AND THE HRD PROFESSIONAL

In addition to the fact that stress affects everyone in the workplace, the following statistics should alert the HRD professional to the importance of understanding stress and managing it in the workplace:

- Approximately 75 percent to 90 percent of visits to physicians are estimated to be stress related.

- Between 11 percent and 14 percent of all workers' compensation claims for occupational diseases are stress related.

- Claim benefits paid for stress average $15,000—twice the amount paid to the normal physical injury claim.

- Executive stress is estimated to cost between ten and nineteen billion dollars a year; stress-related illness in general has been estimated to cost $150 to $200 billion per year because of absenteeism, disability, and lower productivity.

- Alcohol abuse, considered to be stress-related, costs businesses approximately $44.2 billion a year.

- Nationwide, 15 percent of executives and 45 percent of managers suffer enough stress to affect their job performance and the job performance of others; 46 percent of workers find their jobs highly stressful and 34 percent are contemplating quitting their jobs because of stress; 61 percent of workers in high-stress jobs say that stress undermines productivity.

In addition to these statistics, stress is believed to cause increases in child abuse, drug consumption, and violence—and this is the tip of the iceberg. The real problem may be broader and deeper than current statistics reflect. If this situation is not addressed, increasing numbers of workers' compensation claims for stress can be expected; along with this will come an expansion in the ability of employees to sue for emotional distress and an adoption of stress into the definition of workplace safety rights. In fact, it is predicted that regulations governing allowable amounts and levels of workplace stress will be instituted within the next five years (Visions, 1991).

What is the impact of all this for the HRD professional? First is the personal impact. One million professional and managerial jobs have been eliminated nationwide, with threats of more layoffs yet to come. As a result, the average professional work week is now estimated at 52.2 hours. Clearly the HRD professional is bound to be exposed to personal stress. Additionally, the HRD professional's role has been expanded to the point that "today [he or she] has responsibilities for maintaining the health of the organization that go far beyond the traditional functions of a decade ago" (Landon, 1990, p. 37). The majority of the responsibility for workplace stress reduction will be placed in the hands of the HRD professional. The second impact is professional. If the organization counts on the HRD professional to care for its people and its corporate culture and also contribute to the bottom line, that person must be committed to managing personal and organizational stress.

CURRENT STRESS-MANAGEMENT EFFORTS

Stress-management efforts can be categorized according to organizational interventions and individual interventions. Organizational interventions address stressors by taking management action to reduce the harmful effects of stress. Primarily preventive in nature, such interventions center on eliminating or reducing stressors before they can function as sources of stress. Individual interventions address stress reactivity by teaching activities that can be used by individuals acting on their own, regardless of what the organization does. Primarily curative in nature, individual interventions focus on relieving stress once the individual experiences it. Organizational interventions include such programs as the following:

- corporate restructuring/job redesign/job enrichment
- compensation/reward systems
- participative decision making
- team building/outdoor leadership courses/executive retreats
- management and supervisory training
- recruitment/orientation and organizational socialization
- job fit
- performance management/goal setting
- career development
- communication and organizational policies/survey feedback systems
- change of workloads and deadlines
- change in work schedules/flex-time/summer hours/sabbaticals
- casual-dress days
- wellness programs/fitness centers
- employee assistance/counseling programs
- community involvement

From this variety of organizational interventions, goal setting, participative decision making, job enrichment, change in work schedule, and survey feedback systems have some scientific proof of effectiveness (Matteson & Ivancevich, 1987a). Qualitative positive results have been found for sabbaticals, flexible work schedules, summer hours, casual-dress days, executive retreats, outdoor leadership courses, fitness centers, and community involvement in the companies who used these methods of reducing organizational stress (Landon, 1990; Losey, 1991).

Stress-management training is one of the primary methods used by organizations to offer their employees an individual means for coping with stress. In 1989, stress-management training had decreased in organizational popularity; by 1991 it had risen again. In a survey of a local chapter of the American Society for Training and Development (ASTD), 53 percent of the forty-seven respondents said their organizations did not offer stress-management training; however, 96 percent thought that it should be offered.

Individual stress-management interventions include training in such knowledge and skill areas as diet, exercise, time management, assertiveness, support groups, relaxation/meditation, biofeedback, autogenic training, and cognitive restructuring.

Of the variety of individual techniques available, exercise, relaxation and meditation, biofeedback, support systems, assertiveness, time management, and cognitive restructuring have been found to have positive stress reduction effects (Matteson & Ivancevich, 1987a; Higgins, 1986; Norvell, Belles, Brody, & Freund, 1987; Nelson, Quick, & Quick, 1989). However, in terms of long-range results, relaxation was found to lower absenteeism for the first year only (Murphy & Sorenson, 1988) and only those who were trained one-on-one spent increased time in managing stress after training (Jenkins & Calhoun, 1991). In a study of nineteen work-site stress programs, of which 80 percent used relaxation/meditation, the most common finding was that subjective feelings of anxiety were reduced, while physiological measures did not show continued benefits. The authors concluded that these programs seem to lack an understanding of what works in reducing stress and the costs attached (Pelletier & Lutz, 1991).

Having reviewed the various organizational and individual interventions available, this article will now focus on a cognitive-centered stress-management training program.

WHY FOCUS ON THE MIND?

Given that individual stress-management training may avoid a hard look at organizational policies and procedures that need to be changed, and given that other individual interventions seem as useful as cognitive training,[1] why focus on the mental aspect of stress reduction?

There are five compelling reasons to use a cognitive-centered stress-management training program. First, inasmuch as stressors occur on and off the job, and inasmuch as people carry their own individual levels of stress reactivity around with them, a program that assists them in all life areas is useful. In other words, a cognitive-centered stress-management training program is generalizable to any situation and stressor (Matteson & Ivancevich, 1987b). Cognitive training is portable; it can be carried with the person to use before, during, and after a stressful event.

Second, a cognitive-centered stress-management training program can be administered with ease and at low cost. People can be taught how to think differently with few materials other than pencil and paper; the rudiments of changing perceptions and consequent thoughts can be taught in a short time. Compared to equipment required for biofeedback, facilities required for fitness programs, and typically huge costs associated with organizational interventions, cognitive training is highly cost effective.

Third, a cognitive-centered stress-management training program has face validity; it makes intuitive sense to people. Participants can easily identify with

---

[1] Cognitive training involves three ways of thinking differently about a situation. *Cognitive appraisal* involves gaining perspective about the seriousness of an event. *Cognitive restructuring* involves understanding that one's thoughts about an event stimulate reactions and then learning to change thoughts in order to change reactions. *Cognitive rehearsal* involves mental practice in managing a stressful event before it occurs. (Matteson & Ivancevich, 1987a).

examples of how their minds have an influence on their emotions and reactions, both positive and negative.

Fourth, there is strong evidence of the effectiveness of cognitive training in arenas other than the organization. Studies applied to a number of groups have indicated positive results (Burns, 1989; Matteson & Ivancevich, 1987a). Indeed, a change in cognitive style can change pessimism into optimism and helplessness into hopefulness (Seligman, 1991).

Fifth, a tremendous amount of testimony exists as to the mind's power to effect change and deal productively with stress. Sources as ancient as Epictetus ("People are not disturbed by things, but by the view they take of them"), the Bible ("For as he thinketh in his heart, so is he"), and Shakespeare ("Nothing is good or bad, but thinking makes it so") testify to the mind's ability to determine behavior. The following current testimony from stress literature is supportive of what has been concluded for ages:

- The "more mastery or control a person feels he has over circumstances, the less stress he's apt to feel, even if his control extends no further than the power to decide how he's going to feel about change" (Farnham, 1991, p. 72).

- "In the final analysis, most causes of stress stem from our thought processes." The "impact of life change will be as intense and chronic as you perceive and allow it to be" (Girdano, Everly, & Dusek, 1990, pp. 60, 72).

- "The most powerful—and the most controllable—stressor in the world is the human mind" (Matteson & Ivancevich, 1987a, p. 156).

Taken alone, each of these reasons may not prove sufficient for encouraging organizations to adopt a cognitive-centered stress-management training program as an important intervention to reduce stress. Together, however, "in terms of time, dollar costs, and effort expended relative to benefits," cognitive approaches may be one of the best stress-management investments an organization can make (Matteson & Ivancevich, 1987b, p. 27).

REQUIREMENTS FOR A STRESS MANAGEMENT TRAINING PROGRAM

A cognitive-centered stress management training program should meet the following requirements (Girdano, Everly, & Dusek, 1990; Matteson & Ivancevich, 1987a; Greenberg, 1990; Pelletier & Lutz, 1991):

1. The program should be capable of addressing both intraorganizational and extraorganizational stressors; it should be individualized enough that participants can focus on the stressors that presently affect them.

2. The program should be multidimensional in addressing various coping or stress-reduction techniques to combat stressors, stress reactivity, and stress consequences.

3. The program should be multisensory, using visual, auditory, and kinesthetic processes.

4. The program should use terms and concepts that are meaningful to the participants.

5. The program should attend to potential consequences to job performance by demonstrating links between coping techniques and job performance.

6. The program should be thorough; it should assist participants to understand how stress works, to identify stress symptoms, to identify stressors, to learn coping techniques, to explore resources and obstacles, and to allow for incorporation into life style patterns by an action plan.

7. The program should take place over time, with small numbers of participants (twelve to fifteen), so that learning can solidify, generalization can occur, and progress can be monitored.

8. The program should be evaluated for its long-term results.

COGNITIVE-CENTERED STRESS-MANAGEMENT TRAINING PROGRAM

The following program, although focusing primarily on cognitive training, also incorporates other stress reduction techniques that will allow the participants to explore additional helpful coping mechanisms. This program consists of the following ten "D's": define, discuss, dig, and delineate "how to's": decide, detach, declare, dispute, dream, and do.

Define

A variety of approaches can be used to introduce the program, including the following:

- Present some of the statistics provided in this article.

- Ask participants to estimate their current stress levels on a scale of one to ten.

- Ask participants to estimate their abilities to deal with their current stress levels on a scale of one to ten.

- Share cartoons, jokes, or "war stories" about stress.

- Have participants briefly share stressful situations that brought them to the program (this also establishes their expectations of what they hope to learn from the workshop).

- Administer a pretest to assess participants' conceptual knowledge of stress.

- Introduce the workshop goal as producing hardy individuals who can handle stress successfully, explaining that the difference between the hardy and nonhardy is not in the events that occur, but in how individuals appraise them. Hardy individuals do not deny their reactions to incidents. They simply appraise them differently as interesting natural changes that have some meaning to them; in other words, they transform the experience (Rosenbaum, 1990).

After the usual sharing of expectations and objectives of the program (the knowledge, attitude, and skill components involved in these ten modules), the facilitator should define stress and its related concepts.

Any of the definitions used previously in this article are adequate; the more technically-oriented the participants are, the more the definition should be scientifically based. The facilitator should define stress or stress response, stressor, and stress reactivity and distinguish among them, as was done in this article's introduction.

The following formula, tying these three concepts together may be useful:

STRESS + STRESS REACTIVITY = STRESS RESPONSE

Also, the concepts of positive and negative stress (eustress and distress) should be distinguished. Figure 1 depicts a simple model that demonstrates that people need some challenges that require adaptation in order to remain vital (optimal stress) (Girdano, Everly, & Dusek, 1990, p. 4).

Optimal Stress

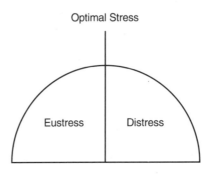

Figure 1. Optimal Stress

Finally, stress can be related to coping skills (stress prevention and reduction techniques), by the following layman's definition of stress: "the physical and psychological distress that we experience when our day-to-day problems exceed our abilities to solve them" (Flannery, 1991, p. 1).

If there is sufficient time and the participants have an interest, the concept of burnout can be defined, related to stress, and explained briefly in terms of its stages. Burnout occurs when the stress of feeling helpless to meet expectations destroys motivation (Watts, 1990); "when people can't or won't do again what they've been doing" (Levinson, 1990, p. 69). Burnout progresses through the following three stages (Lauderdale, 1982):

1. Confusion: Feelings of anxiety and minor health problems stem from a sense of expectations not being met without having the answer to "why."

2. Frustration: Feelings of anger and hostility and more pronounced health problems stem from a sense of being unappreciated and unrewarded.

3. Despair: Feelings of inadequacy and physical and emotional fatigue stem from thinking that actions have no meaning and a sense of depersonalization (being treated like an object).

Discuss

Having defined the terms necessary to understand stress, the facilitator's second step is to discuss how stress works by explaining its causes and symptoms. The model that follows (Figure 2) is a simple yet complete view of how stress occurs; the model relates the terms to the process and gives an overview of stress causes and symptoms (Greenberg, 1990; Matteson & Ivancevich, 1987a).

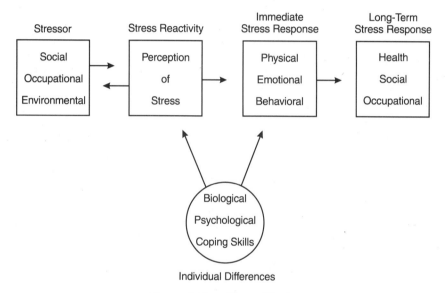

Figure 2. How Stress Works

First, a stressor occurs. A stressor is usually thought to be something that occurs outside of a person. For example, a change in work schedule (occupational), puts a person in a noisier location (environmental), and requires seeing less of his or her family (social). However, the notion that people can manufacture their own stress also should be introduced here. For example, an internal need to be perfect can operate as a stressor even when nothing external occurs.

Stress reactivity then combines with the stressor: The event is perceived as stressful. If it were not perceived as stressful, the process would terminate here. For example, if a change in work schedule were viewed as rewarding and positive, little stress would exist. Adaptation would be necessary, but would occur more quickly because of the optimistic perception.

Stress reactivity is influenced by individual differences. Individual differences have three forms: biological, psychological, and coping. An example of a biological difference is an individual's biological rhythm; if the individual is alert and energetic in the morning, a second or third shift assignment would be stressful. An example of a psychological difference is the need to control. An individual with a high need to control will react to a different work schedule with stress because the change was beyond his or her control (Girdano, Everly, & Dusek, 1990). An example of a coping difference is an individual who has learned and will apply knowledge of nutrition and exercise to ease the adaptation to a different work schedule.

The stressor, combined with stress reactivity, leads to an immediate stress response. An example of a physical response to stress is a headache. An example of an emotional response to stress is irritability. An example of a behavioral response to stress is overeating. Individual differences will continue to influence and can determine whether there will be long-term stress responses or effects.

If nothing changes (the stressor or stress reactivity), short-term stress effects will become long-term stress responses. An example of health effects is ulcers. An example of social effects is marital problems. An example of job effects is absenteeism. The most extreme long-term effect would be death.

Causes of Stress

To review, the two basic causes of stress are external and internal. Three external causes of stress are social, occupational, and environmental. The chart that follows (Figure 3) provides examples.

Social	Occupational	Environment
Marriage	Change in job responsibilities	Noise pollution
Divorce	Lack of training	Overcrowding
Death in the family	Poor relationship with boss,	Temperature
Major loan	co-workers, subordinates	Lighting
Problems with children,	Urgent deadlines	
in-laws, neighbors	Overload of information	
Trouble with the law	Lack of information	
Beginning or ending school	Lack of financial rewards	
Isolation and lack of social	Lack of career guidance or	
support	opportunity	
	Discrimination	
	Introduction of new	
	technology	
	Mergers or takeovers	
	Job insecurity	

Figure 3. External Causes of Stress

Internal causes can be based on biology or personality. Again, examples are provided in the chart that follows (Figure 4).

Biology	Personality
Biological rhythms (morning or night person) Nutritional health (intake of caffeine, alcohol, nicotine, etc.) Body fitness (presence or absence of an exercise program or physically active hobbies) Genetic tendencies (metabolic rate, predisposition to disease, etc.)	Level of self-esteem (feelings of worth, confidence, etc.) Need for control Locus of control (feeling that others are the cause of events) Patterns of behavior (Type A—impatient, aggressive, competitive, depressive; Hardiness—committed, feeling in control, liking challenges, etc.) Belief system ("I must be perfect," "I must be respected," etc.)

Figure 4. Internal Causes of Stress

In ending this section on causes with the personality, the facilitator can reinforce the importance of the belief system as the most important filter through which events are perceived (Girdano, Everly, & Dusek, 1990). Again, the mind's power can be emphasized with the following quote: "We learn how to scare ourselves to death, worry ourselves until we're distraught, and catastrophize even the most harmless situation" (Girdano, Everly, & Dusek, 1990, p. 57). This leads directly to a discussion of the symptoms of stress.

Stress Symptoms

Symptoms can be categorized as short term or long term. Short-term symptoms can be physical, emotional, or behavioral, as shown in Figure 5.

Physical	Emotional	Behavioral
Headache Backache Skin problems Stomach and intestinal problems	Apathy Anger Anxiety Impatience	Irritability Decreased attention span Substance abuse Overeating Withdrawal

Figure 5. Short-Term Stress Symptoms

Long-term symptoms of stress can have health, social, or occupational consequences, as shown in Figure 6.

Health	Social	Occupational
Ulcers	Relationship dissatisfaction	Absenteeism
Heart disease	Relationship termination	Turnover
Respiratory infections	Removal of support	Accidents
Allergies	Withdrawal into isolation	Decrease in quality
Insomnia		and quantity of work
		Reduced decision-making
		effectiveness
		Burnout

Figure 6. Long-Term Stress Symptoms

At this point, the facilitator may move on to the next section or continue with the discussion provided in the appendix of this article, which offers a more in-depth understanding of the physiology of stress.

Dig

After discussing the process and the causes and symptoms of stress, participants can be helped to analyze their own levels of stress. Many inventories exist to assist participants in analyzing their own levels of stress; representative examples are discussed in the section that follows. All inventories use the self-report technique; although they are not all scientifically produced and validated, they can still serve as useful discovery and discussion tools for the participants in a workshop.

External Causes (Stressors). The Holmes-Rahe Social Readjustment Scale (1967) is a popular inventory for assessing "life-change units," or the amount of occupational and social stress to which a person has had to adapt. Participants use a checklist to indicate changes that have occurred in the previous year (such as a new job, a change in living situation, and so on) and total the numerical values provided for the items. On this scale, the higher the individual's score, the more susceptible he or she is to illness.

The Hassles Scale measures "daily hassles," which are thought to contribute more to stress and be more effective predictors of health than life events (Lazarus, 1981, 1984). The hassles are analyzed according to frequency and severity. A corresponding Uplifts Scale also rates positive occurrences for their frequency and intensity (Kanner, Coyne, Schaefer, & Lazarus, 1982). When combined, these two scales measure overall stress level. An additional focus can be on life roles and the stress that conflict or imbalance among them may create.

Focusing specifically on work stress, the Stress Diagnostic Survey (Ivancevich & Matteson, 1983) measures both organizational (macro) and job related (micro) stress. The Maslach Burnout Inventory (Maslach & Jackson, 1981), a widely used and researched instrument, measures the frequency and intensity of burnout in terms of depersonalization, personal accomplishment, and emotional exhaustion. Self-assessment exercises to measure occupational stress and burnout can also be found (Girdano, Everly, & Dusek, 1990; Pareek, 1983; Warley, 1992).

Internal Causes (Stressors). The variety of scales and inventories for internal stressors cover the different personality aspects that affect perceptions of stress and stress reactivity, including the following:

- Locus of control instruments measure where participants believe control over events resides (Greenberg, 1990; Pareek, 1992; Rotter, 1966).

- The Hardiness Scale uses three subscales that measure the components of hardiness: commitment, control, and challenge.[2]

- Type A personality instruments measure responses to situations that might trigger competitive, impatient, or hostile responses (Friedman & Rosenman, 1974; Haynes, Levine, Scotch, Feinleib, & Kannel, 1978; Matteson & Ivancevich, 1982; Wright, 1991).

- The State-Trait Anxiety Inventory measures anxiety as either a personality attribute or a fleeting experience (Spielberger, Gorsuch, & Lushene, 1970), while the Taylor Anxiety Scale measures how anxious one is and how anxiety is manifested (Taylor, 1986).

- The Alienation Scale measures perceptions of social support versus isolation (Dean, 1961).

- The Self-Reliance Inventory measures acceptance of self-responsibility and willingness to establish support systems (Quick, Nelson, & Quick, 1991).

- The Optimism Scale measures how people explain both positive and negative events to themselves (Seligman, 1991).

- The Beliefs Inventory (Davis, McKay, & Eshelman, 1982) measures the number and strength of irrational beliefs a person holds.

Symptoms. Inventories and checklists are available to measure symptoms of stress. The Physiological Reactions to Stress Inventory covers a wide variety of physical symptoms (Ebel, et al., 1983). A quick checklist of physical as well as emotional symptoms can be found in *The Relaxation & Stress Reduction Workbook* (Davis, McKay, & Eshelman, 1982).

Lifestyle. Some inventories measure more than one stress dimension; these take a broad view of the person's quality of life and cover everything from sleep and nutrition to sense of purpose. The five scales in the Personal Stress Assessment Inventory (Kindler & Ginsburg, 1990) measure individual predisposition, resilience, occasional work- and personal-stress sources, ongoing work- and personal-stress sources, and health symptoms. The Health-Behavior Questionnaire ("Health

---

[2] In a personal communication with Kobasa, Rosenbaum explains that a new 50-item version of the Hardiness Scale has been developed. This scale encompasses five different scales: Alienation From Self and Alienation From Work Scales (Maddi, Kobasa, & Hoover, 1979); Locus of Control Scale (Rotter, 1966); Powerlessness Scale (Maddi, Kobasa, & Hoover, 1979); Security Scale (Hahn, 1966); and Cognitive Structure Scale (Jackson, 1974).

Style: A Self-Test," 1981, in Greenberg, 1990) covers the lifestyle behaviors of smoking, alcohol and drugs, nutrition, exercise and fitness, stress control, and safety.

Coping Skills. A final type of measure examines the coping techniques a person uses to combat stress. The Ways of Coping Scale (Lazarus & Folkman, 1984) measures which cognitive and behavioral strategies people use to cope with specific stressful events. Lists of potential coping techniques identified by stress researchers can serve as checklists for participants to assess the number and type of techniques they use (Girdano, Everly, & Dusek, 1990; Sailer, Schlacter, & Edwards, 1982). The "Coping Strategies: Managing Stress Successfully" exercise (Gregory, 1992) allows individuals to list and then to discuss successful and unsuccessful means of coping with stress. Time-management (Douglass & Douglass, 1980; Lakein, 1973), self-control (Rosenbaum, 1990), assertiveness (Bower & Bower, 1976; Rathus, 1973), and support-system (Prokop, 1992) inventories allow participants to explore their competence in specific stress-management techniques. Depending on available time and participant interest, the facilitator can choose which instruments to use in the workshop and, if the design allows, as homework.

The entire digging step, regardless of its depth and breadth, can help participants to see where they deviate from balance, whether it be in perspective, roles, or coping techniques (Selye, 1984).

Delineate "How To's"

With the foundation of definition, discussion, and personal analysis of stress, the participants are ready for practical coping techniques.

Decide

The first step in coping with stress involves recognizing a stressor or one's stress reactivity and then committing to do something about it. Stressors and stress reactivity can be identified from the material presented and from the participants' lives. Additionally, participants can be encouraged to recognize a stress reaction immediately—"In general, if your heart rate is more than 100 beats per minute, beware....if you're aware of your heart beating fast, calm down" (Bernstein & Rozen, 1989, pp. 91, 92).

Detach

To become calm requires detaching from the stress reaction by a shift in focus. Shifts in focus can be accomplished visually, mentally, and physically. A visual shift in focus requires looking at something else. For example, if low figures on a sales report induced a stress reaction, the person could look at a picture on the desk or wall. A mental shift in focus requires thinking about something else. In the preceding example, the person could think about a comedy show that was on television the previous night. A physical shift in focus requires that the person do something else. The physical shift in focus appears to be the most powerful and can be accomplished in the following ways:

Gross-muscle movement will aid in using up the stress products that have been generated by the stress response (Girdano, Everly, & Dusek, 1990). In the example above, the person could take a quick walk to get coffee or deliver a message instead of making a phone call. These short and quick energy breaks can also be used preventively. Exercise, although time consuming, is highly recommended for detaching from a current stress stimulus and also for decreasing stress reactivity over time (Girdano, Everly, & Dusek, 1990). A sales manager who regularly uses the lunch hour to jog would get immediate detachment as well as long-term benefits.

Relaxation quiets the physical and psychological internal environments and therefore aids in reducing arousal level (Girdano, Everly, & Dusek, 1990; Matteson & Ivancevich, 1987b). One can relax immediately and quickly by starting to breathe slowly and deeply. The sales manager could simply sit back for a few moments and focus on breathing. A regular program of relaxation is preventive as well as curative if participants practice the "relaxation response," outlined by Benson (1984), which follows:

1. Choose a comfortable position.

2. Close your eyes.

3. Relax your muscles.

4. Become aware of your breathing.

5. Maintain a passive attitude when thoughts surface.

6. Continue for a set period of time (twenty minutes are recommended).

7. Practice the technique twice daily.

Additional research by Benson (1984) has demonstrated that if the above technique is practiced with a phrase or word that reflects the person's basic belief system, then relaxation and its curative powers will be enhanced. Some examples of phrases used in teaching the expanded relaxation response are "My peace I give unto you" (John 14:27) or "Shalom" (the Hebrew word for peace) (Perlmutter, 1991a). This relaxation procedure thus incorporates meditative techniques that have also been found useful in managing stress (Byrum, 1989).

Mindfulness is a user-friendly mini-meditation that promotes paying attention to the present moment and not being distracted by constantly demanding stimuli (Perlmutter, 1991b; Findlay, Podolsky, & Silberner, 1991). The notion of a mini-technique seems quite appropriate to a training session geared toward generally fast-paced participants. Most of these techniques can be demonstrated in less than five minutes but still allow the participants to witness immediate results from shifting focus.

This can be explained as conditioning the mind to reduce arousing and increase calming thoughts, thus lowering stress reactivity and the consequences of stress (Girdano, Everly, & Dusek, 1990). The facilitator can also introduce the model that follows, which demonstrates that the stress response is a result of the perception of stress.

Many people view the event or stressor as causing the stress effect or response, as in Figure 7.

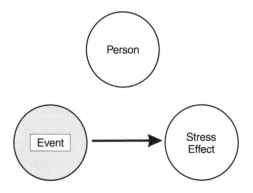

Figure 7. A Common Perception of Stress

A more useful approach, which puts the individual in charge, is viewing the person's perception as causing the stress effect or response (Figure 8).

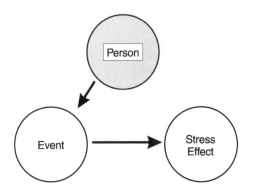

Figure 8. A More Useful Perception of Stress

Declare

The next step is to teach participants how to reduce stress by making positive statements, called affirmations. An affirmation is a positive thought, a specific prescription that you consciously choose to produce a desired result by immersing that thought in your consciousness (Ward, 1984). Affirmations should be phrased positively, actively, and simply; be phrased in the present tense; include the person's name; and refer only to the individual's behavior. Some examples for the sales manager might be as follows:

"I, Chris Hamilton, now see profits increasing by 10 percent."

"I, Chris Hamilton, now find ways to increase sales."

"I, Chris Hamilton, now manage the most successful sales office in the region."

It is useful to have participants pick a stress-related goal, develop some affirmations for it, choose the most appropriate affirmation, and write it down. Although affirmations are more powerful when they are written down at least ten times a day in the first person ("I"), in the second person ("you"), and in the third person ("he or she"), the facilitator may find that the participants resist the time they see this process consuming. In reality, the process takes only about fifteen minutes; however, the facilitator will be dealing with people who believe they do not have that much time. In meeting this objection, the facilitator can take two approaches. The first is to ask participants if they can give fifteen minutes a day to reduce their stress and preserve their health. The second is to provide some alternatives such as writing the affirmation on a card and looking at it frequently or recording it on an audiocassette and playing it while traveling in the car (Byrum, 1989).

Affirmations can be preventive, "I, Chris Hamilton, now can handle calmly and productively whatever sales report faces me" or curative, "I, Chris Hamilton, now know methods for increasing sales in the next month." Because there is little scientific proof that affirmations change mood or achievement level, participants may object to the process as naive. However there is intuitive force and numerous case examples behind the notion of "what you think is what you'll get" (Baldwin, 1985). Additionally, the use of specific coping statements, such as "I can do this," while not in affirmation format, have been found to contribute to athletic success (Roshies, 1991). Similarly, hardy students have been found to use more positive thinking than the nonhardy (Allred & Smith, 1989).

Dispute

The facilitator will need to acknowledge that negative thoughts will surface in the initial process of affirming. For example, in response to "I, Chris Hamilton, now see profits increasing by 10 percent," thoughts may surface about "Who are you kidding? The economy's been down for months now and the outlook is grim." However, participants can be taught to dispute these negative thoughts.

This step can be used in response to negative thoughts about affirmations, or it can be used whenever any negative thoughts appear in response to a situation. Before participants are taught the disputation method, the facilitator should explain the notion of explanatory style.

Explanatory style is the "manner in which [one] habitually explain[s] to [oneself] why events happen" (Seligman, 1991, p. 15). After defining explanatory style, the facilitator might have the participants think of both a positive and a negative event, write down how they explained the events to themselves, and how those explanations affected their feelings and actions.

Explanatory style influences an optimistic or pessimistic outlook on life and therefore has an effect on stress reactivity. After years of research, Seligman (1991) concluded that optimists take credit for success and blame things outside themselves for failure, while pessimists reverse the explanatory procedure. He is also quick to assert that a positive explanatory style does not negate taking responsibility; it simply increases control over how one perceives negative events.

Explanatory style is understood along three dimensions: permanence, pervasiveness, and personalization. The *permanence* dimension determines how long a person will feel helpless and want to give up; the *pervasiveness* dimension determines what aspects of one's life will be influenced; and the *personalization* dimension determines what one feels about oneself.

The optimist would explain a positive event in terms of permanence, universality (pervasiveness), and internal causes (personalization); a negative event would be explained in terms of temporariness (permanence), specificity (pervasiveness), and external causes (personalization). In the example above, an optimistic sales manager would think, "It's only temporary that figures are down. Besides, costs for the region are down and that offsets a profit loss. It's the recession and everyone is going through it." A pessimistic sales manager would think, "This situation is terrible and there's no end in sight. I must be a lousy manager. I'll probably have to go back out to the field. I guess I'm just a failure." When the profit increases, an optimistic sales manager might think, "Well, things have really turned around now. Life is great and I'm a great sales manager to get those people out there selling again." The pessimistic sales manager might think, "Thank goodness we have some relief this month, though it probably won't last. The economy's going to do what it will do." With examples such as these, participants can quickly identify their own thought processes and easily see how explanatory style contributes to stress. Participants can also be asked to share what they wrote about their positive and negative events and how they could now rewrite their explanations.

Once explanatory style is identified conceptually and personally, the facilitator explains how to turn a pessimistic style into an optimistic style. The primary method is disputation (distraction is the secondary method, which has already been discussed in the section about shifting attention and focus). Disputation involves arguing with oneself, and it can help one detach from a negative internal dialogue.

Disputation uses four steps. The first is *evidence,* demonstrating that the negative thought is factually incorrect. The second is *alternatives,* scanning for all possible causes and emphasizing changeable, specific, and impersonal ones. The third is *implications,* asking how likely the imagined negative consequences are to occur. The fourth is *usefulness,* questioning how functional it is to maintain the present belief and exploiting ways to change the situation in the future. In the example above, the sales manager might dispute as follows: "It's not true that I'm a lousy sales manager. I've recruited more successful sales representatives than any of my predecessors. Everyone knows it's the economy, and that could change tomorrow. It's not at all likely that I'll have to go back to the field. The national manager is pleased with my work. Thinking this way just isn't helpful to me, although there are probably some ways I could better support my employees. Maybe I'll start going on some calls with them." The result of this self-argument is feeling better and having more energy to make changes in the existing situation.

After explaining the disputation process, the facilitator can ask participants to practice disputing negative statements.

Dream

The next step is to dream or to visualize. After composing positive statements about a stressful situation and disputing negative statements that arise, participants are ready to imagine themselves being calm in a stressful situation. This section can be introduced by a quote from Dick Rutan, Voyager pilot, "What you can do is limited only by what you can dream" (McGee-Cooper, Trammell, & Lau, 1990, p. 283). Used primarily for preventive purposes, visualization is a powerful stress-management tool because the mind does not know the difference between fantasy and reality. In other words, the vision of calm is equivalent to the actual experience.

Already acknowledged as a powerful tool for organizational change and used effectively by managers in a variety of situations, visualization is becoming a widely used and researched area in stress management (Girdano, Everly, & Dusek, 1990) and training in visualization is increasing (Ungerleider, 1992). It is most often recognized for its success in sports psychology (Zilbergeld & Lazarus, 1987; Cox, 1991; Roshies, 1991) and in clinical settings for stress-related problems (Pelletier & Lutz, 1991).

Visualization can be used receptively to relax the mind and body or it can be used actively to consciously imagine a desired experience. For example, the sales manager could use receptive visualization to imagine a relaxing experience, such as sitting by the ocean and hearing the waves, feeling the breeze, and seeing the sun sparkle on the water. Or, the sales manager could use active visualization to imagine an experience that he or she wants to occur, such as sharing productive ideas about how to increase sales with sales representatives.

Visualization can also be internal, whereby the person visualizes himself or herself coping with a stressful event or succeeding at some task (that is, being inside one's body looking out); or external, where the person watches himself or herself as an observer (that is, being outside one's body looking in). Internal visualization is considered to be more powerful because it stimulates actual muscular activity (Cox, 1991).

Effective visualizations have many of the same characteristics of effective affirmations: They are positive, active, simple, and repeated, and they are used to replace negatives experiences with positive ones. They are also controlled by the visualizer and are intrinsically rewarding. An additional benefit of visualizations, like affirmations, is that repeated use has generalizable effects; it changes not only the reaction to a specific experience, it can also change the way one views oneself and one's ability to cope (Zilbergeld & Lazarus, 1987).

Participants can be asked to visualize themselves handling their particular stress situation effectively. Because each participant will have a different situation in mind, it is helpful to ask each to write out the image, including what he or she sees, hears, smells, touches, and tastes in the vision, before the facilitator provides time for the participants actually to practice visualizing. This allows the participants to include all of their senses for the richest possible experience. Depending on the comfort level of the group, participants can be asked to share their visions with a partner or volunteer to share their visualizations aloud. Helpful questions to guide the participants in forming positive visualizations are as follows:

- Where are you?
- Who is with you?
- What is going on?
- What else do you see?
- What is the other person saying?
- What else do you hear?
- What might you want to touch, taste, or smell?
- How do you want to respond?
- How do you want to feel inside?
- What do you want to do?
- What do you want the response to be?

Do

The final step is to assist the participants in carrying out what they have developed to this point. Conceptualizing and completing an action plan helps participants step out and act "as if" they will manage stress effectively. Such contracting is useful in changing behavior because it involves a commitment to action. For example, the sales manager might contract to go on calls with each sales representative and to develop three new ideas for increasing sales within the next month.

This final step can be introduced to the participants with the following quote (Myers, 1992, pp. 44-45): "Don't worry that you don't feel like it. Fake it. Pretend self-esteem. Feign optimism." Participants can be told that even one step will be useful because each time they act, they reinforce and solidify the underlying thoughts; attitudes follow actions and new habits replace the old by creating new mental paths, which lead to new behavioral paths.

An action plan can assist in reinforcing the process or the participants can be allowed to choose one step on which they will focus. It is recommended that the complete list of steps be included in an action plan because they build on and reinforce one another.

A sample action plan is provided below:

1. The situation in which I will use the six steps (decide, detach, declare, dispute, dream, and do):
2. What I will do to decide to deal with the stress...
3. The method I will use to detach...
4. The positive statement I will declare...
5. The statements I will use to dispute negative thoughts...

6. The dream I have about success in this situation...

7. What I will actually do...

8. When I will do this...

9. I will know I've been successful when...

10. The obstacles that I expect to encounter...

11. The resources that I can use...

12. I will celebrate my success by...

It is most important that action plans be followed up. If the stress-management program is only a one-time occurrence, it can be predicted that not much change will occur because participants may be returning to an organizational environment that does not support these stress-management techniques. The techniques are powerful instruments for individual change and for increasing one's ability to handle stress productively, but the techniques must be reinforced. It is advisable to have a follow-up session after one month in order to share successes and difficulties, to rework action plans or make new ones, and to support the participants in and motivate them to continue the changes.

The program can be concluded in one of the following ways:

1. Participants can share action plans and contract with a partner or share with the group.

2. The pretest can be re-administered to demonstrate gains in learning.

3. Participants can re-estimate their abilities to deal with stress on a scale of 1 to 10.

ADVANTAGES AND DISADVANTAGES

The organizational and individual benefits of cognitive stress-management training have been previously cited: generalizability, face validity, low cost, administrative ease, testimony, and evidence of effectiveness. The generalizability of the skills must be re-emphasized. The ability to change one's perceptions, to change one's mind about a situation is an essential element in empowerment. As the world moves toward the twenty-first century, people in organizations will need this critical capacity to operate in self-directed work teams and to contribute to participative management. Authority and responsibility will need to be perceived in new ways to meet future challenges and changes. Cognitive training in stress management can contribute to empowerment in many other organizational areas.

There are also advantages to the HRD professional involved in such a program. Personally, the professional can benefit from learning or further enhancing these cognitive stress-management skills in his or her own life. Professionally, the HRD professional has the opportunity to serve as a better model for adapting to change and its accompanying stress, both in the training room and in the organization.

However, some argue that individual stress-management training does not address organizational causes of stress and may encourage blaming the victim (Pelletier & Lutz, 1991). Such criticism does not render the training ineffective; rather, it points out that multiple efforts are needed to reduce organizational stress. If there were only organizational responses to stress, the organization would still stand to lose from employees improperly armed to face the changes ahead.

The charge could be made that the program is not comprehensive. As it is presented here, it is not; the intention of this paper was to focus primarily on cognitive skills. However, other stress-management techniques, such as exercise, relaxation, and support systems, were mentioned and could be expanded at will. There is nothing to prevent this program from being enhanced by the addition of such topics as nutrition, assertiveness, conflict management, and time management.

Finally, in comparison to some stress-management techniques, cognitive training may appear to be inactive. With the suggested exercises, the participants can be fully involved in examining and learning methods to better deal with stress.

In summary, this article has provided a cognitive-focused stress-management training program that will have organizational and individual benefits. The individual employee is assigned a primary role "in the perception and management of disturbance. Rather than being the passive victim of environmental forces....[one] is seen as...actively monitoring his or her relationship with the environment and seeking to maintain or improve it" (Roshies, 1991, p. 420). However, just as learned optimism does not relieve people from responsibility for their actions, providing a solid, individually based stress-management training program does not relieve the HRD professional from the responsibility to explore organizational causes of stress and to work to overcome them. With appropriate organizational changes, the employee who knows how to change his or her thinking will be even more empowered to contribute to the organization's financial success and quality of life in the next decade.

REFERENCES

Allred, K., & Smith, T. (1989). The hardy personality: Cognitive and physiological responses to evaluative threat. *Journal of Personality and Social Psychology, 56*(2), 257-266.

Baldwin, B. (1985). *It's all in your head: Life style management strategies for busy people.* Wilmington, NC: Direction Dynamics.

Benson, H. (1984). *Beyond the relaxation response.* New York: Harper & Row.

Bernstein, A., & Rozen, S. (1989). *Dinosaur brains: Dealing with all those impossible people at work.* New York: John Wiley & Sons.

Bower, A., & Bower, G. (1976). *Asserting your self.* Reading, MA: Addison-Wesley.

Burns, D. (1989). *The feeling good handbook.* New York: William Morrow.

Byrum, B. (1989). New age training technologies: The best and the safest. In J.W. Pfeiffer (Ed.), *The 1989 annual: Developing human resources* (pp. 183-209). San Diego, CA: Pfeiffer & Company.

Cox, R. (1991). Intervention strategies. In A. Monat & R. Lazarus (Eds.), *Stress and coping: An anthology* (3rd ed.) (pp. 432-474). New York: Columbia University Press.

Davis, M., McKay, M., & Eshelman, E. (1982). *The relaxation and stress reduction workbook* (2nd ed.). Oakland, CA: New Harbinger.

Dean, D. (1961). Alienation: Its meaning and measurement. *American Sociological Review, 26*(5), 753-758.

Douglass, M., & Douglass, D. (1980). *Manage your time, manage your work, manage yourself.* New York: American Management Association.

Ebel, H., et. al. (Eds.). (1983). *Presidential sports award fitness manual* (pp. 197-98). Havertown, PA: FitCom Corporation.

Farnham, A. (1991, October 7). Who beats stress best—and how. *Fortune,* pp. 71-86.

Findlay, S., Podolsky, D., & Silberner, J. (1991, September 23). Overdosing on stress, and on the 101 ways to relieve it. *U.S. News & World Report,* p. 74.

Flannery, R. (1991). Stress: The secrets of stress-resistant people. *Bottom Line, 12*(13), 1.

Friedman, M., & Rosenman, R. (1974). *Type A behavior and your heart.* Greenwich, CT: Fawcett.

Girdano, D., Everly, G., & Dusek, D. (1990). *Controlling stress and tension: A holistic approach.* (3rd ed.). Englewood Cliffs, NJ: Prentice-Hall.

Greenberg, J. (1990). *Comprehensive stress management* (3rd ed.). Dubuque, IA: Wm. C. Brown.

Gregory, A. (1992). Coping strategies: Managing stress successfully. In J.W. Pfeiffer (Ed.), *The 1992 annual: Developing human resources* (pp. 9-13). San Diego: Pfeiffer & Company.

Hahn, M. (1966). *California life goals evaluation schedule.* Palo Alto: Western Psychological Services.

Haynes, S., Levine, S., Scotch, N., Feinleib, M., & Kannel, W. (1978). The relationship of psychosocial factors to coronary heart disease in the Framingham study: I. Methods and risk factors. *American Journal of Epidemiology, 107*(5), 362-383.

Higgins, N. (1986). Occupational stress and working women: The effectiveness of two stress reduction programs. *Journal of Vocational Behavior, 29*(1), 66-78.

Holmes, T., & Rahe, R. (1967). The social readjustment rating scale. *Journal of Psychosomatic Research, 11*(2), 213-218.

Ivancevich, J., & Matteson, M. (1983). *Stress diagnostic survey.* Houston: Stress Research Systems.

Jackson, D. (1974). *Personality research form manual.* New York: Goshen Research Psychologists Press.

Jenkins, S., & Calhoun, J. (1991). Teacher stress: Issues and intervention. *Psychology in the Schools, 28*(1), 60-70.

Kanner, A., Coyne, J., Schaefer, C., & Lazarus, R. (1982). Comparison of two modes of stress measurement: Daily hassles and uplifts versus major life events. *Journal of Behavioral Medicine, 4*(1), 1-39.

Kindler, H., & Ginsburg, M. (1990). *Stress training for life.* New York: Nichols.

Lakein, A. (1973). *How to get control of your time and your life.* New York: New American Library.

Landon, L. (1990, May). Pump up your employees. *HR Magazine,* 34-37.

Lauderdale, M. (1982). *Burnout: Strategies for personal and organizational life.* Austin, TX: Learning Concepts.

Lazarus, R. (1981, July). Little hassles can be hazardous to health. *Psychology Today,* pp. 58-62.

Lazarus, R. (1984). Puzzles in the study of daily hassles. *Journal of Behavioral Medicine, 7,* 375-389.

Lazarus, R., & Folkman, S. (1984). *Stress, appraisal and coping.* New York: Springer.

Levinson, H. (1990). When executives burn out. *Harvard Business Review, 68*(2), 69.

Losey, M. (1991, February). Managing stress in the workplace. *Modern Office Technology,* 48-49.

Maddi, S., Kobasa, S., & Hoover, M. (1979). An alienation test. *Journal of Humanistic Psychology, 19*(4), 73-76.

Maslach, C., & Jackson, S. (1981). *The Maslach burnout inventory.* Palo Alto, CA: Consulting Psychologists Press.

Matteson, M., & Ivancevich, J. (1982). Type A and B behavior patterns and self-reported health symptoms and stress: Examining individual and organization fit. *Journal of Occupational Medicine, 24,* 585-589.

Matteson, M., & Ivancevich, J. (1987a). *Controlling work stress: Effective human resource and management strategies.* San Francisco, CA: Jossey-Bass.

Matteson, M., & Ivancevich, J. (1987b). Individual stress management interventions: Evaluation of techniques. *Journal of Managerial Psychology, 2*(1), 24-30.

McGee-Cooper, A., Trammell, D., & Lau, B. (1990). *You don't have to go home from work exhausted.* Dallas, TX: Bowen & Rogers.

Murphy, L., & Sorenson, S. (1988). Employee behaviors before and after stress management. *Journal of Organizational Behavior, 9*(2), 173-182.

Myers, D. (1992). The secrets of happiness. *Psychology Today, 25*(4), 38-45.

Nelson, D., Quick, J., & Quick, J. (1989). Corporate warfare: Preventing combat stress and battle fatigue. *Organizational Dynamics, 18*(1), 65-79.

Norvell, N., Belles, D., Brody, S., & Freund, A. (1987). Work site stress management for medical care personnel. *Journal for Specialists in Group Work, 12*(3), 118-126.

Pareek, U. (1983). Organizational role stress. In L. Goodstein & J.W. Pfeiffer (Eds.), *The 1983 Annual for Facilitators, Trainers, and Consultants* (pp. 115-123). San Diego: Pfeiffer & Company.

Pareek, U. (1992). Locus of control inventory. In J.W. Pfeiffer (Ed.), *The 1992 annual: Developing human resources* (pp. 135-148). San Diego: Pfeiffer & Company.

Pelletier, K., & Lutz, R. (1991). Healthy people—healthy business: A critical review of stress management programs in the workplace. In A. Monat & R. Lazarus (Eds.), *Stress and coping: An anthology* (3rd ed.) (pp. 483-498). New York: Columbia University Press.

Perlmutter, C. (1991a, June). Pray for peace. *Prevention,* pp. 42-45.

Perlmutter, C. (1991b, June). Take a moment to muse. *Prevention,* pp. 38-41, 121.

Personal-stress assessment inventory. Pacific Palisades, CA: Center for Management Effectiveness.

Prokop, M. (1992). Supporting cast: Examining personal support networks. In J.W. Pfeiffer (Ed.), *The 1992 annual: Developing human resources* (pp. 15-27). San Diego: Pfeiffer & Company.

Quick, J., Nelson, D., & Quick, J. (1991). Self-Reliance Inventory. In J.W. Pfeiffer (Ed.), *The 1991 annual: Developing human resources* (pp. 149-161). San Diego: Pfeiffer & Company.

Rathus, S. (1973). A 30-item schedule for assessing assertive behavior. *Behavior Therapy, 4*(3), 398-406.

Rosenbaum, M. (Ed.). (1990). *Learned resourcefulness: On coping skills, self-control, and adaptive behavior.* New York: Springer.

Roshies, E. (1991). Stress management: a new approach to treatment. In A. Monat & R. Lazarus (Eds.), *Stress and coping: An anthology* (3rd ed.) (pp. 411-431). New York: Columbia University Press.

Rotter, J. (1966). Generalized expectancies for internal versus external control of reinforcement. *Psychological Monographs, 80,* 609.

Sailer, H., Schlacter J., & Edwards, M. (1982, July-August). Stress: Causes, consequences, and coping strategies. *Personnel,* 35-48.

Seligman, M. (1991). *Learned optimism.* New York: Alfred A. Knopf.

Selye, H. (1974). *Stress without distress.* New York: New American Library.

Selye, H. (1984). *The stress of life.* (2nd ed.). New York: McGraw-Hill.

Smith, E., Brott, J., Cuneo, A., & Davis, J.E. (1988, April 18). Stress: The test Americans are failing. *Business Week,* pp. 74-76.

Spielberger, C., Gorsuch, R., & Lushene, R. (1970). *Manual for the state-trait anxiety inventory.* Palo Alto, CA: Consulting Psychologists Press.

Taylor, S. (1986). *Health psychology.* New York: Random House.

Ungerleider, S. (1992). Vision of victory. *Psychology Today, 25*(4), 38-45.

Visions. (1991, April). Workplace stress. *HR Magazine,* pp. 75-76.

Ward, D. (1984, May). *Using affirmations and visualizations to increase training results.* Paper presented at the ASTD National Conference, Dallas, TX.

Warley, W.R. (1992). Burnout inventory. In J.W. Pfeiffer (Ed.), *The 1992 annual: Developing human resources* (pp. 121-134). San Diego: Pfeiffer & Company.

Watts, P. (1990, September). Are your employees burnout-proof? *Personnel,* 12-14.

Wright, L. (1991). The type A behavior pattern and coronary artery disease: Quest for the active ingredients and the elusive mechanism. In A. Monat & R. Lazarus (Eds.), *Stress and coping: An anthology* (3rd ed.), New York: Columbia University Press.

Zilbergeld, B., & Lazarus, A. (1987). *Mind power.* Boston, MA: Little, Brown.

Beverly Byrum-Robinson, Ph.D., *is both a professor of communication at Wright State University in Ohio and the president of her own company, The Communication Connection. Dr. Byrum-Robinson conducts seminars on topics such as interpersonal skills, team building, stress and time management, and assertiveness. As a consultant, she facilitates team-building sessions in organizations. She has written one book, has co-authored three others, and has published articles on interpersonal and group communication and training.*

APPENDIX: THE PHYSIOLOGY OF STRESS

Although not all participants will care about the physiology of stress and will be attending the training program primarily to determine how to deal with stress, the facilitator needs to be prepared to offer explanations of the physiology that is involved in stress.

A simple and memorable explanation of the stress response involves relating it to the fight/flight/freeze response. Participants can be asked to think of a stressful situation and to recall what happened to their bodies. Their responses can be matched to the list that follows, which details what occurs when the response is triggered (Smereka, 1990, p. 72):

- Digestion slows
- Breathing quickens
- Heart rate increases and blood pressure soars
- Sugars and fats pour into the bloodstream
- Muscles tense
- Perspiration increases
- Eyesight and hearing become more acute

A more detailed and scientific explanation can be offered for people who desire it. The facilitator should be prepared to give this type of explanation with highly technical or scientific people. The facilitator begins by explaining Selye's (1974, pp. 25-27) *general adaptation syndrome,* whose three stages illustrate that the body's ability to adapt to continued stress is finite.

1. *Stage One: Alarm Reaction.* The body shows changes that are characteristic of its first reaction to a stressor. Resistance is diminished.

2. *Stage Two: Resistance.* Resistance continues and increases as the body adjusts. The bodily signs that are characteristic of the alarm reaction disappear.

3. *Stage Three: Exhaustion.* Adaptation energy is exhausted. Signs of stage one appear; now they are irreversible, and death results.

More specifically, a perceived stressor sets off a reaction in the hypothalamus (in the brain's subcortex) to initiate the stress response through two pathways. One pathway is stimulation of the sympathetic nervous system and the adrenal medulla; this is the alarm stage of the general adaptation syndrome. The second pathway is stimulation of the pituitary gland and adrenal cortex; this is the resistance stage of the general adaptation syndrome.

The hypothalamus initiates the alarm reaction by instructing the sympathetic division of the autonomic nervous system and the adrenal medulla (in the adrenal gland) to secrete catecholamines (epinephrine and norepinephrine), which supplement and prolong the sympathetic responses. The visceral effectors (cardiac muscle, smooth muscles, and glandular tissue) respond immediately to

Pfeiffer & Company

mobilize resources for physical action and to stimulate a number of stress responses. The heart rate and contraction of cardiac muscles increase to circulate blood quickly to needed areas. Skin and visceral blood vessels constrict, decreasing blood to unneeded organs, while blood vessels in the skeletal muscle, the brain, and the heart dilate to route blood to organs needed for the stress response. The spleen discharges stored blood into general circulation to provide more blood; red blood cell production is quickened as is blood-clotting ability. The liver changes stored glycogen into glucose and releases it into the bloodstream to provide additional energy. The breathing rate increases and bronchial tubes dilate to handle more air and to give the body more oxygen. Saliva, stomach, and intestinal enzymes decrease because they are not necessary to the stress response.

The resistance reaction is stimulated by regulating hormones secreted by the hypothalamus: corticotropin releasing hormone (CRH), growth hormone releasing hormone (GHRH) and thyrotropin releasing hormone (TRH). The CRH stimulates the pituitary to increase ACTH (adrenocorticotropic hormone), which in turn stimulates the adrenal cortex (in the adrenal gland) to produce more corticoids. The mineral corticoids result in sodium retention, which leads to water retention, which maintains high blood pressure. The glucocorticoids increase protein breakdown and conversion of amino acids into glucose to provide an energy supply after immediate glucose has been used. The glucocorticoids also sensitize blood vessels to constriction and inhibit inflammation. Finally, glucocorticoids are thought to suppress production of the protein in T-cells that assist in immunity.

The GHRH causes the pituitary to secrete human growth hormone (HGH), which stimulates the breakdown of fats and the conversion of glycogen to glucose. The TRH stimulates the pituitary to secrete thyroid-stimulating hormone (TSH), which, in turn, stimulates the thyroid to produce thyroxine, which increases the breakdown of carbohydrates.

Arousal can be further prolonged because the limbic system (responsible for emotion, memory, and homeostatic regulation) responds and the cerebral cortex contributes perception and conscious thought about the stressor.

The following bodily systems can develop conditions related to stress. The muscle system produces such symptoms as headaches and backaches. The gastrointestinal system produces dry mouth, difficulty in swallowing, gnawing or nauseated sensations in the stomach, diarrhea or constipation, and ulcers. The cardiovascular system produces increased blood pressure and atherosclerosis. The immune system produces such diseases as the common cold, cancer, asthma, and rheumatoid arthritis.

CONTRIBUTORS

Pamela Adams-Regan
Consultant
Psychological Management
  Resources, Inc.
2615 Camino Del Rio South, Suite 300
San Diego, CA 92108
  (619) 291-1500

Arlette C. Ballew
Developmental Editor
Pfeiffer & Company
8517 Production Avenue
San Diego, CA 92121
  (619) 578-5900

Jean Barbazette
President
The Training Clinic
645 Seabreeze Drive
Seal Beach, CA 90740
  (310) 430-2484

Beverly Byrum-Robinson, Ph.D.
Professor of Communication
Wright State University
Dayton, OH 45435
  (513) 873-2710
  (513) 873-2145

Jacque Chapman
Director
Leadership Lamar Institute
P.O. Box 10006
Beaumont, TX 77710
  (409) 880-8441

Ozzie Dean, Ph.D.
President
Diversity Plus
10696 Arboretum Place
San Diego, CA 92131
  (619) 566-9787

Rita Dunn, Ed.D.
Director
Center for the Study of Learning
  and Teaching Styles
School of Education
  and Human Services
St. John's University
Utopia Parkway
Jamaica, NY 11439
  (718) 990-6335

Deborah M. Fairbanks
Training Specialist/
  Instructional Designer
13223 Black Mountain Road, #272
San Diego, CA 92129
  (619) 484-5324

Arthur M. Freedman, Ph.D.
Organization Development Consultant
1000 Lake Shore Plaza, Suite 24C
Chicago, IL 60611
  (312) 440-0864

Claire B. Halverson, Ph.D.
Professor of Organizational Behavior
School for International Training
Brattleboro, VT 05301
  (802) 254-6098

April G. Henkel
Director of Program Development
Margaret Lynn Duggar & Associates, Inc.
1018 Thomasville Road, Suite 110
Tallahassee, FL 32303
  (904) 222-0080

Joanne Ingham, Ed.D.
Academic Advisor
Office of Academic Attainment
Adelphi University
Garden City, NY 11530
  (516) 877-3150

Bonnie Jameson
Consultant
1024 Underhills Road
Oakland, CA 94610
(510) 832-2597

Homer H. Johnson, Ph.D.
Director
Center for Organization Development
Loyola University
820 N. Michigan Avenue
Chicago, IL 60611
(312) 508-3027

Neil Johnson
Managing Partner
Ollander-Krane/Johnson
201 W. 70th Street, #42-L
New York, NY 10023
(212) 873-5631

Mary Harper Kitzmiller
Managing Editor
Pfeiffer & Company
8517 Production Avenue
San Diego, CA 92121
(619) 578-5900

Robert J. Marshak, Ph.D.
President
Marshak Associates
11920 Frost Valley Way
Potomac, MD 20854
(301) 340-0191

Mike M. Milstein, Ph.D.
Professor of Educational Administration
College of Education
University of New Mexico
211 Faculty Office Building
Albuquerque, NM 87112
(505) 277-5932

Timothy M. Nolan, Ph.D.
President
Innovative Outcomes, Inc.
13202 W. Cleveland Avenue
New Berlin, WI 53151
(414) 786-4700

Jason Ollander-Krane
Managing Partner
Ollander-Krane/Johnson
2215-R Market Street
San Francisco, CA 94114
(415) 282-4771

Marian K. Prokop
Senior Editor
Pfeiffer & Company
8517 Production Avenue
San Diego, CA 92121
(619) 578-5900

Gaylord Reagan, Ph.D.
Independent Management Consultant
Reagan Consulting
704 Hackberry Court, #3106
Bellevue, NE 68005
(402) 292-0723

Cheryl Repp-Bégin
Total Quality Leadership (TQL)
  Management Specialist
Department of Management Services
State of Florida
243 Carlton Building
Tallahassee, FL 32301
(904) 922-7014

Michael Lee Smith
Director of Training and Development
Metcalf & Eddy Companies, Inc.
Route 22 West and Station Road
P.O. Box 4300
Somerville, NJ 08876
(908) 685-4530